Any Child Can Write

**Other Books by
HARVEY S. WIENER**

On Composition:
Creating Compositions
The English Skills Handbook
The Writing Lab

On Reading:
The Reading Skills Handbook

Anthologies:
American Literature 1
American Literature 4
Emerson and Thoreau
The Short Prose Reader (in press)

DR. HARVEY S. WIENER

Any Child Can Write:

HOW TO IMPROVE YOUR CHILD'S WRITING SKILLS FROM PRESCHOOL THROUGH HIGH SCHOOL

McGRAW-HILL BOOK COMPANY

New York   St. Louis   San Francisco   Bogotá   Düsseldorf   Madrid
Mexico   Montreal   Panama   Paris   São Paulo   Tokyo   Toronto

Book design by Kathy Peck.

Copyright © 1978 by Harvey S. Wiener.
All rights reserved. Printed in the United States of America. No part of this
publication may be reproduced, stored in a retrieval system, or transmitted in
any form or by any means, electronic, mechanical, photocopying,
recording or otherwise, without the prior written permission of the
publisher.

1 2 3 4 5 6 7 8 9 0 D O D O 8 9 8 7 6 5 4 3 2 1 0

Library of Congress Cataloging in Publication Data

Wiener, Harvey.
   Any child can write.
   Includes index.
   1. English language—Composition. I. Title.
LB631.W387   808′.042′071   77-26707

First Paperback edition, 1980

ISBN 0-07-069039-1 (Paperback)

*To my wife, my
mother, my father,
and my sister,*

**for helping
writers grow.**

Contents

Foreword   xi

Acknowledgments   xiv

1. Introduction: *The Second "R"*   1
Writing As Exploration
What's Happening in School
Some Basic Thoughts about Writing
Poor Writers: On the Question of Blame

2. Notes, Signs, and Shopping Lists: *How Can a Parent Help?*   8
Setting the Example
The Tools of the Trade
"I've Got a Little List"
"Keep Out!": A Sign for Room or Door
Let's Leave a Note
Writing and Reading, Hand in Hand

3. Experience and Creative Expression   18
A View of Creative Expression
Autobiography: The Child's Experience
The Parent Sets the Stage
Mothers and Fathers as Storytellers

4. Pictures, Words, and Sentences: *Laying Foundations*   24
Words and the Young Artist
Pictures and Words: Making Connections
Accent on Sentence Sense
Avoiding Bits and Pieces
Scissors, Paste, and Sentences
Seeing the Skill Advance

5. The Senses at Play: *Images As Building Blocks*   37
Sense Words Up Front
Four Writing Games and Variations
Two Longer Efforts
Comparisons for Solid Imagery

6. Correctness, Part 1: *An Outlook for Young
Writers at Home*   57
The Fever of Correctness
How Do Writers Write?
Reacting to Error
Your Code of Ethics: Writing for School
Proofreading, Hedge Against Mistake
Spotlight on Writing in the Grades

7. Correctness, Part 2: *Word Games and Word and
Sentence Craft*   82
Building Vocabulary
Words As Chameleons
Guesswork in the Limelight
Spelling Skills and Word Hot Spots
Sentences to Play With

8. Snapshots of Special Places   108
One Place: The Senses, Front and Center
Opinions in Focus
Subjectivity Leads the Way
Cameras and Crayons
Description Described

9. One Person in the Floodlights   118
One Person, One Sentence
A Party Riddle
Photo Into Words
Self-Portraits for the Very Young
Expanding a Picture of Someone Close

10. A Moment Reborn in Language   131
What Is Narration? What Is a Moment?
The Moment in Focus
A Sense of Sequence
Narration: Sensory Language Leads The Way
Playing With Dialogue
A Short Story: Fiction for Thirteen-Year-Olds

11. Adventures in Make-Believe   147
Riddles and Games on Paper
Visits with Make-Believe
Animals on Parade
"I Am a Pizza": Personification and Delight
On Your Own in Fantasyland

12. A Child's Message Through the Mails   161
Using the Mails

Creative Letter-Writing
"Come to my Party"
Let's Write Letters
Business Letters for Home-Bred Dynamos

13. **Words in Focus:** *Creative Definitions for the Young Writer*   174
What Does It Mean? How Does It Feel?
Writing Clear Definitions
Personal Meanings, Personal Words

14. **Language Singing** *The Child as Poet*   186
Talk-to-Me's and Word Whackies
What's Wrong with Jingling?
Language Singing, Sharp and Clear
Shapes and Rhythms for the Poet's Song
Why Poetry?

15. **A Report for School**   206
A Project in Stages
"What Do I Do?" First Questions First
Shaving the Topic Down
Your Friends: The Encyclopedia and Other
   Source Books
Getting Things in Order
Enter the Finished Product
Using Your Will Power

16. **An Afterword for Too-Busy Parents**   223

Appendix A.   **One Hundred Ideas for Writing at Home**   225

Appendix B.   **A Parent's Primer on Correctness**   228
Sentence Completeness
One Hundred Words Most Often Misspelled
Words Often Confused
When to Use Capitals
Some Punctuation Pointers

Appendix C.   **Books for the Home Shelf**   241
Children's Word Books
Language Skills Books for Parents

Index   249

Foreword

When the cry of back-to-basics hit full force in the mid-1970s, friend after friend stopped me on the street, telephoned, and scrawled hurried postscripts to letters; all voicing concern were parents who wanted to help their children advance as writers. What steps could a mother or father take to influence a son's or daughter's writing capabilities?

I looked in the libraries and the bookshops. But, in spite of what educators had already begun to call the "writing crisis," I could not find a single volume to tell parents what to do to help the child develop competence in that key skill.

It was not long before I knew that I had to write such a book. As a parent and a teacher I had to share with other parents my ideas for a fruitful, enjoyable home program in writing. Such a program starts in the building of attitudes and moves through simple, varied, and practical experience with the written word. A mother or father can direct such a program with confidence, and can help a youngster develop abilities somehow overlooked or not adequately attended to in school.

Of course, it's clear to me that parents are not—nor should they be—teachers in the formal sense. If you have visions of marking up your sons' and daughters' papers at home the way your English teacher red-inked *your* painful efforts, forget them!

And yet, you are without doubt your child's teacher, the best kind in many ways, because you love the one you teach, share the joys and suffering of your child's attempts, and want desperately to assure his success.

My suggestions in this book take into account a parent's busy schedule and other constraints; but they also speak to the parent who is willing to give up some time to help his or her child from losing out on a chosen college or career because of a failure to master the basic, but essential, skills of writing.

There *are* things you can do—and you can have fun doing them.

In planning this book I am indebted to many people for their ideas about good writing and about how inexperienced writers learn best. Many of my suggestions are not original; I learned them from teachers, poets, counselors, tutors, and parents. My friend Professor Don M. Wolfe, who died in 1976, taught me most of what I know, and often our ideas are so alike as to be one man's thoughts. To other friends and colleagues—Mina Shaughnessy at CUNY*; Ronald Buckalew, Carolyn Eckhardt, Robert Worth Frank, Jr., Martha Kolln, Bernard Krimm, William O'Donnell, Audrey Rodgers at Pennsylvania State University; Marian Arkin, Dan Georgakis, George Groman at La Guardia Community College; Don McQuade at Queens College; Charles Bazerman at Baruch College; Fillmore Peltz, Noel Kriftcher, Fred Cohen at the New York City Board of Education; Francis Greenberger, Carol and Joel Anderson—I am indebted for ideas, advice, encouragement, and support. I am especially grateful to Bob Habich for his help. Sally Close did a first-rate typing job, and I thank her.

But the people to whom I am most indebted for the book are the children whose writing demonstrates what young talent, when tapped, can produce. Accordingly I want to thank the following young writers: Sharon Adler, Kathy Apfel, Twyla Boardley, Pamela Bonavoglia, Karen Bracy, Judy Brewster, Helen Cohen, Angela D'Apica, Terry Dause, Mike Davis, Marie Della Porta, Patricia D'Esposito, Brian Donovan, Valerie Drafts, Sherri Dubner, Patricia Durante, Michael Eannelo, Karen Sue Evans, Ruth Feder, Alayne Finkelstein, Leo Finkelstein, Stacy Goldstein, Ellen Greneman, Leslie Gross, Harold Gruber, Joe Havens, Eliezar Havivi, Janet Hutter, Lauren Hutter, Rose Jachter, Nancy Jones, Gary Kimball, Gina Kirsch, Hedy Klein, Sharon Klein, Vivian Krasner, Michelle Landburg, Robin Leach, Denise Leonard, Albert Leone, Mark Levine, Mindy Levine, Myra Leysorek, Sonia Markmann, Dar-

* City University of New York.

rin McGowan, Theresa McGraw, Shelly Modlin, Caroline Narby, Scott Norkin, Frank O'Connor, Carol Orefice, Debbie Osher, Jeffrey T. Pope, Mona Rosenfeld, Etta Rybstein, Beth Ross, Tony Schott, Erica Sher, Andrew Siscaretti, Eddie Southern, Carl Stearns, Rosemary Tyson, Charles Walker, Donald Walters, Myra Weiser, Melissa Wiener, Beth Ann Winters, Carol Zubatkin. To these and others I am grateful for showing conclusively that any child can write.

Acknowledgments

The author acknowledges the use of the following previously published material:

The Bobbs-Merrill Company, Inc.: Selections from pages 83, 131, 159, and 129 from *Language Arts and Life Patterns: Grades 2 through 8,* by Don M. Wolfe. Copyright © 1961 by The Odyssey Press, Inc.; copyright © 1972 by the Bobbs-Merrill Company, Inc. Reprinted by permission of the publisher.

James I. Brown, "Master Word Chart." Reprinted by permission of James I. Brown.

Grolier Incorporated: Entry on "Hibernation." Reprinted from *The New Book of Knowledge,* 1974, by permission of the publisher, Grolier Incorporated.

Indiana Writes: Selections from pages 60 and 67. Copyright © 1976 by the Trustees of Indiana University.

McGraw-Hill Book Company: Selections from pages 45–46 and 173–174 and adaptations of pages 13–17, 45–50, 89–92, and 249–254. From *Creating Compositions, Second Edition,* by Harvey S. Wiener. Copyright © 1977 by Harvey S. Wiener. Used with permission of McGraw-Hill Book Company and the author.

The Macmillan Company: Excerpt from "What Is Pink" from *Sing-Song,* by Christina Rossetti. Copyright © 1924 by The Macmillan Company. Used with permission of the publisher.

Random House, Inc.: Selection from page 95 of *Enjoying English 6,* by Don M. Wolfe, Floy W. DeLaney, Lela T. Hamilton, and Ethel K. Howard. Published by L. W. Singer Co., Inc., 1969. Reprinted by permission of Random House, Inc.

The National Council of Teachers of English: Excerpt from page 97 of *Sentence Combining,* by Frank O'Hare. Research Report 15. Copyright © 1973 by the National Council of Teachers of English. Reprinted with permission; selection from page 660 of "The Single Narrative Paragraph and College Remediation," by Harvey S. Wiener, in *College English,* March 1972. Copyright © 1972 by the National Council of Teachers of English. Reprinted by permission; selection from page 571 of "Media Compositions: Preludes to Writing" by Harvey S. Wiener, in *College English,* February 1974. Copyright © 1974 by the National Council of Teachers of English. Reprinted by permission.

Thomas Nelson and Sons, Ltd.: Excerpt from page 20 of the *Illustrated Dictionary for School and Home.* Published by Grosset & Dunlap Inc., 1972. Reprinted with permission of Thomas Nelson & Sons, Ltd.

Charles Scribner's Sons: Selection from *I Know! A Riddle Book* by Jane Sarnoff and Reynolds Ruffins. Copyright © 1977 by Charles Scribner's Sons. Reprinted by permission of the publisher.

Any Child Can Write

1

Introduction

The Second "R"

Writing As Exploration

Writing is a magical realm of expression that allows a child to come to terms with the joys and pains of daily living. It is a way for the child to explore his inner self. A few words, a few sentences glow on the page like a little crayon drawing. It is an expression of the child's own vision, his perception of the world as he sees it. It is also a permanent record of experience—words and sentences holding and keeping the essence of a moment in language.

Every day a child's life holds innumerable moments that bombard his senses through what he sees and smells and tastes and touches. Etched in his mind, either conscious or subconscious, these moments dwell in his brain, awaiting language to transform them into experiences that are intelligible and meaningful both to the child and to others.

It is this language of the senses that every child has at his fingertips. And it is this language that any child can, with guidance, transform into writing—to capture forever the special flashes of meaning his life holds.

The key word here is "guidance," and this is where you, as a parent, can play an important role. For if you have looked closely at your child's classroom situation, you will see that many schools fall short in the area of guidance in developing essential writing skills.

What's Happening in School

Consider for a moment your child's grade-school teacher as he leaves the classroom at the end of the day. On the chalkboard behind him he has written the homework assignment: "Read pages 25 to 45 in your social studies book and *write* the answers to the questions on page 46; *write* up the experiment on air pressure we did in class today; *write* sentences for your week's spelling words; *write* a book report on the biography you took from the library." If he's a conscientious teacher, he's gripping a worn leather briefcase that is already bulging with written work collected from thirty children that morning. At home the burden of his students' work haunts him. Reams of paper stand in ugly, reluctant piles on the desk or on the kitchen table. Under such circumstances, how can the teacher do an efficient job when it comes to the instruction and evaluation of writing? How can he build in your child a positive attitude toward written work if he himself, being overburdened, views it as a tedious, unrewarding chore?

He can't.

And that's where you come in. By setting up an atmosphere in your home that encourages creative written expression, you can give your sons and daughters an outlook on writing that will build confidence in their abilities to use language.

And that's where this book comes in: It will help you, who know the importance of written communication in today's world, help your children develop essential writing skills.

Some Basic Thoughts about Writing

By its very nature, writing serves in a number of ways. First, writing lets your children show what they know; and, as such, it becomes a means by which a teacher judges the child's knowledge of subject matter. When the instructor reads the answers to a history test or to a list of questions about science, he checks on the student's mastery of content. But, more often than not, he has decided that if students show they know the answers, it really doesn't matter how successful the writing is. With time limitations and excessive student loads being what they are, rarely will a teacher comment in the margin about sentences or the quality of ideas on a page of social studies homework. If you look at the last few pages of written work returned to your child by his teacher, you won't find much in the way of suggestions for writing improvement.

There are two broad areas good writing teachers think about when they evaluate a child's work. First there is the world of ideas and the way a writer puts those ideas together. Often called "rhetoric" or "composition," this aspect of writing is the product of the way a mind works in dealing with thoughts. It involves invention, discovery, logic, organization of ideas, and style. Second there is the area of correctness, often called "mechanics," "grammar," or "usage." This is the domain of more easily measured skills: A word is either right or wrong, a sentence is either complete or incomplete, an apostrophe is either required or not required.

I often use a comparison between effective writing and the human anatomy to illustrate these two broad areas. Rhetoric, the idea and organizing part, is like a person's body: the blood, muscle, bone, tendons, and nerves. Correctness, the right-or-wrong features of our language system, is like the skin, the outer layer, what we see straight off when we think of the human animal. This analogy is a good one, because it equates the writing process with a living being—but it is helpful only if we keep in mind that both the skin *and* the body make up the whole person. One without the other is incomplete.

Just as skin and body make the human being, so ideas and correctness make writing. Without the clear expression of ideas, the outer layer of correctness has no meaning. Nonsense correctly spelled and punctuated is still nonsense. Similarly, a set of brilliant ideas that follows none of the principles of correct writing falls apart, a heap of fluids and organs without skin. Often, in fact, it is only through correct expression that a writer can make his ideas known in the first place. Of course, when I teach writing in the classroom, I focus first upon the internal organs, so to speak, the expression of ideas by means of effective language. I try to build up to a concern for "the outer layer," or correctness. So the level of sentence construction, the ideas at the heart of the writing, and the degree of error all go hand in hand. Clearly, the process of writing as a form of communication demands that ideas, the language used to explore them, and the conventions of correctness work together as a total form of expression.

Of course everyone is concerned with a person's ability to use written language to demonstrate knowledge of content matter. Every book, letter, memo, or report you read illustrates what the author knows or understands. When a child writes about himself he's also, in a way, showing what he knows. But I am not concerned here with what the written word can tell about how many books on Russia the youngster has absorbed or how meticulously he took notes on the experiment with a gasoline can that demonstrates principles of air pressure. My interest is with the expression of *ideas,* the muscle and blood of writing.

With your help and guidance your children can use the resources of their own experiences to develop that magical ability to express an idea—to capture the essence of a moment.

Poor Writers: On the Question of Blame

It's no news to anybody reading this book that today's school children as a whole are poor writers. College teachers all over the country, pointing to low scores on entrance exams and poor writing samples submitted by freshmen, are stunned at the writers' inability both to express ideas clearly and to use the conventions of correctness in conveying those ideas. Who, they wonder, is at fault? How can generations of youngsters pass through high schools, earn diplomas, and still not know how to write? Why is it that previous groups of girls and boys could write so well, and even master the complex rules of grammar (a demand rarely made on students today)?

What is the answer? Why are our children not learning how to write?

As with all simple questions there are too many complex factors to offer simple answers.

The schools, even with the best of intentions, contribute their share to the problem. Although, clearly, there are many dedicated teachers who approach rigorously their responsibilities to teach students how to write, the portrait I drew earlier of the overburdened elementary school teacher shows part of the problem in the grade schools. In some of those schools which do insist upon writing—there are enormous numbers of literary magazines, class newspapers, and yearbooks churned out each year—instructors often take what students create and rewrite, edit, and correct the material themselves, instead of working with the children to overcome problem areas. Still other teachers, in stressing the free and creative spirit of the writer, will praise badly organized, poorly supported writing because of a sudden flash of insight on the part of the writer. Others, sadly, have no good ideas to give children at all. One sixth-grade teacher confided to me a while back that he taught writing no more than twice a year. Twice a year! "It's frustrating. There's not enough time. And I really don't know what to do."

In the junior and senior high schools, where departmentalized instruction means a teacher's job is to teach "English" only, there's not much attention to instruction in writing either. First, the curriculum is hopelessly overloaded with literary appreciation. Those courses of study that include units for writing are not explicit and are weak in their demands. I might add, incidentally, that English instructors complain little about this: It is only in teaching literature, many feel, that their true mission lies. As important as it is to teach poetry and the Great Western Tradition, the scope and dimension of literature programs in the schools are often beyond the student's needs. Time spent in teaching symbolism, onomatopoeia, and blank verse might be better spent in teaching about topic sentences, supporting details, verb tense. I know I am striking, now, at the life's blood for many teachers. There is something about the personal satisfaction and prestige derived from teaching an appreciation of fiction that is impossible to dislodge from the English teacher's outlook. Unfortunately, that attitude does not accompany the teaching of writing skills.

In college the situation is pretty much the same. Professors moan about the awful state of student writing; but having to teach freshman English instead of literature is, to many, a fate worse than death.

It is true that, in the last few years, English departments in many institutions have turned with imagination and energy to teaching composition. Throughout the country directors of writing programs are making headway in establishing writing as a discipline worthy of rigorous study and investigation. Intelligent approaches to college writing have mushroomed at the campuses of Pennsylvania State University, Miami Dade Junior College, Ohio State University, Cornell, Iowa, and the various colleges of the City University of New York.

In spite of all this, however, the freshman writing course is still the stepchild of the English curriculum.

To overcome this sad situation, one might reasonably ask if a teacher's training ought not to include more study of techniques in teaching writing. But more than *what?* The astounding reality is that few teachers in grade school, junior high, senior high, or college have had *any* training in how to teach composition. How to teach reading; how to teach mathematics; how to evaluate tests; how to teach science—in all of these, yes, but no course in how to teach writing. Now, in response to public outcries, some interesting courses and programs in writing for future teachers of English are developing at schools such as Penn State, SUNY Stony Brook, UCLA, University of Southern California, CCNY, and Columbia Teachers' College, among others. But at the moment your child's teacher probably has had *no* instruction in how to teach composition.

Teacher attitude and preparation offer one clue to the child's poor achievement in writing, but there are others. Human beings vary in abilities. Some children never develop the skills parents would like them to develop; or they cannot learn in the time frame the schools have established arbitrarily. This is *not* the same as saying each child cannot be brought to his own level of maximal achievement. Putting ideas into written language with ease, grace, and clarity is a skill that is not easily learned. In any consideration of achievement, there is also the question of talent. But writing is just like any other creative skill—painting, drawing, ice skating, swimming, diving. Some people astound the world with their natural abilities to do things others reach only after great struggle. The point is that if we make the struggle we *can* often achieve our goal despite our own limitations. We'll not all turn out like Picasso, Dick Button, Mark Spitz, and Claus DiBiasi; but if one of the skills they command interests us we can learn it, and we can feel pride in our achievement even if we fall short of greatness. It means practice, hard work, and dedication, but if it's important and enjoyable to us, and, especially, if we begin at a young age, almost anyone can learn to draw or skate or swim or dive.

Another reason today's children seem to have poorer writing skills than yesterday's children stems, in part, from the advantages of the modern world. There is no doubt that television, movies, slides, tape recorders, video units, stereos, citizen band radios, transistors, and portable televisions are making the written word in some sense obsolete. Even letter-writing, a form of communication we could have once said with absolute certainty that children would need throughout their adult lives, may now be replaced by the exchange of homemade cassettes or long distance phone calls.

The irony of the seeming obsolescence of the written word in the wake of the media explosion is that written language continues to play a critical role in the way we communicate. People *write* programs to motivate computers; students must take notes on what they learn, no matter what vehicle is used to convey the information to them; and parents still, and shall forever, write letters. Despite their seeming affection for non-written, often nonverbal forms of communication, our children know what awaits them in a career if they lack writing skills. I've seen brilliant young students who are articulate, clever, and personable turn away from professions in law or business management because they believe they cannot write well enough. In many jobs skill in writing and advancement are correlated.

Will *your* children reject law, teaching, management, public relations, government, civil service, editing, advertising, police science, research science, and countless other professions because they question their own skills with written language?

Sadly, many parents, too, fall easy prey to the media which drain the family's time and which keep them away from the written word. In how many households do children never observe parents put pens or pencils to paper? Do you know that a family can keep a shopping list (such a basic writing exercise) without jotting down a single word? Just stick a peg in a wooden board, alongside the printed word for each staple, such as milk, butter, and eggs. How unfortunate.

On the other hand, some children are lucky enough to see mothers pursuing degrees and scribbling the notes for a sociology paper; or, perhaps, they may see their fathers behave like mine: Every Saturday afternoon my father sat in a green club chair working out the New York *Post* crossword puzzle, a tattered copy of *Roget's Thesaurus* at his side, and a yellow pencil locked between his thumb and forefinger. There are innumerable writing experiences for the parent and child to share. They are waiting for you.

And so, this book. As you look at the ways to help your child, you'll be looking at yourself as a user of the written word, too. So be warned, it's not easy. Yet, given the poverty of other resources from which your child learns to write, you, the parent, must get the ball rolling.

2

Notes, Signs, and Shopping Lists:

How Can a Parent Help?

Setting the Example

Children learn by imitation. As soon as my daughter could crawl about freely, she would slip into my study during the early hours when I write, and, watching me carefully as she played, she would demand her own pencil and papers. Long before her second birthday she would sit on the floor near my chair, scribbling on small white sheets she begged from my desk pad. The sight of her father scratching away at his desk each day set the frame for Melissa's own writing activities. Her dexterity advanced so well that when we tried to teach her to eat with a fork, we used a writing implement as our referent. "Hold it like a pencil," we urged. Watching me type, she soon asked for her own typewriter. We bought her a red plastic children's typewriter, and it remains one of her favorite toys. She used it from the day we gave it to her on her second birthday, and continues to use it now in her sixth year.

A cousin of mine recently had a short story published for the first time. His little boy was so excited to see the magazine bearing his father's story that with a feverish pace the child dashed off three little stories of his own!

Of course not every child has a professional writer for a parent. Still, there are countless opportunities for your child to watch you performing simple writing tasks every day. And there are few better ways to establish writing as a vital and enjoyable process than to watch Mommy or Daddy. These observed activities easily become joint endeavors as the child grows older and demands to participate.

In this chapter I want to explore some simple, everyday types of writing that you can set into motion in the home. Even before we get to that, however, you need to collect the simple equipment required for your child's writing experiences.

The Tools of the Trade

It's not a big task to keep available the things your child will need for frequent writing activities. Most households already have many of the items I suggest. Gather them together and make them accessible to the child.

Here's what you'll need:

1. Writing paper. Don't be fussy: any type will do. It's a good idea to offer as many kinds as you can. Loose sheets of different sizes accommodate the child's unpredictable preferences at any given moment. Always try to provide unlined paper as well as lined, and if the lines are narrowly spaced, do not *insist* that the child's writing fit between them. You should encourage, but not demand, writing within widely spaced lines. Variety is the key to paper supply: Your child may want to use 2-by-3-inch note sheets, plain white paper, lined yellow pages, backs of envelopes, index cards, the reverse side of ruined sheets, newspaper edges, napkins, personalized notepaper, all with equal interest and pleasure. A book, a spiral bound pad of pages, or a tablet provide more permanence for the child's work. Spirals suit a youngster's sudden whim to rip out a damaged page.

2. Heavy-duty paper. You will want to make available index cards, oak tag sheets, cardboard from shirts, the backs of pads, cut-up shoe boxes or cartons. These make good homemade signs and resist tearing when they are hung from a wall or door.

3. Stationery. Some notepaper of the child's own and some cards that can be stamped and posted will go a long way in establishing the value of letter-writing skills. If you're lucky, letter-writing practice during the early years (three and four years old) will save you phone bills later on!

4. Writing implements. Pencils and crayons allow children a wide range of expression, according to their tastes and inclinations. Supply and encourage the use of erasers, teaching the child that all writers make mistakes often and that correcting errors has value (much more of this later on). During a trip through Europe we found colored pencils were a wonderful, durable set of writing tools. Making pictures and words in color held our child's interest on train rides where long, dull stretches of landscape and empty coach compartments offered no diversion; and an inexpensive sharpener fixes a broken point simply. Crayons, though more versatile in color possibilities, break easily. However, for many children, the crayon provides fewer manipulation problems than the pencil. If your child is still developing dexterity, supply large thick crayons. I am at a loss to understand a child's attraction to pens (perhaps they think it is "grown-up" to use pens!) but nothing thrills the four- and five-year-old more than writing in ink. As long as you watch your white linen tablecloth or orange velvet couch, pens are fine. If you encourage felt-tip pens—children love their variety of colors—buy only the water-soluble kind so that you can wash the pink and aqua off a ruffled blouse or the back of a thumb or an elbow.

5. Chalkboard and chalk. Chalk and chalkboard in the child's room support writing activities, providing excellent opportunities for experimental writing exercises and for practice with newly learned words. A picture and a few words are easily erased to make way for another presentation. The feeling of the chalk in the child's hand, the different angle of the writing surface from the usual horizontal on the desktop to the vertical on a chalkboard easel or on a wall provide a learning alternative that will reinforce what your child practices on paper.

6. Word books. A variety of alphabet and word books provides more than reading activities. Many books encourage the child to follow dotted or broken lines in order to write out the alphabet or to spell out words, to copy words printed in large letters alongside pictures, or even to write original responses to questions. (The Dr. Seuss–Roy McKie book, *My Book About Me,* is a notable example of this last group.) These are all fine, so long as they remain activities for enjoyment. Nothing will turn a child away from writing faster than "work" assigned to him in a word book by a parent. The older child (fourth grade and up) should have a dictionary, and the upper junior and senior high school youngster will need a thesaurus as well; these are two tools without which a writer cannot work. Inexpensive pocket dictionaries work handily for the older child, but the small type and incomplete definitions often confuse grammar school youngsters. You might want to explore some of the titles listed in Appendix C; but, in any case, your child ought to have an illustrated, children's dictionary. A good, hardbound adult dictionary should stand on a conspicuous shelf; and you, if for no reason other than to set an example, should refer to that book frequently. A good dictionary returns its investment many times over. Start building correct habits as soon as possible. The thesaurus, a word book that names synonyms, not definitions, helps the adolescent and young adult expand vocabulary for writing. Children who suddenly realize its potential love the thesaurus—but it needs careful supervision.

In chapter 7, I will deal more fully with the dictionary and the thesaurus as tools for your child's learning.

7. Miscellaneous. Here are some interesting items that allow the child to spell out words and sentences rather than to write them in his own handwriting.

a. typewriter. For ten to fifteen dollars (some are more expensive), a child's plastic typewriter offers an exciting tool for the young writer. Typing letters in upper case, the children's typewriter allows another medium for written expression. If you have only an adult typewriter available, urge your son or daughter to use it under your supervision (most typewriters are sturdy enough to withstand some rough treatment). Type out a few simple words in a sentence or in a question; have the child copy it or respond to it.

b. label-makers. For about two dollars, a label-maker allows the child to stamp out words and thoughts on plastic tape. Encourage frequent questions about spelling, however; once the letters are imprinted on the plastic there is no way to erase them.

c. alphabet stamps and stamp pads. Using a rubber stamp for each letter and a well-inked pad, young children can spell out words and sentences. This provides a physical involvement different from writing. Rubber stamps help teach alphabet recognition. As you help the child decide upon some simple thing to write, ask him to select the letters, and name them together. The words stamped out on a sheet of paper will spell out the youngster's thoughts.

Now that your home writer's workshop has its supplies, here are three simple writing activities you can nurture with ease at home.

"I've Got a Little List"
The shopping list (that institution challenged by the pegboard!) is one of the most accessible possibilities for simple types of writing. Children of three or four who know their letters and sounds should be encouraged to add words to the list for the supermarket. For those still learning about the alphabet and the sounds letters make, preparing a shopping list offers painless reinforcement. At the grocery shelf, ask the child to read the word he wrote and to select the item—a can of beans, a bar of soap, or, better, a favorite treat, that brown bag of M&M's or sandwich cookies in cellophane.

In general, lists provide substantial writing practice for any age group. You and your child can prepare a guest list for the next birthday party; a list of toys to take on a visit to Grandma's; a list of favorite foods or best friends; a list of things to do on a special day; a list of clothing to buy for school—the ideas are inexhaustible. As the child grows older the list can be adapted to his or her own interests and needs: a list of records to buy from the radio shop; a schedule of activities for after school; a list of expenses to keep track of weekly allowance or money earned in babysitting. You may recall that Benjamin Franklin kept lists throughout his life. During his twenties, his project was to arrive at moral perfection, so he listed thirteen virtues that he believed necessary and desirable. He made a little book, giving a page for each of the virtues; and, drawing red lines to make columns for each day of the week, he marked with a black spot every fault he felt he committed in regard to a specific virtue. To people today this plan for moral perfection sounds strangely oversimplified, but list-keeping does help bring some order to plans or schemes that we see as important. It works for children as well as for adults.

My view of the parent and the three-, four-, or five-year-old working together on a list—the shopping list, for instance—is simple and stress-free. For the child who has not yet mastered the alphabet you, the parent, must write slowly, firmly, and clearly in large letters, saying the letters aloud, then pronouncing the word. Next, you ask the child to say the word. If he shows interest, urge him to copy the word onto a separate sheet or directly alongside or below yours. Right now, you are trying to establish positive attitudes, so do not worry too much about undersized or oversized or incorrect or transposed or mixed upper- and lower-case letters. Praise the child's effort before you point out his error.

For the child who has command of the alphabet, a parent might also encourage list-writing. The youngster without advanced skills can often write his name, can contribute at least that to the joint list-making venture, even if the parent has to write all the other words. You might suggest titles that include the child's name, titles looking like these: "Hilary's Favorite Foods" or "Guest List for Matthew's Party" or "Clothes to Buy for Maria." In preparing the list you should ask your child to suggest items, which he should then try to write. If he has a sense of the sounds letters make, encourage him to say words slowly and to try to figure out the letter or combination of letters that make a sound. Give as much help as needed. After an incorrect guess you might say, "Good try! But here the letter 'S,' not 'C,' makes the sound you want." If the child cannot determine the letter, tell it to him. The goal is to get your child to print an immediate experience in his or her own writing. Once the word stands out in green or red or blue upon a page, it is the child's own, a word to read and to savor, a word for you to read and to praise.

For your next shopping excursion, let your child make a list of things you both need. Be patient; name the letters to spell the words or word parts your child cannot manage alone. After the two of you prepare the list, read the words together—first the child trying to read his own writing and then you rereading the list. Watch the way his eyes light up as you read your child's words!

Here is a list that my daughter Melissa—at five and a half— and her mother prepared one July afternoon before a vacation trip (the pampers are for my son, Joseph):

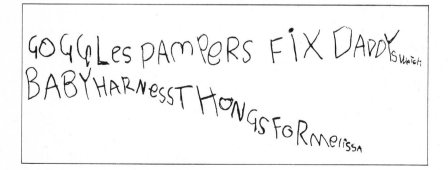

Busy gathering things together, my wife did not supervise the writing, although she did help name the letters as Melissa sat at the kitchen table and penciled in the words. Barbara showed little concern, therefore, for the fact that words ran together occasionally, or that the words were not placed under each other as in a more conventional list. The point is that Melissa wrote the items—many things she wanted for the beach—in her own handwriting, and she knew that the writing would lead to a concrete act. During the shopping trip that followed, Barbara frequently asked "What's the next thing here? Read this for me," in order further to reinforce the vitality of the writing experience.

"Keep Out!": A Sign for Room or Door
Another enjoyable and easy writing experience is making a room sign. After books, one of the early contacts the child makes with written language is the printed sign. Long before they read in any formal way, many children can easily recognize the word STOP in red on the metal octagon near a street corner. Signs such as EXIT, OUT, IN, and even more complex signs like ENTRANCE, CLOSED, MEN'S ROOM make up basic sight vocabulary for many children. In the supermarket, for example, letters scream out SALE or MILK or COOKIES, words that any child can learn to read after some exposure.

If you are a parent who is eager to expand your child's writing experiences, you should draw upon the familiar world of signs that surround him. The sign a child prepares for his room is an indelible mark of his own needs and experiences. Plastic door signs that say *David's room* or *Jennifer's room* are available at any five-and-dime, but why buy such a sign when the child can make it himself? A sheet of paper or cardboard (and perhaps some wood backing), a crayon or pencil, a bit of cellophane tape or a thumb tack—*voilà*—there's a sign-making shop right in your own home.

Aside from naming a room as their own, children can use signs to label objects throughout their rooms. Teachers often make signs to help young children build their vocabularies, but the technique takes on a new dimension when the child himself makes the sign and affixes it to the object. *Window, closet, desk, bed* are words that your son or daughter can easily write. Adding the pronoun MY or the child's name to the sign establishes the object as part of the youngster's own territory. It is *my bed* or *Gloria Liu's closet*. It's no one else's.

Other signs can express the child's preferences for behavior in the room. My five-year-old niece wrote a no smoking sign for her bedroom door because she hated the smell of the cigarettes her parents would forgetfully smoke in her room.

The child might also represent an object, in a little drawing, to accompany the words on the sign. In this activity you can guide your child in a solid language experience: The child identifies some object or impression; writes it down on a sign with your help; affixes it somewhere at home; and has constant opportunity to read the words in his own handwriting.

Let's Leave a Note

Like the sign in the child's own writing, the handwritten note communicates a message. But the note is a more personalized communication than a simple sign. The child prints a message for a select audience, usually only one person. Because a note is such a simple form of writing and because it often brings about some action, it is an exciting activity for the youngster.

I am distinguishing a note from a letter because of a letter's length and formal elements. Of course, letters and notes often have exactly the same parts—salutation, content, closing, signature. I will take up letters later on in a more complete way; but for now I want to think of a note as a brief message to someone, a message with the specific purpose of giving instructions or information.

The chalkboard in a child's room can provide the field for an interchange of daily notes between child and parent. When Melissa started to show interest in words, my wife would slip into our daughter's room as she slept and would write a little note in yellow chalk: "Dear Melissa, I love you. Love Mommy." One morning we discovered that under those words Melissa had copied parts of the message to yield: "Dear Mommy, I love you. Love Melissa." Barbara is still writing chalkboard notes— except that now a line divides the board horizontally, the bottom half for our daughter's responses.

With a little thought you can establish note-writing as a frequent activity at home. The exercise is short enough to engage the attention of young children as well as older ones. Under your supervision, your child can write the note himself, realizing immediate satisfaction from a task successfully performed.

If it is necessary to write a note to the teacher to excuse an absence, why not have the child prepare it? Usually the youngster can write this note easily, in a sentence or two, with your help:

> *Dear Mr. Stevens,*
>
> *I was absent on Monday, May 3, because I had a virus.*
>
> *Sincerely,*

Here, too, show painstaking patience: spell letter combinations the child might not know; help the child to say sounds clearly so that he can determine the letters in a word, especially the consonants. You should sign the note under your child's signature; it will give your stamp of approval to your son's or daughter's efforts (as well as your legal approval to the absence), and the teacher will receive a joint project in writing.

You see the idea, of course—a brief note any child with some basic alphabet skills can write. Leave the classic note for the milkman: "No milk today." Leave a message for an older brother or sister: "We went shopping at Sears." Leave a message for a spouse returning from work or from an errand: "We are in the backyard." Instead of leaving a letter for posting in your mailbox, leave a note for the letter carrier: "Please ring bell for letter," and let the child hand over the mail.

When written communication is related to some desired action and achieves some clear result, it asserts an important, valuable aspect of written language in the child's mind.

Parents with imagination can take advantage of the easy success achieved in writing those kinds of brief messages. Prepare a game to determine the guests' seating plan around the table at your son's or daughter's birthday party (for ages four and up). Seats should be numbered with words, *one, two, three,* and so on, or with numerals, 1, 2, 3 (or both); and, of course, your child will write the words or the numbers, each on a small card so they can be taped to the backs of the chairs. On separate papers (one for each guest) help your child write this message: "Please sit in chair one" (change the number in each note). Fold up the papers. At the party, each guest picks a folded message from a box, matches the word or number in the note with the sign on the seat, and sits down. Aside from the fun at the party, your child performed a task in writing which, because of its repetitive nature and because of its ability to produce action, is a highly positive creative experience. This is exactly the kind of writing reinforcement you can support in the home.

Writing and Reading, Hand in Hand

Experienced teachers prefer to call instruction in reading and writing "language experience" or "language arts" because the two areas, joined with speaking, round out the instructional process. Although reading skills are beyond the intent of this book, there is a close relationship between these two areas, especially in the initial learning stages. For example, to learn the alphabet, the child looks at the letters and also writes them. Part of the ability to recognize a word develops from the ability to write the word and to read it back; for many people, including adults, the tactile aspect of writing is an indispensible feature of the learning process. When I teach reading, I try, wherever possible, to use the students' writings to help me teach the skills. When the context is part of their own lives, students' paragraphs are fertile grounds for building knowledge in reading.

What I'm saying is that practice in writing is a vital part of practice in reading. Underdeveloped readers can advance their skills through the writing process: The child captures an experience in words; he reads back the writing; someone questions comprehension and vocabulary within the framework of that writing activity. Certainly, the youngster needs to read at some time what others write. But in the early stages of language awareness the writing activity is an integral part of reading. I'd like to see someone experiment with a systematic approach to reading through writing. Could not an entire program in reading skills development revolve around directed writing for children? In any case, when Johnny writes something at home and then reads it aloud you're helping him with two critical skills.

I have focused here on those simple, everyday activities any parent, without the slightest training in composition, can use to encourage growth in writing at home. These writing exercises are fun, too, if you follow the approaches outlined here. After all, in building a favorable attitude toward writing, you want to ignore the pains.

Before I go any further, I think that I should establish and examine my philosophy of writing, so that you have a solid base on which to build an enjoyable and successful set of experiences for your child. I hope to offer you a good working definition of "creative writing," often a misapplied term in children's learning programs.

3

Experience and Creative Expression

A View of Creative Expression

When Count Leo Tolstoy, the great Russian novelist, explained the meaning of art, he established a critical relationship between the writer and the written effort. "To evoke in oneself a feeling one has once experienced," he says, "then by means of movement, lines, colors, sounds, or forms expressed in words, so to transmit that feeling that others experience the same feeling—this is the activity of art." It is no less an expression of the creative written process for a child than for any professional writer.

What does Tolstoy suggest? First, you can see the writer, the artist, as a person who experiences things—an event, a momentary flash of time, an action performed or observed, a thought—things that arouse a feeling in him. The writer stores that experience, that feeling within him, and, in order to solidify it in words, he makes it happen again within himself at some later time.

Well, which children do not feel emotional responses to thousands of moments each day, do not lock those feelings within themselves, feelings rooted in the experiences of daily living? Those responses, the experiences, and the emotions that accompany them are a vital dimension of human existence. Combined, they are the earth from which good writing can blossom forth. Surely, your child shares with Tolstoy the origins of creative written expression. Not every child will write a *War and Peace;* but the raw materials—events and feelings, actions and emotions, experiences and reactions—on these, professional artists have no monopoly. Of course, the quality of the experience and the perception of it vary from person to person. Also, those particular experiences a person selects for storing vary from person to person. Thus, five people may share a common moment, but the perception of it, the depth of emotion it arouses, the permanence of the impression upon the mind and body remain unique in each individual.

In Tolstoy's scheme, the artist remembers the experience of some feeling. Then, his purpose is to transmit that feeling to someone else "by means of movement, lines, colors, sounds, or forms expressed in words."

Do you see the continuum? An experience that registers some feeling in the mind makes its imprint by means of the senses. The sounds, the smells, the colors and actions, the sensations of taste and touch provide the passageways for the emotional experience a person stores as memory. To transmit that experience to someone else he uses language that *conveys* those senses. I can illustrate this scheme visually.

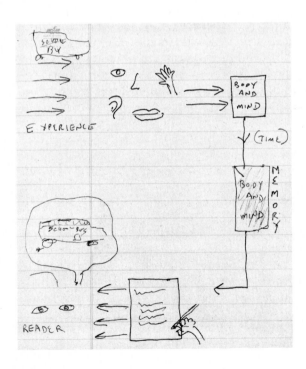

Your child might react to an experience on the school bus, an experience that evokes a feeling and impresses itself upon his mind. The paths the experience travels are the senses. Through the responses of eyes and nose, of hand and ears and mouth the moment registers. The experience takes on special qualities as it remains in storage. When the person translates this stored experience into written words, he conveys through language, as best he can, the same sensory responses that aroused the writer's reaction in the first place.

In finding the right language to portray that experienced emotion, there are wide differences from person to person. There's no promise here that in developing as a writer your son or daughter will capture the artistic skills of a Willa Cather, a Thomas Wolfe, a Leo Tolstoy. There is a promise, though, that given his or her own strengths in confronting daily life and in the use of language, your child can grow and experience success.

Autobiography: The Child's Experience

Going through life, as most children do, with a normal set of sense organs—going through life, *alive,* really—assures a range of experiences and emotions that mark the mind and heart. By using words daily, children develop an endless reserve of language, poised to record feelings, thoughts, and events on paper. A child who looks at his mother rushing off to work in a whirl of red and blue and waving good-by from the doorway; a child who hears the beep of a horn, the squawk of a jay, the scream of thunder; a child who feels sand burn her fingers, who presses a snowflake to her cheek; a child who smells trout frying or breathes in the scent of pine or of the sea or of fumes from a bus on a summer morning, that's your child. And that's a writer waiting to grow.

You can tell that the focus here on written expression suggests a different sense of "creative writing" from the usual one. Most people (especially teachers, for some reason) mean "imaginative" writing when they say "creative." Often in assigning imaginative writing, the teacher asks the child to record some pretend situation. I have read about "My Voyage with Columbus" or "What It's Like to Travel in Outer Space." It's not that I have complaints about imaginative writing (I'll describe some enjoyable activities of that sort later on) as *one* part of the developing writer's program. But to stress it at the expense of writing about personal experience is to turn away from the basic stuff of creativity.

A better synonym for creative writing is "autobiography." Those countless moments in an individual's life—brief, intense stretches of time—stud a child's day and glitter in his mind like diamonds long after the moments pass. By recalling those moments of experience through sensory language—specific, exact, sharply drawn—the young writer can practice the vital skills of writing. So, when I speak of creative writing, I shall mean "autobiographical," my basic philosophy being that you should mine the riches of experiences in every child's world, riches for the pen or pencil to transform into record. In this scheme the parent has a critical role.

The Parent Sets the Stage

The parents set the stage in the home for children to share their experiences, comfortably, and without fear, ridicule, or criticism. This sharing begins with speaking. You need to encourage the youngster, without prying, to talk about moments he wishes to share. "What did you do at school today?" "What did you do outside?" "Who did you talk to on the bus?" Questions like these will start things off. Such talking sessions will provide a pressure valve for the complex events in your child's life as he grows older. In homes where children feel free to examine their experiences, deep, underlying questions and problems can surface in the course of easy conversation. Sadly, in many homes there is not even a possibility for interchange about daily experiences.

However, if you've tried these talk sessions with your youngsters, you know that you can sometimes draw a blank. You might get a one-word response: "Nothing" or "Nobody" or "No." Or, you might get a brief answer without much substance: "I had a fight with Johnny"; "We drew pictures"; "Lisa showed me a frog"; "Mrs. Harris showed us an experiment." What do you do then?

Your first effort should be to draw out the details, to have the child flesh out the story in his or her own language. First show your interest, framing questions whose answers will draw out the experience and its emotions in the child's language. "A fight!" you might say. "Where did it happen? What about? You must tell me all about it!" or "Well, I can't remember when I saw a frog last! What did it look like? What sounds did it make?" Taking cues from the child's narrative, you can ask occasional questions. Show great concern for the details, especially those which demand the child's recall of the sensory experience; ask questions to elicit those details. You want to

know about colors, about sounds things make, about move-
ments and actions, smells and touch sensations, about the
exact words people say. Ask when things took place—afternoon,
morning, before lunch, at recess—because it will help the
child's inner eye to focus upon the moment which he is now
putting into language. The youngest child thrills in giving
these details, and with a little encouragement will even act out
responses. A child who hops about the room with glee when
asked how the frog moves would earn my applause; and then I
would ask, "How would you tell someone who couldn't see you
just how it moves?" I'd hope to hear "He hops" or "He flip-
flops" or "He bounces." What solid, sharp actions! If I heard
"He moves" or "He walks," I'd try to reach out for more exact
words. In later chapters, I'll talk about ways to develop precise
language.

As soon as your child can speak about experiences, you'll
want to begin this kind of creative questioning. At two or three
or four years, the child begins to sharpen the powers of observation that are so critical to effective writing. An awareness
of sensory detail is one of the essential skills you can help your
child to develop. Later as a young man or young woman he or
she will learn of other kinds of details—quotations from reli-
able people, statistics from reputable sources, case studies,
paraphrases from books or magazines—and will adapt these
new details easily to an already established pattern in the
development of ideas.

Mothers and Fathers as Storytellers

If your child does not readily communicate the details of a
particular moment, you yourself must turn storyteller. This
will take pressure off the child, who may feel suddenly intimi-
dated by your request—no matter how gentle—for the story.
Sometimes the emotions evoked by an experience arouse more
pain in the recalling of it than it did during the actual occasion. Back off. Tell your own story, alive in action and setting.
"So you saw a fight, too! Well, I saw two men screaming at each
other this afternoon, right in front of McDonald's. The rain had
turned everything wet and sticky. Well, an old man backed his
Chevy into a new white Oldsmobile. Then a teen-ager in a plaid
shirt leaped out of the Olds and slammed the door. 'Why don't
you watch where you're going, you old goat!' he boomed. 'You
little dummy,' the driver of the Chevy screamed from behind
the steering wheel. 'Why did you park in front of the hydrant?'
Fortunately, a police officer strode up to settle things before

they got ugly!" As you speak, call up your own dramatic energies, changing voices to show how people talk, lacing the tale with whatever excitement, or sadness, or joy it might evoke. In this kind of telling, concrete details set an example for similar experience-sharing by the child. Name places and people (where you can) carefully. Use words that suggest clear actions. Mention colors and sounds and use words for touch sensations. These stories establish a framework and act as models for the child. Using the kind of questioning I recommended you use when the youngster offers *his* story, you can establish a general sense of the quality of details that a good piece of writing usually advances. By supporting the value of the child's experience, you will help remove an impediment to writing I see every day in the classroom: "Nothing interesting ever happens to me" or "I have nothing to write about."

If you need a formula for the kind of atmosphere that leads to effective writing, it is: speak-listen-write. Remember: experience is the heart of creative expression.

4

Pictures, Words, and Sentences:

Laying Foundations

Words and the Young Artist

A child's early attempts at conveying sensory impressions spread out as splashes of line and color on a page. In crayon, pencil, colored pencil, or ink youngsters portray a vision of reality unique to their perceptions and their talents. At first the scribbles and scrawls, the wide arcs, the concentrations of design propose a shapeless landscape of color and texture; then, bit by bit, the components fit together into some partially recognizable whole. There you see a bird with an oversized wing, a beak like a broomstick, one leg; here stands a house, next to a child who is twice as large as the building and spectacular, for an arm shoots from her neck. Next, in a sunburst of light and swirls of red, yellow, green, orange and gold, there is a thing with ears whose crossed eyes look gloomily beyond your shoulder. If your child has easy access to the tools of writing, these scrawls will fill numerous pages, and you'll probably run out of space to hang these little gems. But in how many drawings—especially those created by your two- and three-year-olds—can you actually name the general intent of the artwork, to say nothing of its specific parts?

When, with a flourish, your young artists present their latest works, there's another opportunity to put into practice the principles I outlined earlier, the speak-listen-write approach to creative expression. Don't be one of those parents who, afraid of hurting the child's feelings, only praises and never ventures a "What is it?" about the latest artwork. Of course, it's the way in which the question is asked that determines the nature of the response. But asked without impatience and without a suggestion that the child is either wrong or untalented, a "What is it?" often unlocks a glorious stream of narrative, filled with colors and sounds and glimpses of action that only a child can see. Questions that show interest and which urge a solid attention to details help the child sustain the narration and expand the delight a parent can harvest from the moment. "Why is this boy bending over?" "Where's the driver of that bus?" "Why are there no leaves on that oak tree?" Listen carefully to the responses. Never chide the child for not portraying a person or object in an expected way. Here in the explanation of a picture, your child is sharing an event that marked his consciousness. The youngster's pictures and stories offer snapshots of the child's vision and psychology. Trained counselors can learn a good deal about a child's personality—his problems, talents, fears, and successes—from the pictures that he draws. For you the pictures are yet another starting point for writing activities.

Pictures and Words: Making Connections

In these little talks about some drawing, you establish a critical connection between the picture and the word as means to convey experience. Probably you have begun to caption your child's artistic efforts with a word or two. Like the sign-making activity, this helps to reinforce his reading skills. As you write the word "house" or "girl" or "bicycle" above or below the object, you help the youngster to build his sight vocabulary. You also establish the need for written language early in the communication process. At first, you go ahead and write the words (just one or two for each picture, no more), asking the child to letter just below yours. Later on, when the child knows the letters, encourage him to write the word as he speaks it, helping him with the sounds.

Ultimately your son or daughter will connect picture and word. You'll notice, after a while, that the child will add labels of his own. The degree of correctness for the three-, four-, and five-year-old is not of much concern here. Your first reaction to the child's own attempts at lettering a word should be to offer praise. Read the word or words your youngster writes. He'll love to hear your voice reading it. If you can't read the word, ask the child to read it for you. If the letters are way off target, after praising the effort say something like, "I see what you *tried* to write, but your letters are not quite right. Let me show you how to write that word." With the child's permission, print carefully on the picture (otherwise use a separate sheet of paper). Then ask the youngster to write the word from your model and to read it from his own writing.

But if the words the child attempts, despite errors, convey their message clearly, hang the picture up without fussing over correctness. Remember, you're still building positive attitudes toward writing as a means of self-expression. Do not make the child self-conscious about errors at this stage. You're going to have to use your judgment here—when to make suggestions for correcting incorrect language, when to say nothing. But, on the whole, for the preschool youngster your basic goal is to establish attitudes. Once the child knows that words convey meaningful aspects of experience, correctness has a real purpose.

As I suggested earlier, the drawings and the words, which expand and enrich the meaning of the drawing, provide an outlet for the child's concerns. When we decided to sell our Long Island home, we greeted an endless stream of possible buyers. Melissa, not yet in kindergarten, tried on her own to represent the event in drawing and in words:

In talking with her about the picture, my wife and I learned that she had not really understood what selling a house meant. "Who will sleep in my bed when they buy the house? May I take my toys?" Melissa asked. We tried to clear up her misunderstandings, which might have smoldered unnecessarily. Of course, in the words she wrote, we paid no attention to the errors (those vowel combinations plague children straight through the fifth and sixth grades). As parents, we were full of praise for her independent efforts, grateful to talk about a problem our daughter revealed through pictures and words.

Accent on Sentence Sense

As soon as you feel that your son or daughter has a reasonable sense of letters and sounds (this sense can begin as early as three, depending upon the exposure to language and to alphabet skills), you want to move the child from the use of single words to the use of full sentence captions. This is another stage in the young writer's development. Though the one- or two-word statement may have value as a caption, it is insufficient in establishing the range of information that a sentence can offer. The sentence names a subject, certainly; but it also tells what that subject is doing or what is being done to that subject. It communicates a series of details that expand and alter a basic idea.

The earlier you can help your child establish a "sentence sense," the fewer the problems in complete expression later on. One of the major writing errors that starts early and persists well into college themes is the production of incomplete sentences. Though later chapters will explore correctness more fully, I want to spend a little time here in considering sentence sense, so that you have a realistic frame of reference as you plan to help your child. I don't think children in school receive enough attention in this area of their writing development.

Research into language patterns over the last few years indicates (believe it or not) that when people speak, they usually do speak complete and complex sentences. This idea challenges old notions that spoken language often lacks correct grammatical form. The very young child, of course, communicates in words and clusters of words that frequently lack the formal elements of correct sentences. But once the youngster feels comfortable with spoken language, you'll be impressed with his ability to form what we call "grammatical" sentences, sentences generally complete in their construction. One of my colleagues tells her students that they are incredible sentence machines, that they know grammar much better than they think they do. This knowledge can help you establish an approach at home: Don't assume that the child cannot construct complete sentences, because all evidence suggests that he can.

You are not trying to teach him what he already knows. But you will attempt to offer practice in *writing* complete sentences so that the child extends his skill in speaking to the page and develops a sixth sense for *written* grammatical language. Despite the child's ability to speak grammatical sentences, writing complete ideas with correct punctuation turns into a game of chance, and the sentence becomes something permanent, which the immature writer shudders to change.

Of course, in daily speech both children and adults frequently use incomplete sentences:

> "Hi, Margarita!"
> "Hi, Beverly. Where's your brother?"
> "Sick in bed."
> "Why?"
> "Oh, nothing terrible. Just a bad cold."
> "Too bad."
> "Yeah. No football practice."

In the dialogue above, one can argue that there is only one complete sentence: "Where's your brother?" Part of the very nature of spoken communication—its speed, its demand for immediate response, its request for action, its dependency upon questions —insists upon fragmentary utterances. Certainly, there's nothing terribly *wrong* with speaking in fragments as part of everyday conversation.

The interesting thing, however, is that not many fragments on children's papers resemble those you might hear in daily speech. The fragment I most often see is one in which the writer has lopped off an incomplete unit from a complete one. He's cut off a dog's tail and is telling everyone that it's a dog, too. Some people contend that a child's writing contains many incomplete ideas because he is used to hearing speech fragments, but I've not seen enough proof of that to convince me.

When children begin to read, they will be exposed to incomplete sentences in written language. The signs that surround them—*Exit, No smoking, Sale*—though clear enough to convey information, are not complete sentences. In their attempts to catch the eye quickly and to sear an idea or a product into the mind, newspaper and magazine ads scream out "Newest, fastest way to order"; "Value event"; "Right now . . . Movie Flights to Florida Only on Airline X." This stylistic use of fragments undoubtedly makes an impression on inexperienced writers. Certainly newspaper headlines and magazine ad copy read like the kinds of incomplete sentences I have seen on children's papers.

In spite of their abundant use in our spoken and written language, fragments do not earn respect as examples of correct and mature writing. One of the certain ways for your high-school- or college-aged son or daughter to fail an English course is to write essays that contain sentence fragments! Teaching students how and why to avoid sentence fragments and how to correct them are a teacher's constant chore in the classroom.

Parents should encourage children to speak about their own pictures and, through questioning, invite them to express whole thoughts in full-sentence responses. When the child's statement does not name a person or an object; when it does not tell what that person or object is doing, ask for more information. I know that questions by their very nature invite incomplete responses; and I know it's perfectly legitimate to speak in fragments—everyone does it and gets along fine in communicating ideas. I suggest, however, that we prod our children to speak complete sentences. This is not to tell them they're doing something *wrong*, but to provide them with speech models that they can use later in writing. For this reason, good teachers, knowing the value of the complete sentence, insist on oral responses that express complete thoughts. I don't think that enough teachers pursue this goal with any vigor. Also, a good part of their students' lack of attention stems from the teacher's poor questioning techniques. Too often teachers ask questions whose answer can be only *yes* or *no*. When teachers do this, they prevent children from making sustained responses.

Avoiding Bits and Pieces

In grade schools, on bulletin boards, in hallways, in rooms, in scrapbooks made by children, and on notebook pages, you can often see incomplete statements accompanying illustrations. I once saw a beautiful series of Bible pictures that were drawn and colored by children. Each picture included a few words about the illustration and when hung alongside each other they told the story of Joseph and the coat of many colors. The drawback was that some of those captions were sentence fragments. For example, the words above a picture of wonderful brown camels laden with packs and accompanying men in red, green, and yellow robes read: "Going across the desert." That's not a full sentence! There is no subject. It doesn't tell who is making the journey. Nor do we have the words *are* or *were* to accompany *going*, words required to make the sentence grammatically correct. I could determine those missing details by looking at the picture, but that vital information necessary to the structure of the sentence should appear in the caption. Furthermore, from the lower grades on, students are taught that all sentences start with a capital and end with a period. By putting a capital letter "G" on the word *going* and a period after *desert,* the teacher reinforces the student's incorrect belief that this fragment is a complete sentence.

Now you may argue that a statement accompanying a child's picture is a title and, as such, does not need a complete sentence. If so, then the title should have capital letters for the beginning of each major word: "Going Across the Desert."

Certainly, it is important to learn to write titles for pictures, paragraphs, and, later on, stories and essays. It's a good starting point, as I have illustrated, for young writers. However, I believe that in our attempts to develop skills, title-writing often does more harm than good. By its fragmentary nature, the title does not encourage the idea of the complete sentence as the key element in clear writing. Inexperienced writers often use titles unwisely. Instead of using the title as an invitation to read on, a young writer will often depend on it as a part of the composition itself. For example, in a piece called "My Saddest Morning," a child may begin his first paragraph, "It all happened one day last June." Instead of establishing the point of the essay in the writing itself, the young writer refers immediately to the title.

I am suggesting that you move your child away from those one- or two-word titles. When he or she begins writing words to accompany pictures, encourage the preparation of a complete statement. You can look at a picture such as the "House for Sale" illustration on page 26 and say, "Whose house is this that's for sale?"

"Ours."

"See if you can speak a sentence that tells what your picture is trying to show."

You may very well get: *Our house is for sale* or *This is our house for sale* or *We are selling our house.* If you do, with the child's permission, write the sentence directly on the drawing. Say the words as you print them; then encourage the child to say the words. Better still, help the child write the sentence himself. If you do not get a sentence response at all, *you* offer the sentence.

Another way to help children develop skills in speaking and writing full sentences is to remind them to use words from your question in a response. When you say, "What is this a picture of?" about an illustration and the response is "A house," you can say, "Come on, Beverly. This time tell me in a whole sentence. Use some of my words if you want to. Let's try again. What is this a picture of?" You might hear, "This is a picture of a house." No matter how impatiently the child offers that complete thought, praise it, and get it on paper!

I worked this way with my daughter, Melissa, on her little stick drawing that appears below (she was barely three and a half for this one).

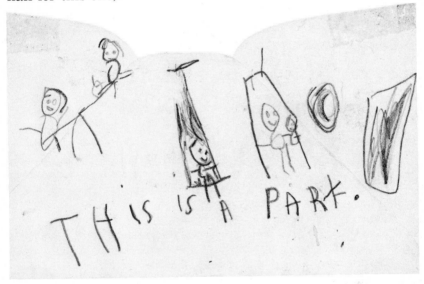

"When I asked her what the picture was, she answered, "A park." (The picture really did become clearer when she pointed out the see-saw on the left, the child on the slide next to it, the big girl and little girl on the swings, the ball, and the sandbox.) Using the kinds of questions mentioned above I managed to get the complete sentence: "This is a park." With my help over the rough spots, Melissa wrote the sentence herself. She printed in all capitals, so I didn't mention that a capital letter should open a sentence. But I did call attention to the period at the end. To this day she loves making that dot at the end of a sentence!

Imagine my delight in seeing this independent effort of Melissa's before her fourth birthday. For days, she questioned me about her imminent annual visit to the doctor because it included, as she recalled from her last birthday checkup, a finger-prick to draw blood for testing. I comforted her as best I could but, as usual, she needed to work this one out for herself. On the morning of the visit I found her at her desk with this before her:

At first I thought she had jumbled some letters together. But she explained: "I took my baby to the doctor and she was sad. The doctor wrote on his pad 'Do not be sad' and gave it to her. So she felt better."

The point I made earlier, that creative effort provides a pressure valve for the child, a means of confronting and working out pressures, fears, and doubts, certainly holds true in this drawing and its supporting language (notice the line under each eye in the figure on the left—tears!). Although the words run together without space between them, they spell out a sentence. Correct vowels do *not* appear, except in one case. This happens because the vowel, alone or in combination, offers such a wide variety of sound possibilities that it is troublesome to a child. In some words the vowel has no sound at all but serves merely as a bridge between other letters.

Despite its problems, this picture and sentence stand as an independent effort by a three-year-old. I want to point out what I see as its strongest features: First the letters representing consonants are all correct: the *d, n, t, b, s, d.* Next, the words offer a full sentence. Without any systematic exposure to sentence sense, Melissa might simply have penciled *happy* over the left picture and *sad* over the right. However, she revealed the fullness of the experience she was attempting to convey in the sentence she wrote. Here, in a nutshell, are all the possibilities for an entire narrative. If I wanted to help Melissa expand the picture and sentence into a paragraph, this production would offer lively results. But the most remarkable quality of this creation is that it suggests an awareness of written language as an important means of communicating experience. Here the sentence works along with the picture, acting as a commentary on it. No simple labeling of parts in a drawing, the words represent an attempt to go beyond the limits of visual representation by using a written statement. A sense of the power of words and sentences is exactly the kind of awareness that you can help your child build.

Scissors, Paste, and Sentences
Whenever you can, try to encourage your sons and daughters to write sentences that tell the ideas behind the pictures they have made. I have talked about drawings because they often grow from a child's spontaneous doodling. More formal attempts, such as finger painting, watercolors, and cut-and-paste creations, are also good starting points for written language, especially for the child who draws reluctantly or too self-consciously.

Every child enjoys cutting pictures out of newspapers and magazines and then pasting these cutouts on sturdy paper to make collages. You should encourage this activity. "Why don't you cut out the prettiest room you can find?" or "Cut out as many pictures of red things as you can" or "Go through the magazine and cut out the things you find that start with the *b* sound." After the child's artistic effort is complete, listen for a sentence response to your "What is it?" question and try to get the child's verbal statement in his own handwriting on paper. Help the child write a full sentence underneath his work: "This is a large happy room" or "These things are all red" or "All these things start with *b*." You can relate this activity to holidays, seasons or months of the year, parties or celebrations, special events at home or at school.

As the child grows older, the possibilities for relating visual and written communication expand. Pamela, one of my students, submitted an exciting photo essay to me. She cut pictures out of magazines and mounted each one in an order she had determined. She placed the photos in a sturdy binder and

wrote a title on the cover: "Life in Harlem's Ghetto." Each picture captured a moment of Harlem, its humor, anguish, ugli-
ness, and delight. The assignment required only the visual
component. Later on I intended to ask the students to write
about their pictures. But Pamela needed immediately to clarify
the meaning of the picture. On the back of each photograph she
wrote an explanation. For a picture of buildings blanketed in
smoke and showing tangled hoses stretching like tentacles
from firetrucks she wrote: "Buildings are so ruined and just get
burned down." Another photograph was of a boy of twelve or
thirteen, who had a wide gash in his forehead; he stood beside
a policeman who gripped the boy's plaid jacket. The caption
was: "Some rob, steal, and kill to make it." The last picture in
the sequence of twenty-one shows a man in a leather jacket on
a rainy night. He sits like a heap of junk in a wire refuse pail
on a nameless Harlem street corner. Pamela's caption reads:
"Loneliness, problems, depression, lost, 'I can't seem to find the
way out.' "

I recommend the photo essay as a wonderful activity for parent and child on a rainy afternoon. It's the kind of creative play
that, once begun, holds a boy's or girl's interest. First talk
about some overriding theme for the project—"violence in the
city," "spring is here." "Christmas is a happy time"—and then
suggest that the child write one sentence to offer the main idea
of each picture. If you have an old tin box of family pictures,
or if you encourage your youngsters to use cameras to take
their own photographs or slides, this creation will be great fun!

Seeing the Skill Advance
Once you help your child rely upon full sentences to convey information, you will, no doubt, observe some interesting things.
First the youngster will want to squeeze more and more verbal
information into one sentence. If he or she does, you can suggest the use of two or three sentences rather than stringing
together ideas with "ands." Here, five-year-old Melissa prints
two thoughts in separate sentences (see facing page).

There is a great deal of activity in this picture: two children
(Melissa on the right, she insists, because *she's* wearing the
bikini); the lifeguard in the middle; one child in a face-down
float. Our question and answer session led to the first sentence;
it tells the basic idea of the drawing. The second sentence is
rather complex and describes the most important detail, from
the child's point of view. Melissa was eager to write the sentences you see (I helped with spelling and with working out

THIS IS A SWimming Lesson.
I WAS AFRAID TO GO
UNDER FOR PENNIES.

sounds); but she quickly lost interest and rushed off to play. Had she remained, I would have helped her turn other parts of the picture into sentences that build a narrative. Later on you'll see how a similar drawing can set the ground plan for a more sustained writing effort.

It's interesting to notice that a child who learns to use sentences early and to rely upon sentences as the key means of conveying information soon tends to subordinate pictures to verbal expression, rather than the other way around. Earlier, I showed how the child tries to convey his messages through pictures, and how you can help build sentences from the pictorial elements. Now look at parts of a little book made by five-year-old Matthew. He tells his story in sentences, but draws only one page of illustration. First he writes "Matthew and Rachel can run." On the next page he states "Matthew can run faster than Rachel." The next two facing pages look like this:

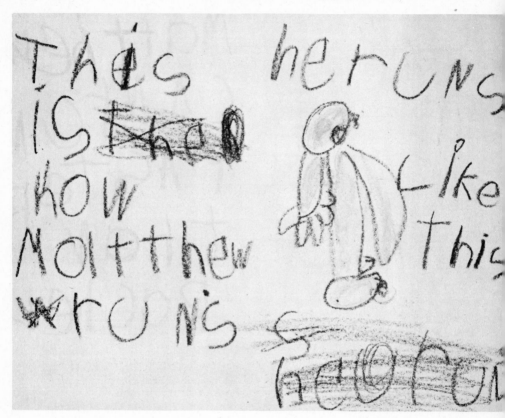

Matthew uses drawing to supplement his writing. We cannot tell just what special features of his running the picture attempts to dramatize, but clearly, he sees the picture as a way to demonstrate some action or event for which he does not have the right words. It is that tendency to pictorialize that you want to tap in order to develop your child's writing skills. With your help the youngster will move from a *drawn* description of his story to a *verbal* description in writing.

The child will learn to use words to create written snapshots of actions, events, and details.

5

The Senses at Play:

Images As Building Blocks

Sense Words Up Front

In this chapter I'd like to tell you how you can help your child use pictorial language by developing his *sense* vocabulary.

You'll need the following definitions: *Sense words* or *sensory language* or *sensory detail* mean words that convey sense impressions: sound, smell, sight (color and action), touch, and taste. Words like *boom* or *whisper, musty* or *piney, squirm* or *leap, orange* or *violet, hard* or *wet, sweet* or *salty* appeal to the reader's senses. For some of the senses it's a simple matter to find word-equivalents for real sensations. Perhaps sound is the easiest to capture because the English language has an enormous variety of words for naming sounds. There are not only words like *shout* and *explode* and *cough*—words for sounds— but also words that make the sounds they name, like *woosh* and *buzz* and *bark* and *click*. Words for color and action similarly fill the language, as do words for touch sensations, though to a lesser degree. Words that name smells are less abundant, and those for taste sensations are the least available.

When I speak of *concreteness,* I mean the degree to which a word names, specifically, the thing it represents. It's clear among these three word choices which is most specific: plant, flower, rose.

Plant names a large and very general group. *Flower* helps narrow down the plant group by excluding vegetables, nonflowering shrubs, many trees, vines, and weeds, and so on. But *rose* is the most exact of the words, the most "concrete," the word that has the sharpest visual quality. Write *flower* and readers need to make their own choices—one person sees a daisy, one a chrysanthemum, another a tulip. Good writers want readers to form exact visual connections, to see things precisely in the way the writers see them. They do not want to allow readers their own selections. After all, it's the *writer's* experience and vision that must be conveyed.

When a single word is expanded upon and modified in order to heighten its specificity, I call that *concrete sensory detail*. By using highly specific sensory language a writer can intensify the picture-taking quality of words. Look at the levels of concreteness in these three attempts at word pictures:

1.	2.	3.
a rose	a yellow rose	a dry yellow rose drooping in a crystal vase

In 1, although the writer by avoiding the word *flower* or some other general word succeeds in limiting the impression, the word *rose,* nonetheless, lacks detail. The reader has an incomplete picture. In 2, the scene expands somewhat with a single appeal to the sense of sight: *yellow* adds a dimension of color that insists upon one color of rose only. (After reading 1, how many of you saw a *red* rose?) Yet in 3 the most complete word picture appears: *dry* names a sensation of touch; *drooping* puts forth a clear, specific sight impression; *crystal vase* sets a location, and the word *crystal* offers an appeal to sight, even touch, if you consider the bumps and lines that mark the surface of such a container.

Through the power of concrete sensory detail the *image* asserts itself. An image is a picture in words, a language snapshot alive in sensory appeal. A successful image creates a clear and exact scene in the mind, leaving no doubt about the author's intent. Smells, sounds, and sensations of touch and taste are just as essential as the visual dimension when advancing specific details of an *image*. It's possible to take the concrete word picture in 3 and expand it into an image of even more concreteness:

In a shadow on the dresser sat a dry yellow rose, drooping in a crystal vase.

A writer who is aiming to capture the essence of a place or an event could expand that sentence to a few sentences, a paragraph, or to several pages, each line striving for sharp images. For example:

> He stood at the edge of her bedroom, a floorboard moaning at his shoe, the scent of her everywhere, lonely and troubled. He knew her by the smell: a light whiff of lemon soap; and then in a winter draft from the window above the bed, perfume, chill and sharp, all the scents from the bottles on the silver tray mixing, suddenly, then vanishing. "Carol?" He coughed, its echo stealing off swiftly. As he stepped into the room he felt on his tongue a thick, sweet taste, something determined, yet frail and fading. And there, there in a shadow on the dresser sat a dry yellow rose, drooping in a crystal vase.

Joseph Conrad, one of the masters of sensory detail and one of the best English novelists, shows how imagery is basic to a writer's purpose; in the preface to *The Nigger of the Narcissus* (1897) he writes: "My task which I am trying to achieve is, by the power of the written word to make you hear, to make you feel—it is before all, to make you *see*. That—and no more, and it is everything." In its intent to present something exactly as the writer perceives it, the image that is strong in concrete sensory detail is everything indeed.

Children are awake to the sensory world; they respond to it, they internalize images of it long before learning the language that will recall it from memory. When naming things for your toddler, right from the start, you must try to find the exact word for an object; *le seul mot juste* as Balzac would say. When reaching out and touching a *leaf,* a child should hear that word along with *flower* or *plant.* The child should hear you say *robin* or *sparrow* as well as *bird,* when he or she hears and sees the flap of wings outside his window. As you help your youngster of five or six to write the word for an object in a picture, help the child find the most precise expression: *elm, bakery, Park Road, skirt* all name more specifically than *tree, building, street,* or *clothing.* In writing there is a magic about naming—especially using proper names—that involves the reader instantly: *Cricklewood Drive, Kings Highway, Hout's Department Store, Grand Central Station* weave a spell that *street, highway, department store,* and *train station* cannot.

Four Writing Games and Variations
After early writing activities like the ones I discussed in previous chapters, you should encourage the use of specific language

by using some of the following games at home. These games can be played with children of seven, eight, and older, depending upon the difficulty of the game and the progress of the youngster.

- *The "What's the Best Word?" Game.* The purpose in this activity is to pick a word that most *exactly* names a particular object. You can do this with real objects or with pictures in a magazine. For example, you might say "Okay, Maria, let's play a word game. I'll point to something in your room and say two words. You tell which word names exactly what the thing is. Ready? *Furniture. Desk.*" Ask her to explain the choice, though it might be a while before she can communicate to you the notion of "general" or "specific." Help the child see that a word such as *furniture* can mean many different things and that *desk* is the better word, because it names precisely what the object is. Below are some other groups of words that move from the general to the specific. Expand the group to three as your child advances in skill.

	I	II	III
1.	fruit	apple	
2.	toy	top	
3.	room	kitchen	
4.	cereal	oatmeal	
5.	book	dictionary	
6.	food	vegetable	carrot
7.	liquid	drink	milk
8.	vehicle	automobile	jeep
9.	meat	beef	hamburger
10.	medicine	pill	aspirin

This is not an easy game, but it's worth your efforts. Even though writing is not involved at this point, the child begins to learn that written language should strive to be as exact as possible. When the child wants to write, scramble the groups, adding where you can, and ask the youngster to copy the words in order, starting with the most general and going to the most exact:

food
↓
vegetable
↓
carrot

Ask for a drawn illustration of the most specific item, to rein-force the precision of the word you're stressing. For *food,* there are too many possibilities; for *vegetable* a choice, too; only *carrot* gives the specific clue to the reader. If you have time to write a separate card for each word, ask the child to arrange the cards consecutively, putting the most specific item last.

An easier variation of this game is to make a list of some general objects (such as *furniture, flower, tree, candy, book, drink, jewelry, toy*) and, as you read them one at a time, ask the child to write down on a sheet of paper a specific example or two of each. Show how to do the first one so there's no con-fusion, and help sound-out and spell the words.

Writing each general object on a separate card allows you or some other person (perhaps another child) to play along. Read one item and have the child write a more specific word; then the youngster will read the general word and you write down the example.

• *The "Name the Action" Game.*   Words for actions also can be named with varying degrees of exactness. You want to help the child to develop a sensitivity to the way some words capture action more exactly than others. This is partly a vocabulary-building activity; but children of all ages have at their command language that names action. Words such as *walk* and *move* can be replaced by much clearer verbs: *run, hop, hurry, trip,* are just a few. I put the word "to be" in all its forms *is, was, were, are, am,* first on a list of culprits that offer especially weak pictures. These are words essential to any vocabulary, but for effective writing they should not be over-used. Some others on the list are: *go, get, have, begin, seems, appears*—for every one of these a word with a more clearly named action will improve the visual connection.

Use the child's innate ability with action language to set up some "Name the Action" games. This one is fun for groups of children: On separate slips of paper write the words for pre-cise actions: *skip, dance, hop, wiggle, jump, drag, crawl, tumble,* and others. Fold the papers and put them in a shoebox or hat. A child chooses a slip from the box and reads the word on it silently. You can help out in a whisper, if necessary. The child then moves across the room and tries to perform the action the word suggests. The other children try to guess the word and write it down. This game works very well even with much older children where the vocabulary is more difficult: *amble, stroll, zip, zig-zag, slink, steal.* With this game it's also possible to teach the child that some words mean the same thing on the surface, but have different qualities. For example, *flee, race,* and *hurry* all mean *to run* in some way, yet each one brings to mind a special idea. *Flee* suggests escape; *race* makes one think of a sport; and *hurry* implies the need to meet a deadline.

• **The "Build an Image" Game.**   This game develops the child's skill at expanding a word by adding details. Start with simple words that add to the sensory appeal of an object, then move to building sentences of high concrete detail.

Examine one word at a time, helping your child to build images in several stages, beginning with the name of an object. You can do it in three columns:

1. Word	2. Add a Color	3. Add a Touch Word
sweater	green sweater	green woolen sweater
table	brown table	hard brown table
sink		
rug		
apple		

If necessary, help the child add the words in columns 2 and 3. Of course you can vary the column headings for different kinds of sensory details:

Word	Add a Smell or Touch	Add a Sound or Color
apple	cold apple	cold crunchy apple

The child shouldn't pile up descriptive words in front of the object; two or three are enough. Later on, introduce a model such as this one, but encourage the child to use descriptive words before and after the object:

Word	Add Color or Other Sight Word	Add a Touch Word	Add a Sound or Smell or Action in a Group of Words
pencil	yellow pencil	smooth yellow pencil	smooth yellow pencil *racing across a page*
sparrow	brown sparrow	cold brown sparrow	cold brown sparrow *peeping on the roof*
orange	wrinkled orange	dry wrinkled orange	dry wrinkled orange *with a bitter smell*

Above, the words in italics have added sensory details to the image; but the details do not cluster in front of the object being described. In the first two groups, the added details start with a word ending in *ing*. In the third group, *with* is a position word that shows relationships (called a *preposition* in grammatical terms) and opens the describing group. If you show them examples, eight- or nine-year-olds should have little trouble following instructions like these: "Now, before you put anything in this last column, try to add the information by beginning with a word that ends in *ing,* for example, *laughing, dancing,* or *peeping.*" Or, "Let's add the details by beginning with a word, such as *with, on, by, near,* or *in.*" Make sure that you can come up with details to fit the object if the child has any question about it—not all words lend themselves to these kinds of describing elements.

After the child has done five or six examples, have him select one and illustrate it on a separate page, writing the description above or below the picture he makes.

Examples are important to this learning procedure. Whenever the youngster practices writing, try to show what someone else wrote about the same thing. That will let the child see how easy or difficult the task is. I've included numerous models in this book, which you can show your children. These examples have been written by young writers like your sons and daughters.

The image games I just described are muscle builders, ways for parents to help inexperienced writers practice turning their observations into language.

Now I want to move toward writing complete sentences that are rich in sensory detail.

   • *The "Sentence Building" Game.* As one of the first activities here, I suggest the changing of an image in the third column in any of the image-building games I recommended earlier. This gives you an excellent opportunity to compare fragments of sentences to whole sentences. Make a fourth column to allow the child to build a full sentence.

I	II	III	IV
Word	Add a Smell or Touch	Add a Sound or Color	Make a Sentence
apple	cold apple	cold crunchy apple	I bit a cold crunchy apple.

or:

I	II	III	IV
table	brown table	hard brown table	I touched the hard brown table.
			or
			The hard brown table stood in the kitchen.

or:

I	II	III	IV
sparrow	brown sparrow	cold brown sparrow	I heard a cold brown sparrow peeping on the roof.
			or
			A cold brown sparrow peeping on the roof flew suddenly away.

In these examples try to show the child the difference between the complete sentence and the grammatically incomplete image in columns I, II, and III. You should talk about the capital letter at the beginning and the period at the end of the complete sentence. Show that by expanding the image into a sentence, the writer has more opportunity to add sensory language. In the second sentence about the sparrow, the word *flew* adds visual dimension. Words like *fluttered, flapped,* or *screeched* would contribute the element of sound if added to the sentence.

In this way, you can aid the youngster of four or five to connect sense words with objects and actions in his or her own world. Plan some activity that will relate language to art. Pick a word that suggests a sensory response; a color such as *red, blue,* or *orange;* a touch word such as *soft* or *rough;* a taste word such as *sweet* or *salty;* an action or sound word such as *fast, noisy,* or *quiet.* Make a list of things that in the child's experience represent color, sound, action, smell, taste, and touch sensations. Ask the child what the word brings to mind. "What color is it?" or "How does it move?" or "What does it smell like?" so that each written item arouses a sensory picture. At first suggest five or six items, then more. (Older children can write their own lists; younger ones will need your help.)

Red

> a sweet, cold apple
> Joseph's frozen cheeks on a March morning
> my new velvet pants
> the numbers that flash on Daddy's clock
> the strawberry jam I spread on crunchy
>   whole-wheat toast

Notice in the example that each item offers details beyond the basic sense word "red," which *does not* appear in any image. If the youngster wants to use the basic word in an image, fine, but encourage him to find substitutes for the word: an older child might use *scarlet, maroon, ruby,* or *wine.*

After your child has produced a list of good sensory details, help him prepare a homemade book. Few games excite the youngster as much as the making of a book with a cover bearing the title and the child's name as author. Using the above list, supervise the creation of a book about red, called *My Book of Red Things* or simply *Red Things.* For each item on the list, the child will draw or cut and paste a representation of the image. At the top or bottom of each page the child should write a full sentence, such as: *Red is a sweet, cold apple.* The child should give each picture a sentence. You can see what a valuable game this is for the very young writer who might have had trouble putting words for images on paper. Using the list as a guide and your sentence as model, the child can create his own sentences by copying the information you helped him prepare.

Let him staple the pages together, and let him give his book to Mommy, Daddy, Grandma, or Grandpa.

Some children who enjoy rhyming can write little jingles of images built from sense words. Here are some rhymes from eight- and nine-year-olds:

> *What is Yellow?*
>
> *Yellow is the sun shining bright*
> *Yellow is an electric light*
> *Yellow is the lemon peel*
> *Yellow is how bright I feel*
>
> *What is Orange?*
>
> *Orange is a pumpkin bright*
> *Orange is a flame that glows at night*
> *Orange is the color of the burning sun*
> *Orange is the fruit that's good for everyone*

Notice how each line in the rhyme is a complete sentence. (I'll say more about poetry later.)

Other sentence-building games start with a complete sentence that has very little sensory concreteness. The child and parent expand the sentences in stages by adding details:

> The dog ran.

Add color and or/touch	1.	A furry brown dog ran away.
Add sound	2.	A furry brown dog ran away, barking noisily.
Name a place	3.	A furry brown dog, barking noisily, ran away down Allen Street.

Some child might suggest changing the word *ran* into a sound word in order to follow instructions. Encourage it! Writers always change words and move their positions. Notice, in sentence 3, the words *barking noisily* stand in front of the word *ran,* whereas in sentence 2 they come after the word *away.* The child will see that sentence elements often shift around and that writers play with words, moving them for their sense or sound or for special effects they might achieve. Thus, sentence 3 could also have been written:

Down Allen Street a furry brown dog ran away, barking noisily.
Barking noisily, a furry brown dog ran away down Allen Street.
Down Allen Street, barking noisily, a furry brown dog ran away.

The last two show higher degrees of complexity, sentences you'd most often find in the writing of children in their teens. Be aware of the fluid elements in a sentence, and encourage your child's experimentation with sentence parts before those teen-age years. I'll talk more about shifting and expanding sentence parts in Chapter 7, when I discuss sentence construction and correctness.

I'd like to suggest another expansion game here. In the "Sentence Staircase" the writer climbs down by adding or changing details to a base sentence. This is an excellent follow-up to what you've been doing with sense images, because it offers a little more challenge. Start with a simple idea and have the child add details according to the instructions alongside each step.

Sentence Staircase

A child played.

Describe the Child	A child *with brown eyes* played.
Tell When	A child with brown eyes played *one crisp winter morning.*
Name a Sound	*Giggling,* a child with brown eyes played one crisp winter morning.
Tell Where	Giggling *in front of his house,* a child with brown eyes played one crisp winter morning.
Use Other Specific Words	Giggling in front of his house, a *boy* with brown eyes *jumped up and down* one crisp winter morning.

With the final sentence you can help shift the parts around:

Giggling, a boy with brown eyes jumped up and down in front of his house one crisp winter morning.

In front of his house, a giggling boy with brown eyes jumped up and down one crisp winter morning.

In any case, the final sentence demonstrates the writer's sensory awareness. Aside from the sound word "giggling," which was specifically requested, he shows action (*jumped up and down*), touch (*cold*), and color (*brown* eyes). He has replaced more general words like *child* and *played* with more specific language.

Here are some simple sentences you might want to use in your "Sentence Staircase" game.

> A man worked.
> The book fell.
> A tree moved.
> The car drove away.
> A cloud passed by.
> A woman danced.
> A girl ran.
> The baby cried.
> The radio played.
> She pulled him.

You can also have fun with imagery in sentences about people or objects around the house. In each sentence your son or daughter should appeal to at least *two* senses with as much concreteness as possible. First, you write one about your son or daughter:

> Melissa squirms on the velvet chair in the living room and coughs into her small pink hand.

Give the child the paper on which you have written your sentence and ask him to read it aloud. Then ask him to write one about you. Here are some examples:

> *In the den Daddy snores on the couch while the fire in the fireplace crackles and turns his face red.*
>
> *The refrigerator hums noisily as I touch its cool silver handle.*
>
> *Mara licks her black paw and then purrs at me with her green eyes in slits.*

These are some good subjects to write about in a single sentence:

> a book
> the telephone
> a doll
> a child's shirt or dress

a closet door
a brother, mother, father, or sister
a neighbor
a pet
the sink
a piece of candy

Two Longer Efforts

For a longer exercise in using sensory detail have the child
practice writing riddles. The riddle should give details of the
object without naming it, so that someone else can guess what
the object is:

How to Write a Sense Riddle

1. Show how the thing moves or how people move
   when they use the thing.

2. Name colors that help us see the thing.

3. Tell the sounds it makes.

4. Tell what we would feel if we touched it.

5. Name a smell that might help us know more
   about it.

6. Do not name the object!

Here are two riddles as examples, the second one written by
an older writer:

This thing is silver and shiny. It has a black piece of plastic
near the top. You must push it down. It feels hot when you put
something in it. It makes a popping noise. It smells of bread.
What is it?

This smooth white rectangle sputters up Polo Road every
evening, with the clink of bells and squealing children down the
street. One youngster steps up to the rectangular object, holds
out a silver coin, and a man in a white hat swings open a door
with a thump. Curls of smoke wind out and the odor of chocolate
and strawberry and coldness fills the air.

In that first riddle about a toaster the conscientious parent
might help the child change his use of the pronoun "it," which
is repetitious. You might say, "Look at sentences 2 and 4. Can
you move some words from the end of each sentence to the
beginning?" Help the child to create sentences like the ones
below:

·   When you put something in it, it feels hot.
·   Near the top it has a black piece of plastic.

Here your attention to clear expression works along with your concern about effective sentences.

Next, have the child write about a scene, relying predominately on one or two senses to form this portrait. Although a writer uses all his senses in such a description, giving more attention to one sense heightens the impact of the picture and serves as a unifying element. Below, an inexperienced writer, barely in his teens, writes about the sounds of a show in which he performed. Note his effort to use color along with auditory detail:

On a sunny spring afternoon, as I waited to perform in a show at the Henry Street Playhouse on Grand Street in Manhattan, the flashing started from the foot and spotlights. People roared and clapped as the curtain drifted open with a small cling and clang. The flashes of yellow beams and orange shadowed themselves onto me. Then the rip and roar of a snappy kind of music echoed and started the purple flashes. The flashes struck, hit, and blinded but yet didn't flatten the lively music. Cling, clang, boom, it shattered, bursting as if everything finally broke loose. Then the click from the light board and red, blue, black, and green showered the stage as I leaped out onto it. The lights moved with fierceness. Then we jumped to heights unknown, swooshing and flying beyond the blur. Pain unbearable came on from a sudden fall in a leap and then suddenly faded away. A dim click broke the silence, then a roar, a smash, a crash, and it all broke loose again, then faded away slowly as before. Lightning legs spun wildly. Finally our flashing day ended as the curtain closed.

Comparisons for Solid Imagery

As speakers, children make comparisons instinctively—it's this movie as opposed to that one, this book instead of that, this restaurant as good as that one. Language relies upon comparison; it allows people to see one object in terms of another, helps them suggest resemblances for clarity and for impact, and sometimes infuses one object with the other's liveliness.

A *figure* is a comparison that helps to produce an image. *Figurative language* is language that compares things: one object is different from the other but a statement relates the two and produces a meaning or an effect that paints a new, vivid, picture.

Our everyday expressions are highly figurative. "He's building castles in the air" compares a dreamer to an engineer or a bricklayer. The comparison is improbable, and when you think of the disaster a castle in the air would be, you see how insubstantial is the dreamer's life—the comparison works! Slang terms like "She bugs me" or "He's a drip" set up comparisons that seem highly improbable, yet they work. Through overuse, comparisons become trite; they lose their ability to bring a picture instantly to the mind.

Children have a remarkable gift for figure. Their language shimmers with comparisons: "Billy ratted on me"; "Hey! Cut it out! I'm not your punching bag!"; "She looks like an old witch"; "Quit your bellyachin'!" "The fur is smooth as velvet"; "My milk is cold as ice."

In great literature and poetry, the good figure opens windows of thought through sensory detail. If you work with your child to develop techniques of comparison, you'll be pleased at the visual impressions he can create.

Any child can produce the comparison using *like* or *as* (called a *simile*). Write out some unfinished sentences, like those below, and have your youngster put in a word, or words, to complete the figure. Don't be surprised if some of the child's responses seem trite. Children haven't enough experience to recognize overused words and phrases. I suspect you'll be delighted at some of your child's precise uses of imagery. Below are responses you might hear from young children:

- She hopped like *a sleepy frog.*
- The bus shook from side to side like *a yellow horse.*
- The kitchen was quiet as *night.*
- My brother makes as much noise as *a hundred popping balloons.*
- The oaks moved like *tall angry men.*

In several of these, the use of sensory language heightens the visual quality of the comparison and therefore the image. You can see color and hear sound; you are given descriptions of emotion and settings. The use of comparison and the use of sense words combine to make a vivid picture.

Let your youngsters try to complete these comparisons:

- The wind blew like _____
- The car started up like _____
- She ran like _____
- When it snows (rains) on our street it's like _____
- He ate like _____

When writers treat nonliving or nonhuman objects as if they had human qualities they use a figurative technique called *personification*. Here the object is compared to a living thing. The writer is not saying "This *is like* this" but instead "This *behaves like* a person." (Notice the word *person* in *personify* and *personification*?) So we have:

> The wind *muttered* through the quiet oaks.
> A yellow floorboard *moaned* at his shoe.
> The morning sun *scattered* gold dust on the grass.

In all these cases a nonhuman object (*wind, floorboard, sun*) performs some task usually thought of as reserved for humans (*muttered, moaned, scattered gold*). Personification adds intense visual quality to an image.

Ask the nine-year-old (or older) to look at or to listen to the following ideas about familiar objects. (Change the proper names to suit things and places in your home or city.) Words in italics you can write in different color from the rest of the sentence.

- The refrigerator *made noise.*
- The light *went on.*
- Our door *opened.*
- A sparrow *flew* by.
- The maple tree *moved.*
- Our Chevy *starts* slowly in the morning.
- Fido *sits* as I open his can of dinner.
- The wind *is* on the desert.
- The crayon *fell* to the floor.
- The television *came on.*

Then say, "Pretend that each of those things moves or talks or acts like a person. Try to change the italicized words to words that show the object acting like a person. I'll do the first one." Next to each sentence in the list write a new sentence that changes the meaning by using personification:

> The refrigerator *made noise.*   The refrigerator *hummed.*
> The maple tree *moved.*   The maple tree *scratched at the window.*

Ask the child to do one or two examples himself. The new sentence should be easy for the child to write because the youngster will use many of the same words as before. Offer help where it's needed, especially in the new elements, but let the child speak his whole new image before he writes it down.

You can also help the youngster of seven or eight develop the skill to personify by asking the child to pretend he is the object. Make it a game, and have the children write (or you help them write) the name of an object on a slip of paper. Then, ask them all to select one of the slips from a box, each child pretending to be the object named. With crayons the child then draws the object being portrayed, and writes three or four sentences to show what the object does or says as if the object were a person. Remind the children about sense words. Here is an example:

> I am Carrie's brown wooden door.
> I squeal when she pushes me.
> I cry when she slams me.
> I shake her hand with my cold silver knob.

Walk around, admiring the pictures in the making and giving all the help you can. Offer comments like: "That's a good sentence, Carrie ["I am Carrie's door."]. Why don't you put in a color? And tell us what the door is made of." After the children finish, have them show their drawings and read their sentences aloud.

Another example of figurative language is the *metaphor:* the comparison that makes two seemingly unlike things equal.

> His eyes, little brown berries, darted everywhere.

In the sentence above the berries *are* the eyes, though clearly the comparison is suggested. *Metaphors* say that each term really *is* the other thing. If I wrote:

> His eyes, like little brown berries, darted everywhere

the word *like* would *compare* the two things. In a *metaphor* the comparison is only *implied.* Metaphors add a fresh, visual quality to written language.

Encourage practice with this kind of comparison. Think about the success, a few years back, of the song from the show *You're a Good Man, Charlie Brown,* "Happiness Is . . ." and the "Peanuts" book by Charles M. Schulz, also called *Happiness Is.* In both of those cases an abstract word—happiness—allowed the writer to imply comparisons between that word and some real object or event by means of sensory language.

Writing images for an abstract word is fun for children as young as eight years old. Here are some examples:

Happiness is going to the doctor and not having to get a shot.
Excited is going to a slumber party for the first time.
Disgusted is my sister breaking my toy.
Scared is seeing shadows in the night.

In each of those examples the child defines a word in terms of an observed event, implying a comparison between the abstract word and some concrete experience. The sentences above, however, lack sensory language. The children who wrote them should be urged to use color, sounds, actions, and sensations of touch and smell in their metaphors. "Which toy does your sister break, Leslie? How does she break it? What sound do you hear when it breaks?" Here's a sentence developed from those questions:

Disgusted is my sister crunching my tin soldier under her shoe.

Already the child has improved the image's sensory appeal. I would say, "Wonderful! I love that word crunch! Now, tell your sister's name, add a color, and maybe some information about where it all happened." See how the writer went on to build a clear and original image by expanding the sensory appeal:

Disgusted is my sister Ivy crunching my tin soldier under her shoe on the gray kitchen floor.

Building image definitions is an easy and fun activity for a child at any age. Look at these by twelve- and thirteen-year-olds:

Fear is sitting in the creaking dentist's chair, seeing only the top of Dr. Rifkin's bald head as his trembling hand tries to zero in on a cavity.

Hope is a blind beggar in a tattered coat who hears a tin coin tinkle in his rusted cup.

Happiness is a small boy, his hands burrowed into the flannel warmth of his pockets, as he presses his nose on the window of a bakery shop.

Life is the questioning blue eyes of my infant cousin, Richard, opening for the first time in amazement to greet a changing world of life and death.

Life is a brown-haired dachsund, spinning frantically in search of his short tail.

   Life is a flock of ducks flying in a wedge in the sky and trying to dodge frightful buckshot from the guns of anxious hunters.

   Life is a rose bush growing in my garden, full of thorns but fragrant and lovely.

   Life is two young children sneakily squatting on the carpeted steps, watching with anticipation the assorted gifts placed beneath the glimmering Christmas tree.

Although there is room for making the details even more concrete in these sentences (Where is the beggar? What's the name of the bakery shop?), they allow the reader to visualize instantly because of their use of sensory language.

   Once a child has learned good sentence sense, you can urge him to develop a series of images that support an abstract or a concrete word.

   After the child has chosen the word (suggest *fear, anger, happiness, red, rain, July* as possibilities), have the youngster write images that the word brings to mind. The attempt here is not so much a comparison between a word and some real picture but a "free association" game. The word stimulates some sensory experience in the child's mind which he recreates in language. Look at the following set of images. Though this writer separates them with semicolons, a listing headed by the word would be fine too:

   Rain: thin strands of brown and blonde hair curling tightly and sticking to my forehead; my slumber disturbed by torrents beating a drum solo on the metal chairs in the backyard; drops splotched recklessly on my window, dribbling slowly to distort my sister Bethy's tricycle hiding from corrosion in the corner of the porch; skipping down Indian Trail to Neversink River and counting the hundreds of salamanders that wiggle near the bank; red and green lights shining wetly down long black avenues; windshield wipers whisking countless drops aside, all in vain; standing under the maple in front of the house with my hands stretched out and my mouth open, and blinking with delight as each trickle saturates my tongue; layers of streaming water blown by the wind like a gray bedsheet wavering on the clothesline; trampling across soggy leaves in Lincoln Terrace Park as water oozes through my sandals; a single stone tossed into a puddle, breaking the rainbow into an explosion of color; worms wriggling from cracks between the squares of cement on the sidewalk on Avenue Z; pouncing on a still puddle in an April downpour.

You can tell from the vocabulary that this is the work of a teenager. Notice how the images vary in length, how the writer strives to reach high levels of specificity, how she taps sensory resources to yield vivid results.

After you help your child establish a comparison between an object and a person, you give that object human qualities using several figurative expressions. A five-year-old can make up the ends to unfinished sentences like the following ones, which you have prepared in order to teach comparisons.

> *The refrigerator is an old man.*
>
> It _____ and _____ all night.
> When it opens _____ .
> When it closes _____ .
>
> (Possible response):
> *The refrigerator is an old man.*
>
> It *coughs* and *trembles* all night.
> When it opens it *breathes out cold air from its mouth.*
> When it closes it *growls.*

Encourage your youngster to supply his own complete sentences and then to personify the object of the sentences.

As parents you can provide the machinery and technique for your child so he can tap the well of senses and experiences stored in his memory. The games and suggestions in this chapter should arouse your child's language awareness and experience and should provide methods of honing writing skills.

6

Correctness, Part 1:

An Outlook for Young Writers at Home

The Fever of Correctness

Correctness and error are issues of extraordinary complexity, not only for their roots in social stigma and mobility but also in their fuzziness as terms about writing. You already know about the interplay between idea and expression, between what a writer means to say and how the writer actually says it. Mature sentence construction is identified with correctness, yet an immature sentence might be mistake-free and still be an example of poor writing. In other cases correctness seems easy to judge. *Coming* spelled with two *m*'s is wrong. The two sentences

I ate peanuts. They tasted salty.

written in either of these ways are wrong:

I ate peanuts they tasted salty.
I ate peanuts, they tasted salty.

the first because no punctuation separates the sentences, the second because a comma is not the kind of punctuation that keeps sentences apart. The sentence *One of the boys are sleepy* is incorrect because the word *one* is the subject and, since it is singular, it requires a singular verb *is* (One of the boys *is* sleepy). But even among those mistakes it's possible to rate different levels of sophistication. So error must be recognized and thought of in terms of sequence, some errors having more importance than others, some errors wisely overlooked at specific stages of development.

Somewhat related, the age variable imposes conditions too: I worry less about *coming* spelled with two *m*'s in a seven-year-old's writing than I do when the word appears spelled incorrectly in a paper of an eighteen-year-old. Even there, complexities abound. Many college writers are writing in a systematic way for the first time, never having had formal instruction in composition skills. Under usual circumstances, a young woman of eighteen would be expected to know how to keep sentences apart correctly and how to spell *coming*. But if, for whatever reason, she has not practiced the craft of writing until now, how can someone judge fairly her degree of achievement? Nevertheless, a strict language code says that a misspelled word is still a misspelled word and sentences run together without suitable punctuation are wrong. So quick or easy judgments are again confounded.

All these muddled thoughts about error burn youngsters with a fever of correctness and arouse hysteria in them against the toleration of mistakes. I have seen a child pushed to tears by the tiniest blemish on a page—a misplaced stroke of pen, a word crossed out, an eraser smear. Children writing at their desks, in a classroom, crumple fresh sheets of paper endlessly. I hear angry crackling, mumbling under the breath, little feet stomping down the aisle to the basket. This preoccupation with unblemished effort murders a child's creative instincts.

But no wonder youngsters have this attitude: Several classroom practices encourage it. Children have learned that erasers are tools of defeat, that crossing out on a page admits stupidity and unforgivable error. On spelling tests, the teacher will judge only the child's *first* written response—changes, erasures, crossings-out disqualify the word from correctness. Some educators see this rule as a protection for the writer who, when changing answers, often changes from right to wrong. Yet many youngsters view the prohibition as a conspiracy against their attempts.

The irony is that a teacher removes *his* mistakes with a quick smudge on the chalkboard, which is a kind of open territory where errors can be snuffed out with a gray felt eraser, a few fingers, or the sleeve of a dress or a shirt. I have watched children trying to create words or sentences on the chalkboard. They surround themselves in clouds of chalkdust, the eraser smearing its way across the slate with frenzy. Letters must be just so, words spelled exactly. Amid all this the child tries to crystallize an idea so that it makes sense in a sentence or two. More unhappy are those unlucky students who must copy answers from their own pages onto the chalkboard. They suffer the glares of seventy onlooking eyes, everyone waiting to attack the first mistake. The hysteria of correctness and neatness often elevates to torture the pressures of performing at the chalkboard.

How Do Writers Write?

Writers are never neat. They are unconcerned with being "correct" when they are creating. The very act of creation sends a pencil or pen all over the place, a thought there in the margin in a hurried scrawl, line after line slashed with gray impatience, a sentence intended for the bottom of the page written *before* earlier sentences which are not yet written. Writers doodle; they jot down notes and even irrelevant reminders on their pages; they misspell with religious fervor; they draw long, snaking arrows from words far down a page so that they know to move those words to other places. The landscape of a page that records creative activity is a battlefield of statements—the scarred, the scratched, and the murdered exist along with those picked to survive. Professional writers, surely, crumple up and destroy sheets of paper at different stages of invention, but no absolute concern for neatness or correctness (in the sense that children perceive it) motivates their actions.

I am not saying, mind you, that writers do not need to follow the conventions of correct writing when they offer their work for someone else to read. Errors in spelling, grammar, syntax, and logic have no place on the final draft. Someone else reading a writer's creation mounts from the start an uncertain stallion, expecting a smooth ride. Error is a burr beneath the saddle; depending on the rider's tolerance, a throw or two from the horse may end the journey. When this happens, the writer has failed.

The efficient writer scours a draft for error *before* preparing the final one. If he types the manuscript himself, he'll work more quickly from an error-free copy. But if he submits the rough copy for someone else to prepare, he must meticulously proofread the retyped draft, because a typist will copy word by word what appears on the original copy. Errors carried from the old copy to the new one can be caught at this stage.

Many young writers focus their energies prematurely on the final stage of their manuscript. To these novices it's not a matter of getting ideas down, exploring them, and working them through, as much as it is putting something down that's neat and correct. This attitude robs the young writer of a key stage in the writing process, the pencil and paper laboratory where experiments and failures should be welcomed.

In your goal to help your child build positive attitudes toward writing, you must defang this monster of correctness. And to help you see what writers go through, here's part of the rough draft manuscript for an earlier section of this book.

Ben Jonson's offhand comment about the way his contemporary, Shakespeare, worked—"in his writing (whatsoever he penned) he never blotted out a line"—may work for pure genius. But, even if Jonson is right, few others (and you can look at rough drafts by Keats, T. S. Eliot, and other great poets to prove it) work without blotches and smears on their pages.

Teach children an easy approach to correctness. When the youngster looks up in terror from a page and whines, "I made a mistake!" look at his work and say, "Good! Isn't it lucky that you found it! Why don't you cross it out and go right on?" or "That's why we have erasers! Fix it now if you want to. But why don't you keep going until you finish, and then I'll help you fix all the mistakes later on." In this way you decriminalize error by refusing to condemn it at the stage where it has little importance. At the same time you establish the value of making corrections *after* the flow of ideas develops into a page of written language.

Here are some more tips:

• *Encourage "rough writing" wherever possible.* To allow thinking and doodling time, word seeking, play, and exploration, the sloppier the page the better. Encourage alterations, cross-outs, and fearlessness about misspelling.

• *Encourage rewrites.* Writing demands *rewriting*—the older the child, the more intermediate drafts you can encourage (two is about right) before any thoughts of final copy. Help the child understand that the rewrite is not a punishment or an indication of personal failure, but a way of making the final copy clear, easy to read, and free from error.

• *Supervise rewrites and correction of errors.* Train your child to *correct* errors, not always to be on the lookout to avoid them, before attitudes formed by school experience develop. Praise the child's efforts even if they are "wrong"; and *then* talk about mistakes. The four-year-old who sounds out the word *barn* to write on top of her picture may write *bran* instead. What do you say? "Well, Ellen, you're trying to write *barn* and you've got all the letters right. Good for you! But you didn't put them down in the right order. Shall I help you fix it or do you want to try yourself?" Once you work through the error, make no fuss; encourage the child to cross out or to erase the incorrect word. If necessary, print the word correctly on the page (with the child's assent), and ask the youngster to copy it. When you first see the error, avoid clucking or an impatient "That's not right!" unless you want that lovely barn with its tilted red silo torn into shreds by an injured child. Furthermore, be prepared for resistance. Despite gentle treatment of mistakes, a child will often say, "I want it *wrong!*" Then you say, "That's all right. It's yours. But if you want someone else to understand and like your writing, you should do it right. It's easy, look. . . ."

Your early responses to error will focus on spelling until the child is eight or nine and begins writing original sentences and little stories in school. However, a parent can build sentence sense and help develop more sustained efforts at a much earlier age. After that you'll be responding to other more advanced kinds of mistakes, and will need a general understanding of the principles of the language. See Appendix B, "A Parent's Primer for Correctness."

Reacting to Error

The painful correction of error after error, especially when accompanied by a parent's impatience, disgust, or anger, squashes the seeds of writing that lie dormant within your son or daughter. It's a delicate and subtle skill to be able to ignore some mistakes while pointing out other more serious ones. In general, don't worry about commas on a young child's paper. For the child of ten or eleven, the use of commas in some easy, familiar places should be no strain: in dates, between city and state in an address, after the salutation in a friendly letter, and so on. Later on, I'll give some very general guidelines about the writing skills your child should grasp at different ages.

Your child's teacher should cover the basics of correct writing in the classroom. If you feel that this is not being taught in your child's class, you'll have to renew your own skills before you start helping. There are many good texts available that will help you learn more about correct writing. Read the child's own language arts book. It can teach you and give you a guide to what his age group should be learning. Don't convey your own limitations, fears, and frustrations about writing through excessive treatment of error. That would obviate any hopes you had of the child's developing good attitudes toward writing. Praise effort at all times with pleasure and excitement; listen without distraction to the youngster who speaks aloud original written sentences, and encourage this kind of reading frequently; fuss over the finished product—hang it in the kitchen on the cupboard, send a copy to grandma, leave it at mom or dad's place at the breakfast table. As the youngster grows older, continue your positive responses to his writing, but show more and more attention to correctness—never so much that it supersedes your interest in the way the child develops an idea and supports a point.

Your Code of Ethics: Writing for School

Just what is the role of the mother or father in seeing that written school assignments are done well? How much should a parent help a child write for his teacher?

The responses vary as widely as the problems faced by young writers themselves. Many believe it is dishonest for the child to receive major help in preparing school work. After all, a piece of writing is something created by an individual, and as an expression of his or her mind at work, it is inviolate. In any large-scale tutoring effort in which the parent plays a major part in the organization and correction of a paper for school, the grade an instructor gives cannot be an honest evaluation of the child's work. Some parents will not help their seventh or eighth grader prepare a report for school, but will type the paper for the child, making corrections as the typing proceeds. Others will examine a paper before it's submitted and will correct any serious errors for the child. Still others, capitalizing on their own strengths, comb the pages for all spelling mistakes, correcting them before the youngster submits the work, perhaps even demanding a rewrite. But all of these attempts may be questioned on ethical grounds. If it's not completely the child's work, what's the point in presenting it to the teacher as such? Following this line of thought, many feel that the parent must ignore the child's preparation of a paper written for school. Others will examine papers *after* the teacher returns the writing in order to help the child understand the teacher's corrections and comments.

Still others believe that providing assistance to writers as their ideas form and develop is a much sounder way to advance skills than to try to help in the correction or revision of a paper already graded by teacher. They think it's best to influence the expression of ideas, and to explore options in sentence and paragraph form at several of the stages the child works through before preparing his final copy. Certainly, some argue, a parent should encourage the child to talk about the writing assignments a teacher gives, so that the work moves along the right track. Then again, shouldn't a parent help a child plan a school assignment, even outline it as it grows in complexity from term to term? Can mothers and fathers really permit a paper loaded with errors to go before the teacher's red pen if there is a chance to correct the mistakes first, to spare the youngster wounded feelings and a sense of defeat?

Weighing these contradictions, what does a parent do? It's hard not to compromise excessively, but truth sits on all borders of this rocky issue. As in any attempts to solve problems edging on dilemma or predicament, the key is judgment, your judgment as a parent and a fair-minded human being who understands your child.

A teacher will not generally expect young children in kindergarten and the first and second grades to prepare extensive written work of an original nature at home, though some simple homework and copying activities may take a child's time after school. That leaves lots of room for you to help your child develop writing skills and attitudes in ways this book suggests, and with a clear conscience! But, as children grow older, as demands on their writing performances grow more and more serious through the grades, you do need to know where to draw the line in offering help on something the teacher will score.

When it comes to aiding your youngster with classroom work *in general* (I'll look at your role in a specific project when I examine the report in Chapter 15), go to see your child's teacher if you have doubts about what's fair. Ask him how much assistance you should give your son or daughter in his or her writing assignments for school. Because attitudes and responses to this issue vary widely, you'll want to clear your position with the instructor. If he says that you should not help the child organize ideas, for example, don't do it for classroom work. One of the good things about encouraging frequent written activities at home is that you can explore problems writers have without having to worry about overstepping some hard-to-define border. This is not to say that I believe it's all right for you to rewrite or to correct slavishly papers children write at home just because no teacher will judge them. The child is still your major concern; it's his or her written work, not yours. Still, for writing at home, you can make your advice more direct, and you can be less concerned about violating the code that work submitted for a teacher's evaluation must be the child's own.

As you try to define your position in your sons' and daughters' writing assignments, I advise you in the way I advise inexperienced teachers starting careers as instructors of English. Teachers of writing are guides and counselors who help writers find the most successful means of expressing their ideas. The best way to achieve that goal is through questioning without putting words in the child's mouth: "What do you mean by this?" "Which ideas do you want to put first?" "What details can you use to support your point?" "Do you see the three spelling mistakes that I see on this page?"

In the list below I've tried to summarize some do's and don't's as you work with your growing children on papers they write for school. Don't worry that I'm recommending some ideas I've not yet explored in this book. I'll talk about things like word choice and sentence growth later on. Again, the child's age, your judgment, and the teacher's demands are the final arbiters. Look this over with special care if your writer is in the third grade or higher.

Tips and Pointers: How Parents Can Help
with Writing for School

Stage	Do's	Don't's
Before Writing	1. Encourage the child to explain the assignment made by the teacher. Ask questions so that you're sure he understands it.	1. Don't interpret the assignment. Don't *tell* him what the teacher wants. Ask questions so the child can figure it out for himself.
	2. Let the child discuss what he wants to write about. Ask questions to make sure he can offer details to support any idea he wants to develop.	2. Don't respond to questions like, "What should I write about?" without making a wide range of suggestions from which the child can choose without feeling obliged to follow your ideas.
	3. Encourage the jotting down of words or ideas as the child thinks the topic through.	3. Don't add details for the child. Ask questions: What color? What size? and so on.
Rough Copy	1. Remind the youngster of how writers write. Show a page of "rough writing" from this book (see p. 60) or better still, a page of your own writing before you turn it into something you'd want to show someone.	1. Don't worry yourself or the child about neatness or correctness.

Stage	*Do's*	*Don't's*
Rough Copy (Cont.)	2. Ignore mistakes. Encourage cross-outs. Encourage skipped lines for information to be added later.	2. Don't push too hard. If the child draws a blank, let him turn to other things. Come back to the writing after a glass of milk, or a game.
	3. Spell out words only if the child asks you. Write them down for the child to copy. Better, help him sound out the words.	3. Don't let spelling get in the way of the writing effort. Let youngsters *guess* at spelling until later on.
	4. Keep an eye on errors so that you can direct the child's learning about some of them later on.	
Reading the Rough Copy	1. Ask the child to read the work aloud. Praise it!	1. Don't interrupt the reading no matter how many suggestions you can make for improvement.
	2. Ask questions: "What color was the house?" "What sound did the door make?" "Would you like to put those words in to give a better picture?"	2. Don't correct the errors.
	3. Show sensitivity to word choice in general. "You've said, 'The shoe *crunched* the glass on the pavement!' What a wonderful sound word!" or "You wrote, 'My sister *walked* to the door.' Why don't you try to find a word that shows a better picture of how she moved?"	3. Don't add any details.
	4. Explain the use of the caret (∧) to insert omitted words. Draw arrows out to the margins, if necessary.	4. Don't show any disappointment about poor writing or about errors.

Stage	Do's	Don't's
Reading the Rough Copy (Cont.)	5. When you see a glaring mistake, help the child find it and correct it himself. After you're both satisfied with the ideas expressed, say, "Oh, oh, I see a place in the first three lines where a sentence should end. Can you find it?" Or, "You have six spelling mistakes. See if you can find them." You'll want to use proofreading techniques here (see the next section in this chapter). You might suggest that the youngster use a different color pencil so that corrections will stand out clearly.	5. Don't make any reference to neatness or sloppiness.
	6. Encourage sentence diversity. Say, "Why don't you put together two sentences toward the end? You can use *and* or *because* or *since* to join them together." Or, "You've used *and* so many times to join sentences. Can you put them together in another way?"	6. Don't expect correctness in areas that the child does not understand or has not yet learned. Again, it's your judgment: If the first few letters of a difficult word tell you what the child means, you may want to ignore the error completely. However, don't allow an attitude of carelessness or indifference to the writing process to develop.
	7. Given the age and attention span of the child, with especially thorny topics or especially hard-to-read rough copies, suggest another draft written from the first.	

Stage	*Do's*	*Don't's*

Copying Over: the Final Draft

1. Encourage the preparation of a careful final copy. Ask about the teacher's instructions on how the page should look. Where does the name go? the date? the title? May the child write on both sides of a page? What margins does the teacher require? Offer hints about good handwriting. Periods at ends of sentences should be clear and firm: the child should leave enough space between the period and the next word. Capital letters should be clearly capitals. With cursive writing, ask that the *i* be dotted directly over the letter and not between the *i* and *e*. Discourage circles as dots for *i*'s.

1. Don't type or write the paper over for the child no matter how "sloppy" he claims his handwriting is.

2. Answer questions about spelling. Spell out the toughest words, writing them down on a separate sheet for the youngster to look at and to copy over. Encourage his use of the dictionary. Look up words together.

2. Don't hang over the child as he copies his paper over. Answer questions if he has any —but this is his effort so don't make him nervous. Welcome questions. You can decide whether or not to answer them after they are asked!

3. Listen as the child reads the paper aloud. Ask him if words sound smooth together, if sentences make sense to him.

3. Don't be embarrassed if the child asks you to spell a word and you cannot. That's what dictionaries are for! A youngster who sees his mother or father reach for a dictionary when a word stumps her or him develops good habits.

Stage		*Do's*		*Don't's*

Copying Over: the Final Draft (Cont.)

4. See that the child proofreads his final draft carefully. Using what you know of previous kinds of errors the child makes, you can help focus the proofreading activity: "Ramón, last time you misspelled *disappoint* and *already*. Let's see if you've spelled those words correctly this time" or "Last time you had trouble with sentence endings. Let's check the paper over so you put in all the periods where they belong."

4. Don't be ashamed if you can't help straighten out problems that both you and your child perceive. Reach for a book if you can, or ask the teacher about a particular sentence (a note attached to the writing when handed in will be fine).

5. Given the child's age, no teacher should expect an absolutely correct paper, especially not for the very young, so don't be overly zealous. The child should apply what he has already learned and what you feel he should know.

6. Don't be reluctant to refuse to help in places when you believe it might be ethically unsound. Say gently but firmly, "Beverly, I don't think Mrs. Wilson would want me to help you with that one. After all, it's your work and you'll get the grade for it. But let's see how you can find out the answer yourself."

Stage	*Do's*	*Don't's*
The Graded Paper Returned	1. Read the teacher's comments together. Make sure the child understands what's said.	1. Don't complain about the grade or the effort. The attitude must be, "Let's see what the teacher says so that you can do better next time."
	2. Talk about discouragement. Explain how in writing people learn by trying and by making mistakes. Tell about how professional writers often have their work severely criticized and refused for publication.	2. Don't challenge the teacher's judgment. It's all right to disagree, but remember that many responses to writing are subjective. The question is, do the instructor's comments explain her evaluation of the paper?
	3. See that the child works carefully on correcting errors even if the teacher does not require it—and this comes before any revision (see 5, below). Suggest a different color pen or pencil as the youngster makes corrections according to the teacher's comments or symbols in the margin.	3. Don't tell the child how to correct errors the teacher points out. Help him find out how to make corrections on his own.
	4. Help the child keep a record of his usual errors. This is especially valuable: first, by giving practice not to make error; and, second, if the child consults his errors before he writes the next paper, he can signal himself about mistakes he often makes.	
	5. Insist that the child copy misspelled words—correctly spelled—onto a list of individual spelling errors (see pp. 231 to 232). If the mistakes fall into	

Stage	Do's	Don't's
The Graded Paper Returned (Cont.)	patterns (that is, *plurals, -ie* mistakes, *suffixes,* and so on), help the child group the errors on index cards or on small sheets. When you can identify patterns, the task of learning about correct spelling is not overwhelming. Make sure the young writer consults the list before each writing assignment.	

6. Many instructors (especially in junior and senior high) will ask for a revision —that is, they expect students to rewrite papers based upon class suggestions for their improvement. Encourage revision along the lines the teacher suggests *after the child corrects the errors.* Otherwise, in revision, youngsters may avoid the words or structures that caused the problems and thereby lose the opportunity to learn how to correct mistakes.

Proofreading, Hedge Against Mistake

Proofreading is the single most valuable hedge I know against error. A shocking number of mistakes presented in a poor composition may be traced to careless proofreading.

What is *proofreading?* It's a term borrowed from publishers who ask people to read over material that has been set into type (called *proofs*) so that the errors made in printing from manuscripts are corrected. Using conventional symbols and following a publisher's style, a proofreader writes his marks on the printed proofs after comparing them to the original manuscript; the printer then resets lines or pages of type to correspond to the alterations. When I use the term *proofreading,* I mean it as a process of looking for errors at various stages of writing. I suggest you encourage the young writer to look for errors at two stages: First, children should read over rough copies before preparing final drafts. In the rough manuscript they will consider broad areas for improvement: word choice and mature sentence structure, as well as spelling, word use, and sentence completeness. Second, they should proofread after the final copy—in which major errors should no longer appear. Here writers find mistakes that slipped past them when they read over their rough copies or mistakes that crept in while they were preparing the final manuscript.

Teachers repeatedly overlook the difficulties children have in performing this task. Frequently I've heard them scold children, "You haven't read this over!" Proofreading is a hard job. To be effective, a writer must do it in a manner quite opposite to the way he ordinarily reads; that is, in proofreading, his eyes must look at only one word at a time, not roam over groups of words in an attempt to take in ideas quickly. Even a first-grader who is barely able to read is led on, pursuing the meaning of the paragraph, as he moves to the end of a sentence. Though he may read each word separately, he is not seeing the word exactly as it appears. He is seeing parts of the word, or maybe he is unconsciously substituting a completely different word that helps him make sense out of the sentence. Familiarity further confounds an inexperienced writer who proofreads; for when reading what he himself wrote, the writer often sees words on a page that are in his head but not really written down. Often I've heard youngsters read words that do not appear in one of their sentences. For example, a child who wrote "She eat by herself" read over and over again, "She *can* eat by herself." I kept saying "What?" and she kept reading the word *can*. It was only when I asked her to touch the word *can* that she saw with great surprise that no such word existed in her sentence!

It's possible to help a child learn how to read for errors—this is a valuable skill that you should encourage. I like to explain the difficulties in proofreading by asking youngsters to read this:

> ASK NOT WHAT
> YOUR COUNTRY CAN
> CAN DO FOR YOU,
> BUT WHAT YOU
> YOU CAN DO
> FOR YOUR COUNTRY.

It's usually a while before they realize that *can* and *you* have been repeated. Why do they miss those errors? People tend to see what they *expect* to see in familiar sentences, instead of what is actually there. Next, they read quickly (having been trained to do so); and with sentences they know people read especially fast. John Kennedy's statement, though certainly familiar, is much *less* well known to the child than his own writing, so imagine how easy it is to overlook mistakes there.

Here are some techniques that will help your child proofread more accurately:

- Read aloud. Listen for words or sentences that sound strange, funny, or "don't sound right."
- Read *slowly*. Read one word at a time. If you use a pencil to touch each word as you read it, you'll slow yourself down.
- Use a ruler or a blank sheet of paper to cover all of the writing below the line you are looking at. In that way your eye is not drawn too swiftly onward.
- For younger children and for those with a number of serious careless errors you might want to follow a suggestion I learned from one of my colleagues. Use an index card with a piece—about half an inch long and as high as a ruled line—cut out of the left corner, like this:

Place the card over the line with part of the first word showing in the space you have cut out. Have the child read only what appears in that space, as he moves the card across the line.

- If you've written more than a sentence, read your writing from the last sentence to the first one. For the older child this technique helps separate ideas, and keeps him from

unconsciously filling in missing details from previous
sentences.

- Correct errors in spelling, capitals, and punctuation
directly on the first draft. If a word has been left out, put
a caret in the sentence where the omission occurs and
write the word above. If there isn't enough room, draw a
line from the caret out into the margin and write the
word. If there are too many corrections on the page, do
the final draft again.

Spotlight on Writing in the Grades

Philosophies and approaches vary so widely from grade to grade,
city to city, state to state that it would be impossible to offer
any accurate representation of specific writing programs in the
schools.

You might ask whether or not there is a sequence of skills
that all schools should follow in establishing a series of writing
courses. There is, certainly, a sequence in word and sentence
recognition usually followed in most *reading* programs. But in
writing, children need to put down ideas and responses based
on experience. Good instruction helps young writers build
vocabulary and exposes them to a variety of sentence patterns;
however, no one can predict exactly which needs come when,
which errors show up at what time, which errors go away
during what year. Further, writing is a holistic process; that
is, a writer at any age needs all the skills to convey whatever
ideas he or she wants to put in writing at that moment. I think
it's impossible to say what skills any writer needs at what age
or grade level. In every grade I taught (including college freshmen), I had to explain about sentence endings, about the rule
for forming plurals of words that end in *y,* and about capital
letters for geographical areas.

Even when accompanied by a strongly worded statement
that children develop as writers at different stages, that re-
gional language patterns make varying demands on skills
development, that home language patterns affect writing
needs, and that no absolute standards of competence may be
established for children in particular grades or at particular
ages, providing a sequence of skills for parents and teachers
is bound to create nervousness about the child's progress. When
parents see lists of competencies arranged by age or grade they
assume that *all* children should have learned the skills by a
certain age. That's nonsense. Writing in the home luckily
avoids the need for looking at set achievement levels. At home,

you can help the child write according to his interests and abilities. And you don't have to worry about suiting an arbitrary sequence. If it's too hard, all you have to do is stop.

Despite these objections to providing a sequence, I think you should have a *very* general sense about the skills some programs help children develop at what points in their writing careers. This information can guide you in knowing what *not* to press on your child, and what to encourage at home and when to encourage it. I want to give you this material in the broadest possible terms so as to avoid as much as I can the "Is my child normal?" or the "What's wrong with our school district?" questions. I hope you will keep in mind, too, that there's a great deal of required repetition and that skills on one level must be reinforced on other levels. Also, writing skills must be part of a total language arts program. Skills in reading, speaking, performing all support the writing area. If you want more specific information, get exact writing goals year by year from your children's teachers or language arts specialists (you're perfectly right to insist that the school have a plan for writing-skills instruction; and your child's teacher should be able to tell you her goals for writing improvement for the class).

As I have already indicated, advancement in writing relates to a complex development of skills, especially in reading and speaking. Children in early stages of reading-skills development cannot be expected to write words independently and fluently if they do not read, use, and recognize them. There is no accurate way to predict by a child's chronological age the stage at which he should be as a user of the language.

In the next chapter we will look at some special word problems children have and at some techniques for expanding facility with words. We'll consider the role of the children's dictionary, and examine some games you can use in the home to build up the child's ability to write good sentences.

·

A General View of Writing Goals in the Schools

Language Skills	Kinds of Writing Exercises and Related Composition Skills

For the Early Grades
(kindergarten, first, second, third)

The *sentence* as a unit that tells or asks

Headings on papers

Capitalization (for beginning sentences, for names of people, the word "I," names of cities, states, countries, names of schools and other familiar buildings like supermarkets or banks, names of holidays, months, and days of the week, main words in titles of stories, salutation and closing in letters)

Sentence sense: recognizing a complete thought

Punctuation: periods and question marks at ends of sentences; periods after initials and simple abbreviations (Mrs., days and months); apostrophes to show letters omitted in contractions; commas in dates and in key places in friendly letters

Plurals: s and *es* endings; exceptional plurals as they arise (*children, pianos*)

Word use: correct forms of words (*brought* not *brung, ran* not *runned,* etc.); seeing differences be-

Words as labels

Sense words

Simple sentence

Two or three simple sentences (to describe an event, a picture, and so on)

Copy work (sentences, words, invitations, messages)

Some independent writing

Dictation: copying a brief story as the teacher reads it

Dictation: children speak a sentence or two as a teacher writes it

Stories using spelling words

Poems

Titles for pictures

Class Effort ⎰ Lists for class shopping excursion
Instructions to follow
Daily plan or log

A General View of Writing Goals in the Schools

Language Skills	**Kinds of Writing Exercises and Related Composition Skills**

tween words that sound alike
(*it's, its; here, hear*); avoiding
slang (*ain't, his'n* etc.) simple
pronoun use

Vocabulary: practice with
new words; changing shape of
words with new endings

For the Intermediate Grades (fourth, fifth, sixth)

Sentence sense: combining sentence elements; writing longer, more complex sentences; relating properly more than one idea in a single sentence; seeing and writing whole sentences; keeping sentences apart; varying sentence openings; how subjects and verbs work together; how verbs show tense

Dictionary use: for spelling, pronouncing, finding meanings

Capitalization: of names, peoples, abbreviations, outline topics, titles of people and books, in first word of quotations, in addressing envelopes, for the deity, geographical regions

Punctuation: quotation marks for someone's exact words, apostrophes to show possession; commas (for pauses as opposed to

Paragraphs: effective opening and closing sentences; good use of supporting detail, especially sensory; correcting sentence ideas with transitions

Writing descriptions

Writing stories of real events that show clear sequence

Writing fanciful, make-believe stories

Original letters to relatives, friends, pen pals

Poems and rhymes

Short plays for acting out

Gathering data

Brief reports on books

Brief reports requiring the encyclopedia

List-writing

A General View of Writing Goals in the Schools

Language Skills	Kinds of Writing Exercises and Related Composition Skills
stops in sentence endings) in series, in quotations, to separate elements in sentences; to set off *yes* and *no,* to set off the name of someone addressed in a sentence	Taking notes
	Diary or journals (individual or in-class projects)
	Fables
Vocabulary: how to build words from parts; selecting clear, specific words; using vivid words; using new vocabulary in writing	Minutes of meetings
	Articles for newspapers
	Brief business letters
	Magazine ads
Plurals: patterns of plural formation (*y* to *i, f* to *v,* some special foreign words)	Television commercials
	Original cartoon strips
Grammar: basic grammatical language, explanation of key terms; functions of basic sentence elements	Original film strips captions
	Filling out forms
	Summarizing materials read
Word use: more on correct verb forms (*choose, freeze, swim,* etc.); comparing with and without *more* or *most;* no double negatives; using correct pronouns; more look-and-sound alikes (*loose, lose; quit, quiet, quite,* etc.), uses of slang	

For the Pre-High-School Years (seventh, eighth, and ninth)

Sentence sense: keeping sentences apart, joining sentence elements; avoiding fragments; experimenting with more and

Paragraphs: narration and description practiced frequently; other paragraph forms introduced and practiced: compari-

A General View of Writing Goals in the Schools

Language Skills	Kinds of Writing Exercises and Related Composition Skills

more sentence patterns; varying sentence length; types of tenses; special subject-verb problems

Capitalization: all uses; distinguishing places which exclude capitals (words for animals, flowers, sports, seasons, directions)

Punctuation: the semicolon and colon; commas after opening sentence element and for parenthetical parts of sentences; parentheses

Dictionary use: for history of word, etymology, parts of speech

Vocabulary: more prefixes and suffixes; thesaurus use to expand word resources; using new vocabulary in writing; continued practice with selecting exact, vivid words

Plurals: all uses

Grammar: more grammatical terminology; recognizing and identifying grammatical elements; using grammatical knowledge to create sentence patterns

Word use: more on tricky verbs; *should have* and *should of; between* and *among;* more look and

son, use of illustrations, simple listings, cause and effect, definition. Paragraphs expanded now in length; details support a clearly stated topic; effective use of transitions

Experiential writing: personal experience revealed through concrete sensory language

Interpreting data from charts and writing down findings

Using secondary sources: books, newspapers, testimony from knowledgeable people

Imaginative writing: dreams, wishes, make-believes

Writing dialogues

Writing up interviews

Essays: longer compositions which argue and analyze

Book reports

Character analysis

Original fiction: stories, poems, vignettes, plays, TV scripts

Writing answers on subjective-type exams

Basic techniques of research: bibliography; using sources properly

A General View of Writing Goals in the Schools

Language Skills	Kinds of Writing Exercises and Related Composition Skills
sound alikes; sensitivity to word choice depending on situation; correct pronouns	Writing about literature: why a poem or story is good; how it achieves a certain purpose
	Business letters: of inquiry, application, complaint
	Making out job applications

High School and Beyond

Sentence sense: continued review based upon error and need

Dictionary: different kinds and how and when to use them

Capitalization: all uses and abuses understood

Punctuation: review all; dash, hyphen, brackets; special uses for apostrophes; italics and underlining as compared with quotation marks; commas in all correct places

Vocabulary: continued review and expansion. Wide use of relational words (*on the other hand, consequently,* etc.), ease and familiarity with abstract language; expanded repertoire of word choices

Word use: practice with and elimination of sticking errors and fine points of usages

Paragraphs: review and practice of previous skills; introduction of new forms: division, classification

Details: review and practice of sensory language and other kinds of supporting details

Longer compositions: how to write introductions and conclusions; how to correct parts of paragraphs; how to hold together paragraphs in a long composition; how to select appropriate forms (narration, comparison) to suit the subject of the written exercise

Using deduction and induction

Arguing convincingly

Analyzing clearly

Responding to books in written essays and reports

A General View of Writing Goals in the Schools

Language Skills	Kinds of Writing Exercises and Related Composition Skills
Grammar: Full exposure to a grammar system; ability to recognize grammatical elements—to identify and to write them; application of grammatical principles to structuring sentences and to determining correct punctuation.	Basic research techniques: gathering data, writing footnotes and bibliography Writing research papers with documentation Writing outlines Preparing résumés Writing expanded autobiographies Understanding when to use personal reactions or objective data Writing essay tests Writing business letters Original fiction: all types

7
Correctness, Part 2:

Word Games and Word and Sentence Craft

When more than 60 percent of California's top high school graduates in 1975 failed a nationally used writing test, the professor who reported the statistics felt that poor previous instruction not lack of intelligence created the problem. He gave three reasons for the failure. Students, he said, lacked skills in correctness of expression, in the ability to organize their writing, and in the ability to choose the right word to complete a thought.

The problem of organization relates to an ability to put together words and sentences that show clear and logical relationships to each other and to provide solid support for ideas. This has always been an especially difficult area to teach because problems in organization vary with each activity. Solutions for one kind of writing do not necessarily work for other kinds. To learn this skill, one must practice different types of writing on various subjects, must read with an eye to the way writers organize ideas, and must practice different kinds of organizational strategies. This is something that children as well as adults *can* learn.

By correctness of expression, I assume, the professor means good grammar, spelling, and orderliness of ideas. When I read the phrase "correct word choice to complete a sentence," I immediately think of vocabulary and ways writers put their words into whole thoughts. How can a parent help expand a child's word resources and his options for using those words in quality sentences? Here as in other areas of writing skills, you can use the home environment to build strengths that prepare youngsters to meet later demands on their writing.

Building Vocabulary

Professor Mina Shaughnessy, a researcher in the most acute problems of inexperienced writers, and author of *Errors and Expectations: A Guide for the Teacher of Basic Writing* (New York: Oxford Press, 1977), gathered sample after sample of poor *college* writing by young adults.

Her findings suggest some of the concerns parents should keep in mind when working with children. In addition to extensive problems in spelling, she shows that these writers lack a variety of words that they can use to name things specifically. In most of the students' writing that she examined there is a great confusion in the use of word endings and beginnings as they change their function in sentences.

Experts agree that a child's vocabulary relates to the nature of his experiences and to the language he hears and uses to explore those experiences. Children have an innate love for words—witness your child's delight as you read aloud the improbable rhymes in Dr. Seuss books or as he or she invents nonsense words. Never lose sight of the pleasure and fun of saying, using, and playing with words in every moment of shared experience with your youngster. A parent accompanied by a four-year-old who watches snatches of activity in a supermarket can direct and influence the child's vocabulary by observing and discussing the words that apply to the supermarket scene. A child may hear and use: *unloading, supplies, stack, crate, special, discount, coupon, container, margarine, aisle, sawdust, manager, refrigeration,* and countless other words that may be new to him or only vaguely familiar. In a natural way you should talk about objects and events, and encourage questions and observations.

After an exciting experience, you can aid vocabulary growth by guiding the child's use of words to describe that experience. A three-year-old rushing in and announcing, "It's snowing" has opened a door for word study. You might say, "Snow? Terrific! Let's see how many words you can use to tell about snow." Parent and child can enjoy this together and make up a list of many words, such as:

icy	dancing	lazy	like white paint drops
cold	white	flaky	playful

fluttering	swirling	wet	like falling sugar
soft	blowing	tickly	fluffy
frozen	shivery	powdery	slippery

All the vocabulary-building books and exercises and all the attempts to commit long lists of words to memory pale beside the invaluable connection of language and experience. The parent acts as a child's dictionary of word resources by naming, constantly, the items that are part of a new or a familiar experience. A visit to the doctor yields: *examination, throat culture, patient, prescription, stethoscope, injection, blood pressure, vaccine, inoculation.* The child who helps with cooking hears and uses: *simmer, steam, blanch, blend, pot, pan, carving knife, dice, beat, mold, cinnamon, yeast, broil, bake.* The youngster who likes to wash the car with Mother or Father considers: *filthy, sudsy, scrub, hubcaps, grid, hood, taillights, headlights, windshield.* A talk about a picture in a magazine uncorks a flow of language. The bedtime story, a program on television or radio, and the motion picture are ample sources of new words too. The question, "What does that mean?" from a boy or girl of any age, who is reading a book or watching television, is an invitation for a conscientious parent to help with vocabulary. Explain the unknown word, give an example, and offer other words that mean the same or nearly the same thing. Often I will "plant" a word using one my child might not know, and then I'll wait for her question about its meaning. Even with simple words, such as *pot* and *pan,* I suggest you make the meanings distinct so that the difference between such familiar objects stays clear in the youngster's mind. Selecting the most specific word from among several and attempting to find more specific words for general ones are other techniques that help children focus upon the *exact* meanings of words. Helping the child name opposites to words also fixes meanings in mind, though this is often difficult because not all words have true opposites and because in many cases there exist several opposites with subtle differences of meanings. However, opposites to words like *day, black, sweet, weak, boy, cold, sad, light, woman,* and *enemy* are simple to find, and children love and learn from the game.

The use of concrete language comes strongly into play here in this discussion of vocabulary growth. Yesterday my wife overheard an instructive interchange between a child and an adult as they waited to see a performance of *Snow White* at the Westerly Parkway Junior High School. One mother, accompanying her young daughter and a group of the daughter's friends, tried engaging each in conversation. To one little girl with brown hair and smooth skin, she said, "Those are really cute shoes you're wearing." The child shook her long brown hair and said, "Uh, uh. They're not cute." "Oh, yes they are, Mary," her friend's mother replied. "They're very cute." "Nope. They're *attractive.*" The woman laughed. "Well, I still think they're pretty neat."

Here the child brought a precise word from her own store-house of vocabulary, one much more valuable in suggesting the grounds for judgment than *nice* or *neat* upon which the older woman insisted. *Attractive* is not as precise as *new leather shoes* or *brown suede shoes,* but it's an improvement over time-weary choices such as *neat* or *nice. Cute* and *neat* and *good, interesting, nice, swell,* and *bad* are vague words, and are as poor for describing as the words *thing, item,* or *object* are for naming, and as *went, walked, was, appeared,* and *seemed* are for showing action.

When you have the chance to explore words with your children, try to select words that suggest qualities as precisely as possible.

"Well, Nicholas, how did you like the book Aunt Clara gave you?"

"It was good."

"Good? What do you mean? I don't think I know what you mean?"

"It was good. You know. It was good."

"Do you mean funny?"

"Oh, yes. It was funny. It was even silly."

As soon as the child taps his vocabulary for a precise word, help him or her explore the wide variety of words that can replace the vague one even more specifically. Make lists of precise words according to the child's interest and age.

Instead of *good* (for a book)		Instead of *nice* (for a person)	
funny	fanciful	friendly	happy
exciting	realistic	helpful	funny
silly	tender	gentle	peppy
unusual	challenging	warm	relaxed
scary	suspenseful	inspiring	lively
dramatic	humorous	good-natured	thoughtful
heart-warming	tense	kind	cooperative
truthful	romantic	generous	fun-loving
adventurous	lively	cheerful	adventurous
imaginative	frightening	loving	strong

Instead of
went or _walked_

rushed	hustled
drifted	limped
scurried	scampered
strolled	galloped
skipped	marched
hopped	eased
sailed	slipped
flew	rolled
jumped	paraded
stormed	hobbled

All these activities encourage the exploration of options and help the child to avoid the overuse of "standard" words—old reliables that are so much a part of the inexperienced writer's grab bag. In a subtle way, you are discouraging the common imprecise favorites: _thing, idea, way; give, make, get, be, put, walk, have, cause; a lot, interesting, important, big, much, many, good._

The following games and those that appear in Chapter 5 will help you develop your own resourceful approaches as you strive to expand your child's vocabulary. If you arrange to share exciting experiences—better still, if you and the child train yourselves to see excitement in even the most ordinary experiences —the language that grows out of such occasions builds and reinforces a valuable supply of words. Your own sensitivity sets the pace for your youngster's lifelong attitude toward language.

Words As Chameleons
Part of the word-building program is to point out to children the way words change to mean different things. Novice writers sometimes see words as unchangeable terms and use them incorrectly. For example, a writer with such a vision will say, "The _describe_ of this person is hard to believe" or "The _fastly_ car won the race."

Yet even a simple shopping-trip excursion with a sensitive parent can inspire a boy or girl to look at the mercurial nature of words. You visit the _bakery_ and see the _baker baking;_ as _shoppers_ you go to the _shop_ to do _shopping;_ see _drivers drive_ into a _driveway._ By saying the words, talking about meanings, and enjoying the fun of hearing changes in word sounds you and your child become aware of the immense flexibility of language.

Help the child to develop lists of words that demonstrate their versatility. For the word *play,* the two of you might write down as many words that use *play* as possible:

Play

plays
player
played
playing
playful
playfulness
playtime
double-play
play-off
playpen
a play

By offering your son or daughter a group of unfinished sentences, you can ask him or her to fill in the blanks with words from the list you just prepared. This will show you if he understands the vocabulary.

1. The children were _____. (*playing, playful*)
2. He _____ all afternoon. (*played*)
3. The pitcher helped in a _____. (*double-play, play-off*)
4. The kitten was _____. (*playful, playing*)
5. At school I like _____. (*playing, playtime*)

Another way to help a youngster see how words change is to start with a base word and to ask the child to create words from it, words that suit the blank space in a sentence. Help out with the tough ones!

Sleep

1. I feel _____. (*sleepy*)
2. Two puppies were _____ on a rug. (*sleeping*)
3. She spoke _____. (*sleepily*)

This discussion of word changes brings me to a consideration of word parts. Experts are divided on just how much the study of prefixes, suffixes, and roots (or stems) helps the child expand vocabulary. Many believe that it is only *after* people know the definition of a word that knowledge of its parts comes into play and that one doesn't learn much about the meaning of a word from unpuzzling its pieces. When coming upon an unknown word, not many people take it apart to discover its meaning. *Expose* comes from *ex* (meaning *from*) and *pos* (meaning *put* or *place*), but applying the definition *put from* doesn't help a reader who is trying to understand the meaning of *expose* when he finds it in a book. Once he knows it means *lay open* or *make accessible* or *make known* the reader can see a connection between the definition for the Latin prefix *ex* and the Latin verb root *-pos*.

The older child, however, can rely upon predictable elements, such as frequently used prefixes and suffixes to expand his vocabulary. Sometimes this reliance is instinctive: *re* as a prefix is often fixed in the mind as *again* and requires no conscious analysis. I think the schools stress this method of language acquisition too much—teachers often require children to commit lists of word parts to memory.

Yet, sometimes taking apart a word *can* help a child to discover its meaning. For instance the words *irresistible* and *uncomplicated* can be broken down into small pieces (into *ir–re–sist–ible* and into *un–com–plic–ated*), each with a meaning or a particular role in the correct use of the word. Once the child has thought about the pieces and has put them all together, he gains insight into the meanings of the words. A young writer who knows the word *appropriate* and understands prefixes and suffixes could change it to a negative word that named a quality: *inappropriateness*.

Just how do you assist your child in learning about prefixes, suffixes, and roots? First, you'd better understand them yourself. A *prefix* is a sequence of letters attached to the beginning of a word, a *suffix* is a sequence of letters attached to the *end* of a word, and both influence its meaning. A *root* or *stem* is a group of letters that make up a base word or part of a base word. Roots often come from Latin and Greek and have special meanings. Letters can be added at the beginning and at the end of the root.

Next, you'll want to help the child see how many words depend upon the use of similar prefixes and suffixes. Youngsters already have a number of these words at their fingertips, and you can help bring the words together to stress relationships. I think you should take your cues from the kind of classroom reading instruction your child receives—word parts are usually taught as word-attack skills for reading. In any case, don't be *too* ambitious in your attempts. You can help children prepare their own groups such as these:

"re-" words	"un-" words	"-y" words	"spect" words
*re*play	*un*happy	happ*y*	re*spect*
*re*write	*un*developed	funn*y*	*spect*acle
*re*ceive	*un*laced	fluff*y*	*spect*ator
*re*act	*un*dressed	furr*y*	in*spect*
*re*claim	*un*cooked	ic*y*	

These words have a reason for analysis because they have been generated from the child's experience. After you have talked about the meaning of each word the child suggests, ask, "What does the *re* do in each word?" "What does the *y* at the ends of those words do?" You establish a personal context for the child's study of language by looking at words that are already part of the youngster's word bank. In this approach, you are saying, "These are *your* words, so let's see how they work for you."

Once the child recognizes the pattern of meaning in the word groups, you can add new words to that group. "You've got it now," you might say. "*Re* means *again*. What do you think the words *reclaim* and *reexamine* mean?"

In working with prefixes, suffixes, and roots you must make your child aware of the problems, inconsistencies, and frequent unreliability of word-part clues. For example, a child who knows that *re* means *again* could sit forever peering at the word *reiterate* and never divine its meaning if *iterate* were a mystery. *Try* has no connection at all with the *y* suffix despite its last letter; *reason* and *really* have no relationship to the *re* prefix.

Knowing the meaning of parts of a given word does not *always* bring about clear understanding. Failing to make sense of a word with discernible parts, a child could easily lose heart, and could question his own abilities. So he or she must learn that studying prefixes, suffixes, and roots provides a valuable means of building vocabulary, but it is only *one* part of a larger pattern of growth and development.

Before we leave this subject, I would like to call your attention to an excellent scheme for vocabulary training developed by James I. Brown and pointed out to me by Mina Shaughnessy. Professor Brown provides a table of fourteen master words made up by twenty prefixes and fourteen roots. What is so astonishing about these words is that, knowing the meanings of the prefixes and suffixes that make them up, one has access to an enormous number of words. I urge you to have a good look at the chart on the next page.

Prefix	Its Other Spellings	Its Meaning	Master Words	Root	Its Other Spellings	Its Meaning
1. de-	....	Down or Away	DETAIN	Tenere	Tain, Ten, Tin	To Have or Hold
2. inter-	....	Between	INTERMITTENT	Mittere	Mitt, Miss, Mis, Mit	To Send
3. pre-	....	Before	PRECEPT	Capere	Cept, Cap, Capt, Ceiv, Ceit, Cip	To Take or Seize
4. ob-	Oc- Of- Op-	To, Toward, Against	OFFER	Ferre	Fer, Lat, Lay	To Bear or Carry
5. in-	Il- Im- Ir-	Into	INSIST	Stare	Sist, Sta	To Stand, Endure or Persist
6. mono-	....	One or Alone	MONOGRAPH	Graphein	Graph	To Write
7. epi-	....	Over, Upon or Beside	EPILOGUE	Legein	Log, Ology	Speech or Science
8. ad-	A- Ac- Ag- Al- An- Ap- Ar- As- Al-	To or Towards	ASPECT	Specere	Spect, Spec, Spi, Spy	To Look
9. un-		Not				
Com-	Co- Col- Con- Cor-	With or Together	UNCOMPLICATED	Plicare	Plic, Play, Plex, Ploy, Ply	To Fold, Bend, Twist, Interweave
10. non-	....	Not				
ex-	E- Ef-	Out or Formerly	NONEXTENDED	Tendere	Tend, Tens, Tent	To Stretch
11. re-	....	Back or Again				
pro-	....	Forward or In Favor of	REPRODUCTION	Ducere	Duct, Duc, Duit, Duk	To Lead, Make, Shape or Fashion
12. in-	Il- Im- Ir-	Not				
dis-	Di- Dif-	Apart From	INDISPOSED	Ponere	Pos, Pound, Pon, Post	To Put or Place
13. over-	....	Above	OVERSUFFICIENT	Facere	Fic, Fac, Fact, Fash, Feat	To Make or Do
sub-	Suc- Suf- Sug- Sup- Sur- Sus-	Under				
14. mis-	....	Wrong or Wrongly	MISTRANSCRIBE	Scribere	Scribe, Scrip, Scriv	To Write
trans-	Tra- Tran-	Across or Beyond				

Guesswork in the Limelight

I want to tie up the basic goal of improving writing skills with a general consideration of how to deal with questions about new words. I think it's very important for you to resist telling your child the meaning of the word straight off. At the early stages of vocabulary growth, you will sometimes provide the answer immediately but as soon as you can, begin to free the child from dependency on you as a source of definitions. Suggest the patterns you follow when *you* stumble on words you don't know.

Most people first use informed guessing as a means of unpuzzling a new word. Don't you try to figure out the meaning from the sentence in which the word appears? Most times you can come up with a definition that's accurate enough to let you guess the meaning; later on you'll check your guess in a dictionary. Children need to practice this guesswork whenever they can.

Suppose your daughter asks you to define a word—for example, *irritated*. You can rely upon the child's love for games and puzzles to urge her to use clues in sentences to figure out definitions. "I know what that means, Gigi. But let's see if *you* can guess what it means when I use it in a sentence. Listen carefully to the hints before you say anything. 'The woman left the party because smoke *irritated* her eyes.' What do you think it means?"

It won't always work! You may have to try other sentences that have more obvious clues. But once the child gets the meaning, it's one she's put together from your clues *into her own language,* and you have helped her to use vocabulary that is already part of her repertoire.

Go on talking about the same word, and suggest sentences in which the word can be used: "Good, Gigi! That's right. It means *bothered.* Suppose I said, 'Mother was *irritated* because I forgot to buy eggs for tomorrow's breakfast.' What would that mean?" You might say "What are some things that *irritate* you?" or "What does your brother look like when he's *irritated?*" Finally, ask the youngster to write the word down and to construct her own sentence using the word. A picture cut from a magazine or newspaper or drawn by the child can illustrate the new word and will provide visual reinforcement.

The dictionary plays a critical role in expanding vocabulary, and serves the writer in many ways. Often, it provides new meanings for words he already uses. Other times a writer seeks the dictionary when he drafts a sentence using a word that strikes him pleasantly or harshly and he is not sure it means what he wants it to mean in the sense he has used it. Or he may be groping for a word, his sentence flow dammed up by uncertainty: Is it *healthful* or *healthy, meritorious* or *meretricious, ingenious* or *ingenuous?*

The writer may be unable to think of the exact word he wants; yet he can look it up because he knows its opposite. Perhaps he uses a word whose meaning fits the sense he has, yet he dislikes the sound of it or it's not precise enough in this instance. So he turns to a *thesaurus* (a word book of synonyms). But he'll come back to the dictionary to look up the meaning of the synonym, which he might not know too well. A writer will use a dictionary to check the spelling of words as he finishes his manuscript before sending it to the typist.

And, of course, the dictionary is a book for reading, whenever the author wishes to take time out from the preparation of his manuscript.

I want to show you how to help your child learn to use the dictionary in a productive way. Teach your child that the dictionary is a resource for expanding word power, a means for learning about new things and ideas, and a way to spend time enjoyably. Set a good example by using the dictionary yourself. How often do your sons and daughters see you with it in your hands, checking the meaning of a cookbook term, a word from the news, or a word you have heard in conversation? Unless the youngster recognizes it as a tool that people use in real situations, the dictionary becomes a text left in the classroom.

School instruction in dictionary use is, by nature, an artificial process. The teacher sets up a situation in which he or she demonstrates the features of a typical dictionary entry. By the third and fourth grade children are already learning about alphabetizing, guide words, diacritical marks for punctuation, entry words, even something about multiple definitions of words. The teacher must also help the child use the dictionary selectively: There is such an abundance of information in it that it is important to be able to *ignore* extraneous material when seeking the one or two details related to one's search. To help develop these skills, a teacher will provide a list of new words or prefixes, and will stage a situation that arouses the need for practicing dictionary skills, selecting a number of words whose exploration in the dictionary will bear fruit. Except to check on the spelling of a word he is writing in a story or composition, a child does not often use the dictionary in school to suit his own specific and immediate needs. However, the home environment can foster that use, and one of your primary goals should be to guide your child's creative use of the dictionary. I suggest you buy children's editions, suitable for your child's age group at different stages of his or her development. Those alphabet books that you have been buying since your son or daughter's first or second year are kinds of primitive dictionaries. Picture dictionaries provide a number of words for each letter; the illustrations usually portray a word's meaning in visual terms. Sometimes the book will have picture explanation of a word's meaning and a sentence to demonstrate that meaning. Below is an example of this approach taken from the *Illustrated Dictionary for School and Home* (New York: Grosset and Dunlap, 1972).

C

a b c d e f g h i j k l m n o p q r s t u v w x y z
A B C D E F G H I J K L M N O P Q R S T U V W X Y Z

cabbage

A cabbage is a vegetable. We have a cabbage with our beef stew. Do you like cabbage?

cake

There is a big cake on this plate. Tim takes a piece of cake with the cherry on top.

camel

A camel is a useful animal of the desert.

camera

A camera takes photographs. Tim's Daddy is taking a photograph of him with a camera. It will be a good picture.

captain

This man is a captain. He is in charge of a ship. There are also captains in the army. Jim is captain of his team. He is leader.

Because of their limited number of entries (Grosset and Dunlap's dictionary offers only thirty-two for the letter *A*, for example), picture dictionaries are used to teach the child the variety and delight of words, and your youngster will certainly pick up information about specific words and will even learn some new definitions. But picture dictionaries are not complete enough to be used as a tool to discover the meaning of unknown words. However, the picture dictionary helps the child establish the important habit of using the dictionary as a source of information about language.

For eight-year-olds and over, there are a number of more advanced children's dictionaries, and you can select from many attractive ones that are complete and clear enough for young writers. Buy one of these for your youngster's bookshelf and help him or her use it. In Chapter 13 I will suggest a number of specific ways you can use the dictionary in a program of word expansion.

As a word book, the thesaurus is a tool a writer cannot afford to be without. It is the writer's book of options. If a word does not convey exactly the meaning that is needed or does not sound right among its neighboring words, the writer can check the thesaurus to come up with several other possibilities. Even an eleven-year-old can grow intoxicated with delight at the endless supply of word choices that exist for unspecific words such as *good, nice,* or *walk.* The simplified pocket thesaurus in dictionary form is a word book that's easy for a youngster to use. A child who looks up the word *happy* finds almost fifty different synonyms! The danger is that the writer might run into trouble if he uses just *any* of those words to replace *happy:* For example, if you look up the word *happy,* you will find that both *delighted* and *blissful* are rough synonyms, but they are as different from each other as they are similar, and are not interchangeable. One can easily spot the inexperienced thesaurus user by the excess of million dollar words he or she uses in place of simpler and more direct ones. On the whole, with guidance the child will learn to use the thesaurus to his or her advantage as a valuable sourcebook for the vast array of words in the language and their frequent interrelationships.

To the eleven-year-old, you can say, "Let's look up *happy* in the thesaurus and see how many words we can list." The child will copy the synonyms onto a page and will ask about meanings and pronunciations for unusual words. You will then ask him to check the children's dictionary, then the adult one, in order to reinforce the interdependence of thesaurus and dictionary. Words supplied by the former are worthless unless the writer knows what they mean. After the list is complete, ask the youngster to write a sentence of five words for each, or ask for an imaginative story of five or six of the words presented by the thesaurus entry. These kinds of language games use word books to build writing skills.

Spelling Skills and Word Hot Spots

To the unprofessional eye, weakness in spelling immediately brands a writer as incompetent. Often the reader of a poorly spelled letter, memo, or job application makes an unfavorable judgment about the intellectual ability of the writer. This is unfortunate because poor spellers can be as intelligent or as unintelligent as good spellers, and competent spelling does not assure skill in sentence structure. However, a page full of spelling errors jars the reader and often disorients him or her. See how long you, as reader, will put up with this piece written by a college freshman with no experience as a writer:

> Wmen's liberation is good in one way, but not in another way. Wemen should be paid the same amount of money as a men, in some field, for example. If wemen have the knowlegde to become nurse, doctor or any other field, wemen should be paid the sam amount of salary. If she doesn't have the knowlegde for that particular field, then she should not be paid the same salary. I think that wemen should have the same rights as a man. Because if a lady doctor is examining a patient, if she doesn't have the knowlegde, the patient eighter will become very ill or die. There are some job's in which wemen cann't work at, for example, sanatation department, plumer's ETC.

This eighteen-year-old author's bad spelling shocks you, no doubt, and leads you to believe that he is severely limited intellectually. That conclusion is untrue—he is a bright and talented young man, yet it's easy to understand why you made that judgment. Of all the writing-related skills children learn in school, they probably suffer most from spelling. You know the cycle in one form or another. First the teacher gives a pre-test on twenty words for the week; during the rest of the week the children examine the twenty words, write each one several times and write sentences for each word; on Friday there is a test in which the teacher reads a word, uses it in a sentence, then asks the children to write the word down on paper, and to spell it correctly the first time. You know this pattern very well because you probably lived through it as a child and because you replace the teacher when your child studies at home.

I have a few insights to offer. First, you ought to know the seventy-five to a hundred words that are most frequently misspelled by children from the third grade through to college. Look at pages 231 to 232 in the appendix where I've reprinted such a list; it should help you be on guard for those words in your child's writing. They are the demons, the spelling headaches that plague most beginning writers and some accomplished ones.

Knowing problem words in advance helps you and your child keep a watchful eye for them. I believe one of the problems in teaching spelling is that letters in textbooks look different from handprinted letters. See the difference, here, between the *a* and *g*:

dragon *dragon*

Usually differences are not so obvious, but the youngster should learn the word in the medium in which he'll write it. When cursive writing begins, the differences among the three types of writing are more pronounced:

dragon *dragon* *dragon*

Of course, the child must also see the word he's learning in type as well as in handwritten print so that he'll recognize it when he reads it. I always find it peculiar that spelling is tied more to reading as a skill than it is to writing. I rarely see a textbook that shows words in a child's handwriting. It seems to me that the mental picture the child makes of the word ought to begin in the way he will *write* the word on a page. For older children and adults with spelling problems the teaching of different words should be attempted through handwritten or handprinted examples.

We should capitalize on the child's ability to create mental images. Therefore, I'd like to suggest another means of examining words. Each word on the list below has a hot spot—a combination of letters that become confused in a writer's mind. What is interesting about these letter combinations is that they confuse *many* people. If you call attention to the hot spot in a memorable way (often with humor) you can help your youngster build up a resistance to the problems these words present. Ask your child to look at five or ten words at a time, then to write them in clear firm letters in his notebook. Underline, circle, or draw a box around the troublesome letters (in the list below the hot spots are printed in italics); then play a game in which you and the child try to figure out a way to remember the hot spot, writing down the advice alongside the word. Here are some examples for the eight- or nine-year-old:

afr*ai*d	Give *aid* after the *r*.
am*on*g	No *u* in this word—just *on*!
be*lie*ve	Never be*lie*ve a *lie*!
co*m*ing	Only one *m* in this word.
di*nin*g	Only two *n*'s in this word.
fr*ien*d	*I* am your fr*ien*d to the *end*.
ho*p*ing	I *hope* you remember only one *p*!
pleas*an*t	Do you see the *ant* in pleas*ant*?
s*en*t*en*ce	Three *e*'s! No other vowel!
s*ur*prise	Say "Sir," but write *sur*. What a surprise!

You and the child will come up with countless others: "Look at *pa* in se*pa*rate"; "Rely on two *e*'s in sinc*ere*ly"; "No *e* in truly," are examples. These little memory tricks will go much further than rules or lists in helping your child with difficult spelling words.

If your youngster returns from school with many words marked "incorrect" on a spelling test or in a piece of writing, you must be supportive yet firm. It's easy for a child to develop a sense of hopelessness about spelling—problems poor spellers have are various and resistant to instruction. But they *can* improve if the writer is determined. As a parent you must encourage the kind of attitude that says, "Spelling improvement is possible."

How do you help the child build skills? First, develop a record-keeping system for misspelled words. Suggest that your child write words on index cards, and store them in a "Spelling Box," a homemade shoe-box affair; or you can suggest a list or chart format. Any of these is excellent procedure for the child to use for study. No matter what approach you take, follow the same kinds of steps you took when looking at spelling demons with the youngster (see pages 231 to 232). Here is a typical chart that focuses upon individual mistakes:

My Spelling List
by Claire Anderson

Word	Hot Spot	Word With Hot Spot Underlined	Way to Remember
all right	two l's, two words	all right	Think of *all wrong*
across	only one c	across	a + cross
it's	apostrophe s	it's	it's = it is

Encourage your children to write their own sentences or little stories using the words that appear on these private lists.

Professor Shaughnessy suggests that writers group their mistaken words so that errors demonstrate a pattern. Using such a procedure, you may find that ten or twelve errors on a child's page will reduce themselves to four or five types of mistakes.

If the child asks you how to spell a word, spell it slowly and carefully, watching as the boy or girl writes it down. After the youngster finishes writing say, "Now let's put all those words you had trouble with on your own spelling chart so you'll know them for next time." Even a four- or five-year-old who loves to write little stories will respond to this kind of game of hunting out words and writing them down on a list. Of course you must exercise judgment about which words to bother with: A preschooler who struggles with a four syllable word doesn't have to learn that word at this time.

As your youngster grows older, you will be inclined to advise, "Use the dictionary" when he asks you how to spell a word. I want to caution you about how frustrating this response can be to a poor speller. First, stopping to look up a word during the process of writing derails a writer from the track his thoughts are taking. If he must break his thought to look up a word in a dictionary, he might never come back to exactly what he wanted to say. When they use dictionaries, writers usually check spelling selectively, having been trained by practice to know just where to question the letters in a word. However, I have watched inexperienced young writers sitting with dictionaries on their laps at story-writing time: They will stop at every third word to check their spelling. This is a terrible procedure, but teachers rarely point out its shortcomings.

Countless times I've heard: "If I can't spell it, how can I look it up?" That *is* an intelligent question. It is also a good reminder of how little we have done to show the child how to use the dictionary in such a situation. What do you answer?

Your conversation should run something like this: "Okay, here's a word that might cause you some problems in spelling: *crime*. Suppose you wanted to use the dictionary to check it. You've got to look under several possible spellings. The sound of the word might tell you to look it up in these ways:

cryme
kryme
creim
krime
krhyme
crime
crhyme

If you can't spell the word, you might have to check them all before you found *crime*."

With such a discussion you give the child some good tips about the way dictionaries help spellers.

In fact, you should offer the child other kinds of advice about how to spell, advice which helps in the long-range acquisition of skills. Remind your sons and daughters about these steps toward better spelling:

- Listen carefully as someone says the word.
- Say the word yourself as you look at it.
- See if you can find the hot spot.
- Run your finger over the letters, saying each letter as you "write over" it with your finger.
- Close your eyes and try to see the word.
- Now write it down.
- Look at each letter. Check the word you have written against the word you were looking at. Did you include all the letters? Did you put the letters in the right order?
- Write the word again. Write a short sentence that uses the word.
- If you missed the spelling, put the word on your own spelling list.

Such procedures will help the child establish a program of learning.

I've not encouraged working with spelling rules for several reasons: First, though the rules seem to work in teaching the child about word families, they do not seem to help him avoid misspelling a word he usually misspells. Second, very few rules stay with the child for enough time to be practical. How many spelling rules can *you* remember today? (*Maybe i* before *e* except after *c*—and I bet you still have trouble applying it!) Teaching rules to young children assumes that the child has the ability to see and to use the relationships among parts of words. Most poor spellers have trouble seeing word-part relationships, so they cannot use the rules when trying to spell a word. The best way to use rules is to ask the child to state one in his own language each time he has spotted a pattern of misspelling among several words.

Sentences to Play With

If misused or misspelled individual words knock a reader off the horse, a trail of individual sentences on a page can similarly make the trip a pleasant or a nasty one. A paragraph of sentences that all start the same way, have about the same length, and follow pretty much the same pattern make a boring ride, a journey across a changeless landscape. In paragraphs where relationships between ideas never focus, and where thoughts tangle, fragment, and run together, the journey becomes intolerable, and ordinary readers refuse to go further—they stop reading.

The problem of structuring sentences, of putting words together in ways that are clear, varied, and directly related to the idea intended for expression is called *syntax*. This arrangement of words in a sentence is difficult for many writers. An astonishing thing about immature college writers is that their spoken language is often rich in varied structure—they put words together in complex, highly related forms—but their written language shows remarkable inexperience with the options syntax allows. That's from lack of practice. Since effective writing is often measured by the writer's use of mature structures, you will want to increase your child's experimentation with sentence patterns. What I mean by mature sentence structure will grow clearer when I show you some samples, but at this point, just keep in mind that there's nothing *basically* mature or immature about the syntax of a given sentence. The reason should be clear: The structure a writer chooses must be the *best* possible one to put forth the meaning he intends. Sometimes a simple sentence of four or five words reveals the writer's intention better than a more complicated pattern. Other times, because of the play of ideas and the crosscurrents of related meanings, writers join elements that might better stay apart.

Look at this and see if you have a reaction to the structure of the sentences the writer uses to advance her meaning:

> I held my friend Carol's new baby, Jim. I enjoyed the experience very much. We rested on a worn red easy chair in the warmth of the living room. I fed Jim his nighttime bottle. He was too tired to drink. The television screen cast flickering shadows on the ceiling and walls. Jim strained to watch the screen. He licked the nipple with a tiny pink tongue. His head rested in the curve of my elbow. He gurgled with contentment. He fell asleep. I carried him into his room gently.

This writing is choppy, even childish, in its needless repetitions and in its resistance to structures that allow ideas to interrelate for clearer meanings. The vocabulary makes good sensory appeal, but the writer's sentence patterns work against her effective use of language. Below the paragraph has been revised:

> When I held my friend Carol's new baby, Jim, I enjoyed the experience very much. Resting on a worn, red easy chair in the warmth of the living room, I fed him his nighttime bottle, which he was too tired to drink. As the television screen cast flickering shadows on the ceiling and walls, Jim strained to watch it. He licked the nipple with a tiny pink tongue, his head resting in the curve of my elbow. Then he fell asleep, gurgling with contentment. Gently I carried him into his room.

In this sample you can see a greater maturity of expression, because the writer has made the events of the narrative interrelated through the use of sentence structure. The first sentence makes a logical connection between the event and the writer's appreciation of it. The second sentence suggests simultaneous action (resting *and* feeding); in the first paragraph you read those as separate actions. Further, the second sentence uses the word *which* to relate the baby's tiredness and his inability to drink the bottle. Notice how in sentence three the writer shows a clearer relationship between the flickering television and the baby's straining: one action depends upon the other. In the fourth and fifth sentences actions again depend on one another. You can see the tongue licking *as* Jim rests in the writer's arm; and you can see the baby falling asleep while he gurgles at the same time. In the last sentence the use of the word *gently* creates a new emphasis and then provides a new sentence pattern, one not used before in the paragraph.

It's easy to see that in the second paragraph the writer expresses her thoughts more maturely by using sentence patterns that state her ideas in clearer ways and which keep more to her purpose in writing.

Although numerous studies have found that instruction in grammar has little bearing on writing growth, teachers continue to teach grammar as if it *did* influence writing skills. Others support the kind of plan followed by men like John Milton and Benjamin Franklin: Sentences that have been written by masters become models that developing writers copy for style and structure. Some relatively recent research (1969 to 1973) suggests a new approach, which its originators call "sentence combining." Here a child, following directions, replaces one sentence element with an element from another sentence in order to create a tighter structure. By working with language supplied to him, the child shifts, replaces, and alters words and word groups. The assumption is that once he creates a sentence of complex syntax, he can then recreate that structure in his own language. Results from experimentation with school children by Professor Frank O'Hare at Florida State University bear out that assumption and demonstrate that such sentence-combining practice is not dependent upon a formal knowledge of grammar.

Look at this combining procedure, which is often called *embedding* because the writer inserts (embeds) an idea from one sentence into the sentence that comes before it, changing forms of words as necessary. These practices of combining sentences are called *transformations;* and the grammar system which describes the way the language operates through embedding is often called *transformational grammar.* It's really simple. In each of these groups, notice how the sentence (or sentences) in 3 results from combining features of 1 and 2.

1. The child cried.
2. The child was hungry.
3. The child who was hungry cried.

1. The old man tapped his cane.
2. The old man hobbled down Oak Lane.
3a. The old man hobbling down Oak Lane tapped his cane.
3b. Hobbling down Oak Lane, the old man tapped his cane.

I don't intend to suggest that you become *teachers* of this sentence-combining activity. That would be too time consuming for the average parent and would require too much training. You'd need to invent countless sentence examples in groups which could be effectively combined into a final sentence that made sense. Further, you'd have to be able to write clues for the child so that the combining elements provided practice with various syntactic forms. Professor O'Hare's exercise for a group of twelve-year-olds would look like this:

A. The slave cried out for mercy.   (ing)
   The slave threw himself at the Sultan's feet.
   The slave had been caught in the harem.   (WHO)

B. Crying out for mercy, the slave, who had been caught in the harem, threw himself at the Sultan's feet.

Notice how the *ing* and the *WHO* in parentheses direct the youngster to perform special kinds of operations in combining the sentences. That example, like most of the others Professor O'Hare uses, is lively and well thought out, obviously requiring more time in construction than any parent (no matter how willing) would reasonably be able to give.

However, you can adapt a number of these sentence-combining ideas into games young children can play with great fun at home. In the first place, I suggest you provide examples that ask youngsters to use their *own* language as they perform certain embedding activities. Next, you can offer a sample that shows the kind of new sentence which might be created. You will not come anywhere near a complete examination of possible sentence combinations, but I will indicate the kinds of activities you might set up so the child can practice sentence patterns.

Establish two columns for combining. Then ask the child to embed an item from Column B into a sentence in Column A, so that the result makes sense.

A	**B**
The car broke down.	who lives in Texas
My cousin owns a horse.	that I love
Carrie's book dropped with a clatter.	which fell from her desk

Once the youngster writes a sentence like this one:

My cousin who lives in Texas owns a horse

you then provide a similar activity in which the child fills in
blanks in a sentence:

My aunt who ————————— writes ——————————.

I call this the Jigsaw Sentence—it is a puzzle with some
pieces in place and others waiting for the child to create. Its
advantage is that the child can use in a new syntax words that
are based in his own concrete experiences. The child is writing
about a real aunt, thus using his acquired combining skill to
give us information relevant to his own life. After inventing
pieces for the Jigsaw Sentence, the child can then follow these
instructions: "Write a sentence about your sister and use *who*
the way you did in the Jigsaw Sentence."

In the chart below you'll find examples that you may copy
with your own words and set into columns for the child to combine into a sentence. Remember, each item represents a type of
combining. To be effective, you'll need to make up several
examples for each, so that the boy or girl has sufficient practice. I'd say eight- or nine-year-olds could manage these games
nicely—from the combining of elements in the two columns,
through the Jigsaw Sentence, to an original statement of the
youngster's own.

A. Main Sentence	B. Word Groups for Combining	C. New Sentence	D. Suggested Jigsaw
We ran through Sunset Park.	because we were late (Similar words to start word groups for combining in this way: *although, since,* *after, so,* *that, when,* *whenever,* *if, how*)	Because we were late we ran through Sunset Park We ran through Sunset Park because we were late.	Because ———— ———————— ————, we looked ———— ———————.
The sparrow shivered.	sitting on the roof (Similar words— almost any that end in *-ing* work in this instance— to start word groups for	Sitting on the roof, the sparrow shivered. The sparrow sitting on the roof shivered.	Dancing ———— ———————— ————, the child ———— ———————.

A. Main Sentence	B. Word Groups for Combining	C. New Sentence	D. Suggested Jigsaw
	combining in this way: *dancing, laughing, running, playing, singing,* etc.)		
Johnny made a snowball.	dressed in a warm red sweater (Similar words—almost any that end in *-ed* work here—are *placed, locked, poured,* etc.)	Johnny, dressed in a warm red sweater, made a snowball. Dressed in a warm red sweater, Johnny made a snowball. (Point out the humor—and the incorrect expression—if the combining element goes in the wrong place: Johnny made a snowball *dressed in a warm red sweater.*)	Placed _____ _____ _____, the doll _____ _____ _____.
Flora baked cookies.	a good cook (Any word group that describes the person or thing named in the main sentence works here.)	Flora, a good cook, baked cookies. A good cook, Flora baked cookies.	Mommy, _____ _____ , bought _____ _____.

Those four examples will help you practice some combining techniques with the child. Though they do not show the youngster how certain elements substitute for others, these sentence games encourage manipulation of sentence parts, which all writers need to practice. If you're ambitious, you might set up groups of sentences, so that the youngster can see replacements and new punctuation elements.

Sentences for Combining	New Sentence	Sentence Jigsaw
The truck struggled up Pike Hill. It shook from side to side. Then the truck stopped.	The truck struggled up Pike Hill, shook from side to side, and then stopped.	The kitten _____, _____, and then _____ _____.

In offering practice in sentence-combining techniques that require replacement, removal, or change of certain elements, provide as many hints as possible for the youngster. In the example above, underlining the words tells the child which ones to eliminate. In the example below, the underlined word is to be left out, the circled word is to be changed, and the hint in parentheses tells how to make the change:

The dog chased his tail. The dog(played)in the snow. (Use -*ing*)	Playing in the snow, the dog chased his tail.	_____-ing _____ _____, my friend _____ _____.

I want to repeat that it really will take some time for you to prepare games like these. But even if you don't have the time, it's enough to know about sentence-combining possibilities. A child who presents for your approval a paragraph that looks like the story of Jim on top of page 101 will learn from your comments, such as: "There are excellent pictures here— I can see everything so clearly. But why don't you try to combine some of your sentences? Let's see. Can you put the first two together using *when?* Can you change *rested* to *resting* and then put sentences three and four together? What other combinations can you make?"

Though I've talked quite a bit about how to structure sentences correctly and maturely, you've no doubt noticed that I've not mentioned much about the incorrect sentences children write. I talked about sentence fragments in Chapter 4, but I've deliberately excluded lengthy discussions about sentences that run together, about sentences whose verbs and subjects don't work correctly, and about sentences whose pieces do not fit together sensibly. Children make so many different kinds of sentence errors that it is the trained teacher's job to be able to react to those individual problems. A discussion of grammatical concepts here would take me too far from my purpose, which is not so much to make you competent in pointing out and dealing with language problems as much as it is to give you ideas for developing positive attitudes toward writing, and to help you to guide your child in enjoyable writing activities at home.

For those of you who want more information about specific areas of correctness, I have provided an overview of language instruction in the appendix (see page 228). It will help you deal with the errors your child's teacher points out on a page of schoolwork. I have not written a grammar course, only a sampling of some typical kinds of mistakes inexperienced writers make with sentences, and I follow it with suggestions for correcting those errors.

8

Snapshots of Special Places

From the earliest moments of awareness infants respond to the physical environments surrounding them. As children grow, the intensity of those impressions strengthens through familiarity and repetition (and sometimes through some single yet dramatic event). The places in which the youngster lives, eats, plays, and dreams all make an indelible impression upon the film of memory. It is to these powerful images in the child's mind that you can turn for creative activities in writing. Description is a key skill, one which the child will need to demonstrate frequently, so nurture that skill as best you can in the home.

One Place: The Senses, Front and Center
Which room shall you and the child choose for exploration through word pictures? The choice is limitless really: There's the bedroom, which defines more than any other the child's world—dolls, trucks, and stuffed dogs lining a wall, bits of rocks, crayons, cutouts strewing a desk; there's the bright yellow kitchen, the thud and click of its cabinets, the whirring of the refrigerator and its cold breath, the scent of apples and raisins from the oven where a pie crust lifts and browns; there's the park, not far off, and its creaky swings, its maze of gray metal bars for climbing, the crunch of dry leaves under sneakers; there's the doctor's office, such a mysterious, often

scary place, crackling white paper stretched across an examination table, balls of cotton in round blue jars, that glass cabinet with bottles and boxes and silver tools; there's the grocery or the street corner or the library or a church or an empty lot; there's the beach or the riverside, a living room, a friend's room, the bathroom, a ballpark, a gym, or a bakery. If you've been sharing experiences with your child, been talking and writing in the language of sensory awareness, you'll be impressed with all the possibilities for describing a place.

This is an exercise children of any age can practice with your guidance and assistance—even the child who writes haltingly and who must copy your attempts to put his words into written language or who must ask for words to be spelled with great frequency. It's the rare child who cannot look around a place, name an object, show its color or an action it performs, name a sound it makes or a smell it has or a sensation of touch it conveys. You've been practicing those skills with your child all along, so that when you begin writing about some special place much of it is crossing familiar ground.

Begin by asking your child to describe the room in which he or she is sitting at that moment. With such an activity you have the place in constant focus and you can help the youngster construct sentences or even write them yourself as he or she dictates. Encourage the child's efforts by saying, "Very good! How about adding a color?" or "Let's put in a word to show how the thing felt when you touched it."

For a first writing assignment I often ask a class to describe their classroom as they write. Here is an example by a thirteen-year-old:

> On this October morning I hear the excited murmur of my classmates as Mr. Wiener introduces our theme topic. At once the teacher writes down the requirements of the theme. The milky, white chalk glides across the dusty blackboard. Once in a while the chalk creates a shrill screech, forcing me to tremble and quiver as I feel goose bumps. A gentle, lazy breeze flutters through the room, filling it with a feeling of sluggishness and an air of freshness. Jeff's fingers run quickly through his dark brown hair; a serious expression sits upon his face. Steven bites nervously on the cap of his pen as thoughts leap through his mind. As the teacher plods around the classroom, I hear his black shoes squeaking and shuffling along the floor. A faint tapping rushes from the back of the room sounding much like Indian war drums. I feel the iciness of the desk's iron legs as my feet lean toward them. The smell of the vinyl book cover

floods my nose. Suddenly the bell rings: a quiet classroom turns
into a hullabaloo. And so, another English period has become
part of the past.

An easy way to encourage a youngster to record sense impressions is to play the following little game before the child
actually begins writing his description. On a large sheet of
paper, upon the chalkboard, on separate index cards, or on
pages, help the child develop a table of sense images which
later can be expanded and improved upon in a descriptive paragraph. First the writer indicates the place and time during
which he or she makes the observations, then in each column,
lists sense words and word groups evoked by the place at that
time:

Place: my bedroom
Where: Kings Highway
When: Saturday morning

What I Saw	What I Heard	What I Touched	What I Smelled or Tasted
red and white blanket	the oil burner rumbling downstairs	soft blanket cold pillow and wall near my bed	coffee sweet whole-wheat toast
pink walls	my bed squeak-ing		
black and white picture of "The Country Mouse"	Mom's footsteps		
Barbie doll on the white desk			
yellow sun shin-ing through the shades			

From those collected impressions the writer builds a description of the place:

It is Saturday morning in my bedroom on Kings Highway. A
black and white picture of The Country Mouse is on the pink
wall near the door. I see a red and white blanket on my bed. It
feels soft. My pillow is very cold and so is the wall beside me.
I see my Barbie doll sleeping over there on the white desk.
She does not mind the yellow sun shining through the shades.
I can hear the oil burner rumbling downstairs and my bed
squeaking when I move. I hear Mom's footsteps in the kitchen.

She is making breakfast for us. I smell coffee and sweet whole-wheat toast. I don't like coffee, but the toast smells delicious!

You'll notice in this simple description how the writer relies upon the table of senses she prepared. The words, "I see," "I can hear," "I smell" help provide starting points for full-sentence images. Encourage simple and direct statements that urge the child to write sustained sensory images. Even if all the sentences in these early efforts begin "I see" or "I hear," applaud them. Notice, too, how this writer combined sense impressions of different types and how she connected the ideas in her writing with words like *beside me, near the door, over there, downstairs.*

Below I have listed some goals for this writing exercise. It's an excellent idea to discuss this list with the child before writing begins. I've found that the clearer the expectations and aims for an activity, the better the youngster performs. With such a list at hand, your responses to the child's writing can be specific, more than just empty praise. I present these "goals" in question form as suggestions for effective writing:

What to Aim For: Tips for Strong Descriptions of Place

1. Do you name the place you are describing and tell where it is?
2. Do you tell the time of year or the day or time of day you are looking at the place?
3. Do you tell several colors?
4. Do you name some sounds or actions?
5. Do you tell what things you touched and how they felt?
6. Do you tell what you smelled or tasted?
7. Do you connect the ideas together with words like *beside, near, over there, downstairs?*

These suggestions, coupled with the sense chart, provide a stimulus for the child beginning descriptive writing and later provide a guide for improving the first attempt. "What a lively description you have. But why don't you find a word to name the sound of Mommy's footsteps? Do they *creak, scrape,* or *thump* on the floor?" With clear aims and techniques, such as the sense table and list of goals, you can overcome one of the young writer's biggest fears, that of not knowing what to write about.

Wherever possible, show the child an example of what you mean. You can read the samples from this book to your daughter or son. You might write something yourself! Nothing illustrates better than an example: A child who reads another child's creation has a realistic model at which to aim his own level of achievement. Of course, the goals of an activity are always clearer when weighed against a completed project.

Along with our attempt to help your child heighten and expand the level of sensory diction in his or her writing, talk about building, combining, expanding, and altering sentences. In the piece on page 110, the writer uses a simple structure: She begins most sentences with "I." You might say "In sentence 3 why don't you try to change the sentence around so you don't begin with *I?*" (*On my bed I see the red and white blanket.*) "Now combine 3 and 4 using *which.*" (*On my bed I see a red and white blanket which feels soft.*)

Opinions in Focus

For the developing writer, sustained description rooted in sensory language can grow overwhelming. The more acute the writer's sensory awareness, the easier it is to collect large numbers of details. A weakness often found in an inexperienced writer's attempts at description is that he or she presents a flood of images that have lost their focus when removed from the time and place of their origin and set on paper. The youngster looks around and records whatever sensory impressions strike him. A single place can stimulate hundreds of responses and merely recording those responses fills page after page. The goal is to make the description easier to manage by helping the child select key details that have a relationship beyond their existence in a given place. What I am saying is that you must help the writer learn which details *not* to include as much as you need to show him or her which ones are necessary to the description.

Before the record of sensory images begins the writer should be able to identify some overall impression he has about the room he wants to describe. When he looks at a kitchen is it *messy, cheerful,* or *noisy?* When he responds to the doctor's examination room is it a place that's *scary, tense,* or *pleasant?* Is the bakery a *busy* place? Is the synagogue *quiet* or *loving* or *active?* Is the classroom *tense* or *relaxed?* Is the train station *bustling* or *empty?* By encouraging the expression of some attitude, some opinion, some judgment or point of view about this room, you make a major contribution in the way the child develops as a descriptive writer and as a writer in general. You're helping to give the description focus, and, in a larger sense, you are helping to train the child about selectivity of detail.

I want to consider briefly the notion of objectivity. You may ask about the form of descriptive writing in which writers remove themselves from their subject matter, with the purpose of providing a complete, nonsubjective collection of detail. Scientific or reportorial writers fancy themselves wholly objective; their goal is to collect details, so they *define* things by recording an endless train of impressions. I'm uneasy about that: Distinctions between objective and subjective descriptions often seem to me to be only a matter of degree. You can look at one description when comparing it to another and say, "This is more objective than that." I suppose you would mean that there is less of the writer in that particular piece than in the other. But, as soon as a writer begins to record detail, he's making some judgments about degrees of completeness, about which items to exclude, about which to place first or last in a presentation, about which to stress by means of alternate word choices. Very subtle subjectivity is operating here, one which the writer (be he scientist, news reporter, or industrial manager) may not have identified for himself.

The closest I ever came to "objective" writing was as an undergraduate in a comparative anatomy class at Brooklyn College. In the warm spring months we sat at our lab tables, our white coats smeared and stained, while we examined dogfish lying on black paraffin trays. Those were the days when instructors in every subject area looked upon writing as an essential part of a course, and Professor Coonfield, an austere Southerner with glasses and a small black moustache, terrorized us with his rigorous vision of language. He demanded a formal report, submitted at the term's end, as a record of our anatomical journey through the dogfish shark. The report had to describe fully the object we had dissected and poked at with cold probes for more than seven weeks. We spent a full session talking about how to write our reports, during which he laid down his rules for words and sentences. Our writing must be simple; we must avoid overstatement and overexpressive (what he viewed as "poetic") language; we must be precise. For example—and this was the most challenging and difficult part of our task—we were never to use the word for an anatomical feature (nose, ear, eye) until we had described that feature fully. It was the size, the shape, the color, the position on or in the body that we identified first. Then we might say: "We will call such an organ *the ear*." Professor Coonfield insisted that our word choice be perfect: Do veins really *run* down the thoracic cavity? Are there two *pair* or two *pairs* of arteries? We found ourselves scurrying for dictionaries. Though I grumbled without end, this approach did more for developing my sensitivity to nuance and precision of language than any other course I have known. His purpose was to approximate inductive reasoning in the writing process: We gathered a number of particular details before adducing some general principle, which in this case might be the word of identification for the described object. But his larger goal was to have us describe the anatomical features of the dogfish so completely and objectively that a person who never saw the fish would have an accurate and scientific description of it.

This was a helpful activity for me as a writer—it forced me to look at words and language in a way I never had before—but I see now how short it fell of its purpose. I remember wondering about the innumerable gray bumps along the face of the shark, bumps that ought to be counted and measured (they were, after all, features of the anatomy). Yet, I decided not to list them because they would take too long to record and because, in comparison to the other features of the face (jaw, eyes, nares, teeth, etc.), those bumps paled in importance. I see now how many aspects of the dogfish anatomy my colleagues and I chose to ignore.

Even though factual writing implies a lack of subjective thinking, all this suggests that even in an intense scientific setting, writers exercise selectivity when they present detail. They do not focus this selectivity by means of some judgment or attitude they have about the object; nevertheless, by *some* process of evaluation they report certain details and not others. The doctor who writes a medical report can make it only as complete as his individual judgments allow. And, I think, reporters of fires, robberies, and murders are deceiving themselves when they think that their view is objective.

I am not arguing against "objective" writing, but I am trying to suggest that it is difficult to distinguish it absolutely from subjective writing.

Subjectivity Leads the Way

When your child writes about a place, help him or her use subjective responses to select and order details. Help your youngster zero in on his or her attitude toward that place. You may have to ask a number of questions and to suggest a few possibilities from which the child may choose, such as "What *one word* would you use to show what you felt about the supermarket we visited this afternoon? Was it *quiet, busy,* or *noisy?*"

Once the writer identifies a reaction, he collects only those details that relate to that reaction. Beginning writers should give details of time and place, and should identify their opinion about what they are describing in the first sentences they put down. Encourage first sentences such as these:

- Our kitchen on a Sunday morning looks messy!
- Sitting here in this basic English class on a rather warm Monday morning, my fellow prisoners probably feel the tension of doing their first writing.
- The library on Park Boulevard is very quiet this Tuesday afternoon.

If these sentences served as starting points, a writer would next add details that support his or her impressions about each place. The writer of the first sentence would add details to illustrate the kitchen's messiness; in the second sentence he or she must support the claim that the class feels tension; and in the third sentence he'd add details to picture quietness further.

As the youngster advances, he can create and sustain a dominant impression without exactly stating in a first sentence his opinion toward the place. Notice how this sixteen-year-old creates a mood of despair, almost imprisonment, as he describes the locker room where he must change clothes for work. Look especially at the last sentence which summarizes, brilliantly, the impact of the place.

Five o'clock again and the beginning of another night of work, here at The Kitchen in Green Acres. The punch clock stamps out the time with a thud, like a heavy metal gate falling closed, imprisoning me. The smells of flour and frying fat and the clatter of a hundred dirty dishes in the dishwater fall behind me as I near the dull gray door streaked with grease and soot, the door that leads to the basement and locker room.

The door flies open before I even reach it and Bill rushes out, beads of sweat still on his brow, his face red, his skin shining from body oil, his hand brushing strands of hair into place as he passes. The door closes behind me and before me in a narrow rectangular tunnel descends the long stairway to hell. Halfway down, I feel the heat of the boiler room, and the musty smells hit me, but it's not till I reach the locker room that I first see the Inferno. There stretches before me a long, narrow room, with the left side and rear wall covered by broken lockers painted gray, many with doors permanently ajar or completely torn off, and others with their doors jammed shut. The ceiling, once painted white, now stands dirtied by the soot of years past and scarred by the rust of the pipes running parallel and perpendicular across it. The right wall is made of cinder blocks and in front of it stands a clothes rack; no clothes hangers swing here and only one shirt hangs from a joint on the rack's far end.

Behind the open door sits the bin which holds the dirty checkered pants, usually soaked from soapy water. It holds the dirty shirts and aprons stained with food and bearing the colors of red, blue, black, and brown. By the end of the week the bin also holds the only uniforms left, so that I must pick through this maze of dirty rags to find the cleanest of the dirty.

One broken chair sits at the far end of the room, and many worn shoes lie scattered upon the floor. In the corner between the two lockers sits a box of receipt tapes of years past, forgotten and gathering dust.

Sitting down, I pull my shirt off and reopen my eyes to the dim light shed by one feeble bulb. The room hums with the rumble of the boiler in the next room and the clatter from above. A cool drop of water falls on my hand from a leaky pipe above as I gaze down at the floor, its original color smeared with the black of grease and gum.

I look absently over to the gray door standing open to the room, but mainly to the sign pasted on it reading, "This is your locker room, keep it clean." My eyes now drop to a comment written in reply to the sign and penned boldly in black magic marker directly on the door. I agree.

A roach slowly turns the corner of the doorway, his feeling antennas like hairs blowing in the wind and I feel as though he belongs here more than I.

Cameras and Crayons

Children can command few other mechanical wonders with the ease that they manage cameras. An inexpensive Instamatic lights fires even in the most reluctant writer. After he or she writes a paragraph describing a place, turn the child loose with a roll of film! Keep your instructions simple: "Take ten pictures that show why you feel this room is messy," or, "Take one picture that shows what each sentence in your paragraph describes." Develop the snapshots and have your child paste them on sheets of paper. Then ask your youngster to write a sentence about the action and details in each picture.

You can even start with the camera *before* the youngster writes. From a five- or six-year-old just ask for photographs that will show different features of a place. Ask an older child to portray his attitude or impression of some place with pictures. You can then use those photos to stimulate the child's written reaction in a group of sentences. Whether you use photos before the child writes or afterward, ask for written words to explain each picture.

Our daughter snapped her first picture when she was three years old, and I suspect we might have let her try it even earlier than that. What a thrill, when the photograph your child took comes back from the developer! If you have a Polaroid or one of the other instant developers, there's even more immediate reinforcement. A child snaps a picture and watches the scene develop before his or her own eyes! Your youngster can secure these photographs with a sentence of explanation in a scrapbook entitled *Places I Like*. The child can paste each photograph on a page and write a sentence of explanation under each.

You help your child establish the idea of opinion or attitude as a key to writing by connecting it with some cut-and-paste fun. Make a list of words that one might use to describe a place (*busy, quiet, neat, lively*); then ask your child to cut a picture representative of each word from a magazine. He should choose his favorite picture, then write a description that presents details about the picture he's cut out, details that support his dominant impression. The youngster next uses a large sheet of paper (8½-by-13 inches) and pastes the picture on top of the page. Below it he copies the final draft of his paragraph. An illustration prepared by the child can be used in the same way you used the snapshot with a camera. You can ask the youngster to draw and to color a picture of his favorite place either after or before the writing exercise, depending upon how you want to use it.

In both instances you're relating your child's writing with his communication in another medium. This connection opens countless roads to creative expression.

Description Described

Don Wolfe, a great teacher of writing who died in 1976, wrote that the assignment which asks a child to describe a room "has explosive power to raise standards of writing on every level" and that it "calls forth the use of sensory diction in almost every sentence, the gold of communication, the nearest approach to sound and color films, a vocabulary familiar to the most deprived pupils. . . . It calls for the realistic and imaginative observation that flows immediately into language. It proves to the child that he can paint pictures in words. . . . [It] shows the way to electric communication of the child's deepest feelings and most profound moments of insight."

9

One Person
in the Floodlights

The physical environment is a rich source for the developing young writer, and the women and men who people that world also make excellent subjects for practicing good writing. If you follow the techniques that focus on sense impressions, you can direct the writing of a simple description of a person. Mother, seated in the green leather chair beneath the window, reading the *Times;* Dad scrambling eggs in the kitchen on a sunny Sunday morning; the letter carrier as he strolls from house to house; a bank teller shuffling bills and counting out coins on a wooden counter; the butcher in a long white coat as he cuts a bone with an electric saw; a brother or sister, aunt or uncle, cousin, friend or classmate in a flash of action or a moment of repose, all these become subject matter for a child writer.

One Person, One Sentence
A simple and pleasant writing exercise for a youngster directs him or her to look at a person and to write a single sentence that describes that person performing an action. The word games you have been playing with your child will sharpen the precision of the image he can convey. Activities in choosing a concrete word for a general one, in capturing movement with exact action, in writing sensory language, in expanding and combining sentences help the child succeed in this exercise. Again, you should offer clear directions: "Write a sentence that

tells what _____ is doing. Try to use lively words for action, color, sound, and touch." Read the child an example—one of those below or one you have written to describe someone, perhaps the child himself.

Here are several one-sentence descriptions, the last few written by writers in their early and late teens. You can see how sensory images make the brief portrait come to life.

> Momma sits on our squeaky rocking chair with her soft brown hands on her lap.

> Robert, the newspaper boy, zips by on his bike and tosses the *Centre Daily Times* onto the porch.

> My brother Joseph dribbles on his yellow pajamas as he pokes his teddy in the playpen.

> Staring through wire gold-frame glasses, Jean brushes a soft strand of brown hair off her forehead and then coughs nervously into a trembling hand.

> His hairy arms stretching from black pants pockets, a yellow shirt hanging loosely over a worn leather belt, Danny breathes cold morning air and whispers, "I don't know what to talk about."

> A golden ray of sunlight crept into the room through the window and enveloped Twyla in a spotlight of dust, her blouse reflected in the lenses of her gold-rimmed glasses.

A Party Riddle

At the next party you and the child make, plan to have the guests write riddles as a party game. Every child gets a pencil and a pad of paper. Explain the game: "You all have pencils and paper. We're going to write a riddle. Look around the room and find one person you think you can describe in a few sentences. But don't tell us who the person is! Make your description as clear as you can, so that we can guess from your sentences who your person is. You might want to write about what the person did earlier at the party, something you remember. Be sure to tell us what the person looks like, how she moves, what color her clothes are. Put these four things into your description:

1. Show how the person moves or what he or she does.
2. Use a color and a sound.
3. Show a bit of the person's clothing.
4. If the person talks, tell what the person says and how the person says it."

After you talk about these points, see if everyone understands them. Then read a sample like this one:

> I see a little girl in red pants and a white blouse with red and green flowers. She scratches her short brown hair. In her hands she holds a yellow pencil. She is smiling and her warm brown eyes make me happy. She is my best friend. Who is she?

or this one:

> There is a boy at this party who shouted, "I won! I won!" when he pinned the tail on the donkey. He is wearing brown pants and a gray sweater. He has little brown freckles on his nose. They are hard to see under his blue glasses. He likes green jelly beans only. Who is he?

This games relies upon a child's natural love of riddles and his keen sensory awareness. It's sure to be a hit with any child, and helps your youngster practice key writing skills.

Photo Into Words

That tin oval, the large wooden box, or the tattered scrapbook that holds your photograph collection is a thing of delight and mystery for every child. I have watched children sit for long hours, sifting through a maze of pictures strewn about the bedroom floor, studying familiar and strange faces with concentration, laughing at styles, smiles and actions. This intense interest in snapshots of family, friends, and even strangers can be used for another stimulating writing exercise for your youngster. Suggest that he select a picture of some person from the photo collection, and ask the child to study the subject's face and pose, and the setting of the photo. Your goal is to encourage the youngster to write four or five sentences that will give life to the picture. Ask him to imagine action, sound, and color (if the photo is in black and white) and to try to identify the person in the picture. The picture selected can be of someone he knows well or has never met. What is important is the intensity of the appeal the person in the picture has for the writer. With your guidance, your child can write a visual portrait like one of these:

> My daddy's grandfather has a round face. In this picture he leans against a brick wall. A brown cigar is in his mouth. I like his tiny blue eyes. If he could speak, he would cough like my daddy and say, "I have to stop smoking!"

This is a picture of my mother before she met dad. She is wearing a blue bathing suit at Rockaway Beach. I can see white bubbles from a wave behind her. Her blonde hair looks messy because a wind is blowing. She smiles at me. I can see her straight white teeth. But she can't talk to me because I wasn't born yet.

A collection of these little word portraits makes a lovely scrapbook of family favorites. Help the youngster mount pictures on colored paper or cardboard on one page and the written portraits on facing pages. Ask friends and relatives to comment in the child's presence on the difference in the descriptive qualities of the visual and the verbal pictures.

Self-Portraits for the Very Young

As much as a child can write accurately in sensory language about a familiar person, I find the self-portrait an even more exciting activity. Young children love to look at themselves, to report what they are, and how they look. This first manifests, I think, as little drawings such as the one Matthew drew of himself (see page 36) in order to tell a little story. You must have many paintings that your own children made of themselves.

I'm going to show you one self-portrait Melissa did on her own when she was five and a half.

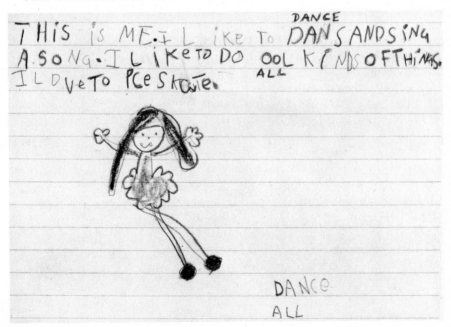

The picture and words are delightful, aren't they? However, I would have guided her to prepare a more sharply visual portrait, set in time and place, and showing much more sensory detail. Nonetheless hers is an instance of the impulse to define and describe oneself and deserves great praise. I asked Melissa to read her words aloud, and we both enjoyed her word picture and her little drawing. She told me about the ballerina dress and the dancer's crossed legs. At this point she had not colored the sketch; it was completely in pencil.

After we had talked about her words and picture, I felt that I could help her use her sensory responses to clarify the verbal portrait. Here's a rough summary of our talk.

"This is such a nice picture! I love the way you told all about yourself in sentences. But I bet you could add some words or ideas that would help make an even better picture of you."

"How? What do you mean?"

"I bet you can add a color word. Where could you name a color to make the picture clearer?"

"I don't know."

"Well, as the little girl in this picture, what color could you see around you, maybe a color of something you're wearing."

"Well, red. Red skates."

"Good! Try to put it in one of your sentences."

"I love to ice skate in red skates."

"That's perfect. Now, see if you can tell about something you can hear."

"What do you mean?"

"I mean a word that gives a sound—as when you're skating."

"*Errrrr.*"

"What's that?"

"The sound of the skates on the ice."

"That's a wonderful sound! How about a *word* that tells a sound?"

"I don't know what you mean."

"Well, you've given the real sound the skates make. That's very good. But I thought you might want to use a *word* that tells the sound. For example, when someone moves across the floor the person can *thump* or *squeak* or *thud*. Those are all *words* that tell sounds."

"Slip? Slip on the ice?"

"That's a good word to show action, though it's not a sound."

"Let's put it in."

"Go ahead. Put it in."

"I slip on the ice . . . and slide. I slip and slide on the ice."

"That's a fine sentence. But don't you want to put in that sound, *errrrr?*"

"I slip and slide and go *errrrr* on the ice."

"I really like that! That's very good. Now, can you put in a word that tells how the ice *feels?*"

"That's easy. Cold! No. Freezing. Let's put *freezing ice.*"

"All right. Good. Do you want to try to find a sound word, too? Can you tell how you sing?"

"What do you mean?"

"Well, do you *shout* or *squeak* or *sing* in a *soft voice?*"

"I sing in a soft voice. No. I sing like a bird."

"Okay. Let's put that in. What kind of bird?"

"A blue jay."

"Well, you've complained about how the blue jay makes such loud noises outside your window. It sings in a noisy way. Is that the way you sing?"

"No. A robin! A robin!"

"Does a robin have a soft song?"

"Yes. It's soft and pretty. A little *peep peep peep.*"

You can see through this little dialogue the way you can encourage a child to explore words and to select only the most precise words that are concrete and sharp in sensory appeal. Melissa had some trouble understanding the concept of "sound word," and I'll continue to help her with that concept when she wants to write. But her wonderful *errrrr* sound is characteristic of a child's original perceptions. I can't see how anyone else would have made that sound! Still, my intent in pressing her further was to try to have her look at legitimate words that name sounds as they show actions. She missed that concept, but she grasped quite a bit, so I didn't worry!

You can see how instinctively she turned to a figurative expression in order to clarify her description. Though not the most original simile from the professional writer's vantage point, it's fine as a child's effort, especially with the highly specific naming of the robin.

As Melissa spoke and made additions to her sentences, I handprinted each one. This is her new story:

This is me. I like to dance and sing a song like a robin. I love to ice skate in red skates. I slip and slide and go *errrrr* on the freezing ice.

Melissa copied my printing. Then she took the page and made the pencil drawing as you see it.

Melissa is not really describing herself in her story but is instead telling about things she can do. I would have encouraged something more like the little paragraph on page 125. But this is her own work brought to me for reading, and within that context I helped her use the skills she has been working to expand. A week later Melissa announced that her kindergarten teacher, Mrs. Coleman, wanted all the children to describe themselves aloud to the rest of the class. When I asked Melissa what she planned to say, she recited her self-portrait, and I was delighted with her use of detail:

> "I am a white face with nice dark red lips. My teeth are shiny and white. My two new teeth are growing in the middle of the bottom. I have rosy red cheeks—well, not as red as my lips. My hair is brown. I usually wear dresses and in the winter I wear pants."

In my discussions with Melissa I dealt first with ways in which she could improve the visual quality of her language and the exactness of her word choice. But in the sentences she first showed me there were some errors with which I wanted to deal. Since Melissa was offering me a finished product, I felt it was necessary to talk with her about some of the conventions of correctness that her sentences didn't follow.

We discussed the expectation that words will be spelled right and that sentences will be correctly written when people read someone's work. I reminded Melissa how periods tell readers when to stop. I read aloud her first sentence—"This is me"—and asked if she could tell what happened to my voice on the word *me*. She heard how my voice dropped; and I pointed out how I stopped reading after that word. Together we established a working rule for the period: It tells when a sentence ends, and it goes where the voice drops and stops when the sentence is read aloud. It's almost as if the voice knows automatically about sentence endings. I put a period after the *me*. She made it darker and rounder. Then I asked her to read aloud from the word *I* to see if she could find where the next sentence ended. She missed it; so I suggested she read more slowly and take note of where her voice went down and of where she stopped reading. She found it and drew in a heavy dot after *song* and again after *things* and *skate*.

One of the chief difficulties inexperienced writers have is keeping sentences apart. So I advise you to seize any opportunity to show children how to separate thoughts in sentences with periods (or question or exclamation marks, depending on the intended meaning).

Next Melissa and I looked at the spelling in her self-portrait. She has had no formal training, but she is a first-rate phonetic speller. Our favorite is her spelling of cucumber in a "vegetable book" she was illustrating. She labeled it *ququmbr*. She spells her words from her own sight vocabulary or by carefully sounding out word parts. I pointed out her spellings of dance (*dans*) and all (*ool*), told her that she had faithfully reproduced their sounds as best she could, but that those were not the spellings people used when they wanted to write those words correctly. I then wrote the words right near hers, so that she could compare the spellings. Then I asked her to write them correctly at the bottom of her picture (you see them over to the right) by copying from mine. There's no guarantee that she'll spell *dance* and *all* correctly next time, but the more practice she has the sooner she'll be able to spell them.

In his book for teachers, Don Wolfe describes a wonderful word portrait in which the child describes what he sees when he looks into the mirror:

> In the mirror I see a boy with black hair and snappy black eyes. His name is Joe Havens. His chin is a large heavy one. On his nose is a bandage where he got hit with a tennis racquet yesterday. On his dark face I see lots of freckles. One big freckle is on the tip of his nose. When he smiles, he shows a couple of big white teeth in front with a space between them. I guess this boy needs braces, but he doesn't want them.

Notice the wonderful specificity in what seems to me the best sentence: "One big freckle is on the tip of his nose." And there are other fine word pictures: "black hair and snappy black eyes," "dark face," "big white teeth in front with a space between them." No child other than Joe Havens could write this. As such, it is a supremely original piece of himself which the child lays before the reader.

I often ask young writers to prepare a collage of themselves. In the collage the writer-artist tries to answer the question "What Am I?" Look at the illustration on the next page to see what I mean:

After the young man or woman finishes the visual portrait I ask for a word portrait to answer the question "What Am I?" Below are two young writers' responses:

"What Am I?" is a question which takes a lot of soul-searching for me to answer. Sometimes I am the sound of an undertaker's voice reciting a eulogy for my father who died of cancer when I was four years old. I am the muffled sobs of sorrow I remember from my mother and the white lace handkerchief pushed against her lips. But I am also the confusion of voices whispering and my Aunt Helen's arms lifting me to hold me close and help me through something I didn't understand. I am the mixture of apology and hope in my mother's gray eyes when I first met my new father-to-be. I am the tension of my stepfather as he tries to read a book in Brookdale Hospital, while my mother is inside having a baby. I am the rough kiss, the whiskers and cigarette smells when my stepfather hears from Dr. Beck, "Congratulations. You have a little boy." I am Michael Barry's cries in the middle of the night, the egg yolk in his breakfast dish, his dirty diapers, and the clean smell of baby lotion and powder after Mother bathes him. I am the noisy bustle of moving to Bayside, the clatter of dishes, the scrape of our old couch on squeaky new floors. I am the giggle of my friend Bobbi when I tell her about Saturday night's date. I am also the oversized black-and-white poster of Bob Dylan that smiles at me from above my bed. I am the pink-and-white daisies on my bedroom wall, the torn white sneakers in the corner, my vocabulary-building book hidden in the closet. I am the quiet moments alone in my room when night comes and I can think.

I am the ringmaster of a three-ring circus formally known as my family. I am the arguments between my brother and the whisperings of my sisters. I am the polluted, grayish-blue sky of Long Island City and the slimy, filthy waters of the East River and Newton's Creek. I am the limp in old Jack's leg or the large red girder that smashed down upon it. To my childhood companions, I was a real Casanova for going out with twin sisters at the same time and to those girls I am a devil. And I am the look that I still receive from their reddened blue eyes. To Mom, I am still her blue-eyed bundle of joy, maybe growing up to wear the black robe of priesthood, while to Pop, I am a future Jim Thorpe sprinting flat races, hurtling over large obstacles with a pole vault, and smacking through defenses for touchdowns. Or am I a future Jerry West, swishing the winning basket at the buzzer? On the football field I am every player to hold a ball, but after ripping my leg open, I change from a growling bear into a purring kitten waiting to die. In the hospital I become the uncontaminated cleanliness and the antiseptic fragrance of the ward. I also become the lethal point of the syringe used to render me into the "world of nod," or the scent of flowers I receive from close friends. While listening to my stereo, I become Eric Clapton strumming "Layla" before close to thirty thousand screaming fans, and I also become the tangy odor of marijuana that permeates Madison Square Garden. I become one of the fans smoking a joint in the front row. My gang thinks of me as just another head in the crowd, but I am still part of each one of them: one person's sneer, another one's smile, I am the hate and the love that exist among them. In the movies I become an Errol Flynn and a John Wayne who rescue the beautiful brown-eyed damsel and slay the cowardly rogue. I am the pebble in a little boy's shoe, a knife in a policeman's back, a dent on someone's car, a Hank Aaron home run, my mother's teardrops, a bubble in Raquel Welch's bath, or a derelict stinking of alcohol. I am all of these things and many more. I am life.

Expanding a Picture of Someone Close

Help prepare your child to write his description of a relative or friend by reminding him or her to set the person in a particular time and a particular place. Suggest that the youngster record bits of detail using a table of sense impressions (see page 110). He or she can begin writing while observing the person in the midst of some action. When you look at the rough draft, ask questions as I did with Melissa in order to focus the child's sensory awareness—and remember, it's important to read an example together first. In the sample below, a young girl describes her sister:

I remember when my little sister Julia first came to live with us. She was just one week old. She looked like a little round beaver. When she wasn't crying, you could see that her eyes were blue. Her nose was like a little bell. Her mouth was a little round ball. As soon as she got home, she began to cry, and did she cry! When she started to cry, her mouth became a big "O." Her hands were tiny, and her fingernails were as thin as eggshells. Julia was always kicking her feet in the air and waving her hands. We were all very proud of our new baby.

In this one a sixteen-year-old describes her grandmother:

On a rainy night, in front of the TV, the roar of a Boeing 707 and the pitter of rain echoed in my ears: in her heavy red fireside chair sat Grandma, intently watching the lit screen. The glow from the table lamp beside her shined softly in her heavy blue eyes, glaring through her thick-rimmed spectacles. Her gray hair, pulled back tightly in a bun, touched the back of her neck. As she sat smiling at a cigarette commercial, her wrinkles deepened and her dimples quivered as she chuckled. Her large hands like shovels sat folded serenely in her lap and her elbows rested on the wooden armrests. A spacious chair surrounded her thin, slumped frame. As an old movie, *The Diary of a Young Man,* unfolded, her head nodded and her spectacles slid down and rested precariously on the top of her nose. On the table before her, a plate filled with orange wedges, dry and wilted, sat waiting. And as she snored loudly, her heavy breath fluttered the handkerchief in the pocket of her worn tan sweater. Then, as I lifted her head onto a downy pillow, she sleepily muttered, "Grazie."

You can tell here how each writer, on her own level, presents sharp sensory images through her own language resources. These are clear pictures indeed.

Yet you can help the child climb beyond this. Once a writer determines the attitude, opinion, or reaction he or she feels toward the subject, it becomes easier to control the details and to make them tell the story as the writer sees it. To do this, the writer eliminates unnecessary details and focuses upon those details that support his opinion. Encourage your child to do this by saying, "What is your main opinion about the person? Is she *carefree* or *attractive* or *strong*? Is he *shy* or *bold* or *serious?*"

Once the young man or women expresses that opinion, you can help sort through the details. "What is there about the way he looks or moves that makes you think he is shy? What does he say or do that says *shyness* to you?"

I call your attention to the piece below in order to show the effectiveness of a portrait in which the writer limits the description. I asked a group of writers to look at one of their classmates, who stood before them as a model, and then to decide on one single impression the person created. Was the classmate *handsome, nervous, playful, cheerful, charming, serious, strange, relaxed, confident?* They were to describe the details about the person that contributed to their impressions. We established the list of hints that follows. Go over these points with your child before he or she writes.

Hints for Solid Description of a Person

- Mention in the first sentence the time, place, and the single impression you have of the person.

- Tell some details of the setting in which you see the person: a piece of furniture, a wall, carpeting.

- Use only those details that contribute to the single impression. *Leave out any details that do not help create the impression.*

- Mention the person's size, color of hair and eyes, and clothing. Use images of sound, color, and touch.

- Write a sentence that tells what the person says.

- Toward the end describe the one feature of the person's face that gives you the impression you have.

In the description below, see how all details support the idea of Richard's *confidence.* Notice how effectively the writer quotes Richard's spoken words (I'll point out the conventions of this technique in Appendix B):

Richie Fries sits confidently atop the brown desk before us on this English theme day in late November. He speaks immediately, brown eyes sparkling at his audience of fellow classmates. His pressed blue shirt stresses his tall straight posture as his hand motions express words. He scratches his neat black hair as if in thought. "Next question!" he says. "Gotta wake you up. Ya look like you're falling asleep." The class watches his every expression, but there is no sign of nervousness in Richard, not a drop of sweat falling from his brow. "Look at me," his apple cheeks shout. "Look at me," his smile says. "Look," his position

at the edge of the table screams. "Look at me. This is my moment
of glory." His actual words race by at record pace. "My father
tells me I should think in seventy-eight and talk in thirty-
three," Rich speedily adds. Susan asks him to smile and change
his position. Propping himself upon his elbow, he leans back on
the desk. "Hey, why isn't this guy in Hollywood?" I think to myself. His eyes dance. They illuminate when he talks and glow
softly when he is silent. His exciting brown eyes hold the class
in a strong grip. They are only brown, same as so many other
eyes, but they twinkle and they bubble and they look squarely
at their audience without so much as a nervous blink. His eyes
smile even when his lips fall. The girls like him: he is lively, has
a good physique—I suppose it is understandable. Michelle asks
where he goes to meet girls and the class giggles squeamishly.
After a long, funny answer, Richie leans back, the edges of his
lips pushing his cheeks up. His brown eyes now stare at no one.
Everybody is writing. He takes a deep breath. Then, in a sudden
leap from the table, Richie returns to his seat like a conqueror.

I doubt that any writing skill is more important than description. Every kind of written activity demands description
of some kind. In a school assignment the young writer must
often explain a process—how a radio works, for example; or
must compare two forms of government; or must explain why
poverty exists. At some point he will have to turn to descriptive techniques. The training I encourage will sharpen your
child's eye, and make him or her a shrewd observer who can
transform observation and experience into written language.

10

A Moment
Reborn in Language

Children have a natural ability to tell stories. In school one student's story may send a class on a visit to the supermarket; another's illustrates a principle of gravity; someone else's instructs the class on the roles of community helpers. Unfortunately schools rarely use children's great knack of telling real events as the core of established writing programs. Recalling a shining event from some particular day is an easy way for inexperienced writers to develop practice in writing skills. When a child burns to communicate a story, the problems of carefully thinking out and inventing what to say and how to say it reduce themselves in a flow of language, a parade of scene. You can stimulate good writing at home, once you understand narrative techniques and how a child responds to narration.

What Is Narration? What Is a Moment?

Narration is the telling of event. It is story-telling—but I hesitate to use the words story-telling because they frequently connote *fiction, make-believe,* and *untrue.* I have nothing against imaginative writing, tales woven from the child's fancy, but the best way to stimulate the faithful recording of detail for beginning writers is through attention to real personal experience. When I use *story,* unless I say otherwise, I mean the telling of a real event.

Narration is an essential writing skill for the school child because it contributes to many other types of writing, such as scientific or historical reports, explanations of processes, and argumentation. In its most simple form, narration is the review of time through language. As such, it may unveil an event that occurred over a long period. Reporters and historians do this when they write about the instances that characterize a crime or a battle. With an enormous base of data at their fingertips experienced writers, by using details, can present an account of an extended occurrence so that readers feel that they are living through the times described.

Inexperienced writers rarely produce effective prose when they narrate events spread out over too vast a period of time. Children are usually given dreadful writing assignments: "How I Spent My Summer Vacation," "What I Do on Saturdays." Can you imagine how difficult it is to squeeze three months or even twenty-four hours onto a single page! To get finished with such assignments, students string occasions together without detail. They write, "First I did this, then I did that, later I did that," and so on. There's little there in the way of interesting material.

A single narrative moment is a successful approach to narration. By means of sense words, the scene and action of a brief period are fully expanded. Don Wolfe first explained that concept to me, and it has proven its value anew every time I have contact with developing young writers.

What is a *moment?* A moment is a single instance, a flash of time which the writer recalls sharply and can recreate in vivid language so that the event comes alive. Description (which we explored in Chapters 8 and 9) must come into play here. The only way to expand a scene that is sharply limited in time is to fill in details of the moment—physical background, characters, actions, and march of events—using concrete sensory language. I see a great overlap between description and narration, although some teachers of writing will insist on "pure description," that is, description that excludes a sequence of events and attends only to physical detail about the object, room, or person.

There's no way to write "pure narration" effectively. If the reader is to travel through the moment with the writer, only descriptive detail achieves that goal. Certain kinds of writing, for instance, a scientific report that records details of an experiment or a business report that tells the history of a corporation, will have few sensory details.

So, all your attention to concrete sensory detail until now prepares your child for another leap into writer's territory.

The Moment in Focus

If you've preschoolers or elementary school children at home, you probably can't stop the endless flow of story after story, little narrative jewels, some fanciful, most real, all told with intensity and animation. A simple, "Why don't you write about that" will often send the child scurrying for pencil and paper.

Encourage the child to talk about the narrative so that by creative questioning you can help limit the event to a brief span of time and can stimulate the youngster's memory for details. Ask when the event took place and encourage the child to name the month or season of occurrence. Did it happen in the morning or afternoon, in December, or sometime during the summer? Ask about colors and sounds, about what people said and how they moved. Say, "How did you feel about what happened? Were you scared? Were you happy? Were you annoyed?"

Any occasion that impresses the youngster is ripe fruit for successful narration. A moment at the breakfast table, at the street corner, on the yellow school bus, in the playground covered with snow, on the stairs to class, in the gym, during snack, at the chalkboard, in the lunch room, and at the supermarket are all possibilities. (See Appendix A for a number of specific suggestions for good narratives.)

To get the youngster talking, *you* might ask about your child's subjective judgment on an event in order to establish a focus that will aid his or her insight.

- "Did you have a good day at school—what was the best thing that happened to you there?"
- "What do you like doing most with your baby brother?"
- "When did your friend Karen make you angriest?"
- "When were you embarrassed?"
- "What was the most exciting thing you did in the snow?"
- "What was the best part of the picnic?"

A youngster's inclination to draw may also serve as a solid means for an experiment in narrative. After Melissa's swimming lesson at the town pool, she would rush to me as I wrote at a nearby table and would beg for paper on which to draw. One morning I suggested she write a sentence about the picture she had just finished. I asked how she felt about the lesson, and she told me it was "good." I inserted the word in her original sentence.

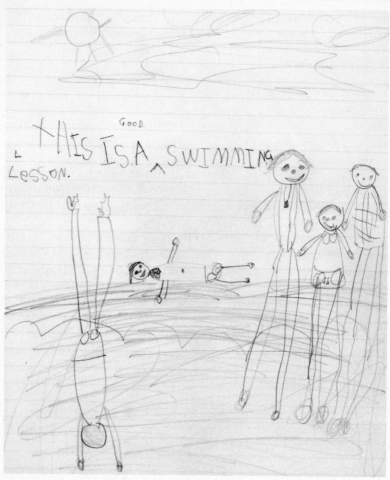

This sentence could serve as an effective opening to a group of sentences that tell a story about the lesson. Melissa explained the picture. As she talked I wrote, starting with the left figure. Later we used carets to add details and to sharpen the exactness of her word choices:

This is a boy doing a handstand. This is me doing a

                      in a red bathing suit.
backfloat. This is Michelle. ∧ She could not float on her

        with black hair
back. A girl ∧ was trying to help her. The swimming les-

      Liz
son teacher, ∧ taught me how to breathe and to swim.

One could argue that Melissa's writing is more description than narration, but I don't think the distinction that important. Despite little sense of sequence, it is the story of a swimming lesson with descriptive details added to show the event exactly as it occurred. Melissa has not pinpointed the action nor has she effectively established the time and place, but I will help her with those later on.

A Sense of Sequence

I want to consider the notion of chronology because it is so essential to clear narrative. Children often have trouble keeping time sequence in order; they often bounce back and forth from one part of an event to another. In Melissa's story you don't really know how the lesson proceeded. However, when she told me about the picture she discussed the events from left to right as they appear in her drawing. She was describing the picture she had made rather than the event that occurred. Time is suspended in the drawing as all the figures perform actions simultaneously. Even when young writers suggest sequence more clearly than Melissa did, you will often read a hodge-podge of events. For example, here is one confusing narrative:

> On Sundays the whole family has a good time. We usually eat lunch of fried chicken and French fried potatoes at a diner on Route 17. My father and I wash the car after breakfast so it looks new and shiny when Dad zooms our blue Chevy down the street to the Garden Parkway. My mother and sister clean up the house first, and then we're off driving in the sun. Of course, we change our clothes because after an hour of car washing we're all sweaty. When we finally get home, we're all exhausted!

The writer needs help to separate one event from another and to guide the arrangement of the events in timely order.

Often a young writer will flash back to earlier times in the midst of a straightforward march of scene. Except in the most adept of hands, the flashback rarely succeeds in riveting the reader to the moment. It is always a digression from a sequence, and even when it is rich in detail, it is a distraction from the main story. Writers usually bog down in a flashback because they use complicated verb forms to keep the time clear, and then imagery pales. One writing teacher calls it "the tyranny of flashback," calling the technique an impediment to a writer's growth. An effective narration calls for the focus on one clear moment, which reveals itself through a march of events described in concrete sensory detail.

Here are some suggestions for easy activities that will help your child build skills in commanding sequence.

- Have the child keep a list of the chronological events of some familiar actions, such as walking a dog, sitting at the breakfast table, leaving for school. These sharply limited actions compel the youngster to look at a brief time span and to consider in correct sequence the events that make it up.
- Have the child explain to you some simple process around the house: how to fry an egg, how to make a bed, how to put on shoes. Tell him or her to list the steps in sequence and then to perform them!
- Ask the child to draw pictures on separate pieces of paper about things that occurred in one day. Ask him or her to talk about which came first, second, and last.
- Show the child different photographs of one person—a member of the family. The photographs should show the person at different points in time. Have the child arrange the pictures in correct time order and discuss each photograph.
- Consider transition words with the youngster. These words serve as bridges from one idea to the next—one teacher I know calls them "sentence glue"—and they help writers tell the order of events more clearly. The important words that bridge ideas through time are: *later, before, afterward, earlier, now, then, some time later, suddenly, in the first place, former, latter, in the next place, once, often, next, first, second, third, previously, when,* and *at last.* Does your child understand these? Consider the child's age and command of language when judging which words to stress. Ask for an explanation of the words. Discuss those the youngster doesn't know, then encourage the child to write a series of sentences using some of these transition words.

By learning the importance of correct sequence in his own writing, your child also advances his or her reading comprehension. A child who knows how to use sequence as part of a story about a moment in his own life will respond to the chronology in a story he reads.

When you first ask a child to write about a sequence of events in order to demonstrate his command of chronology, you might try to follow one of Don Wolfe's good ideas: Ask the child to describe the happenings, one after the other, of the hour after getting up in the morning. Here is one result Wolfe shows:

I woke up at six-thirty this morning and went downstairs and ate. I had bacon and eggs, milk, and toast. After that I got washed and dressed. Then I went down and read the newspaper. After that I took my dog out. He is black and white. Then I got my water pistols, loaded them, and went outside and shot them. Then I went in and put my water pistols away in my desk. Now it was eight-thirty, and I left for school. At school I played "Catch a Fly" and "You're Up." The school bell rang at ten of nine. Then I went into school.

This is straightforward reporting with little sensory awareness and with weak sentence structure, but it is a product that a parent can help his child stretch toward excellence.

Narration: Sensory Language Leads the Way

The two of you should talk about the youngster's story, then prepare for the writing exercise. The child's sensory responses will serve as the means of developing detail to support his narration. Lead the child to record the sounds, smells, tastes, and sensations of touch that characterize the moment through discussion and questions, through bits of detail woven into the sentences after the child jots them down, or through a table of senses such as the following:

Place: Burger King	What I Saw	What I Heard	What I Touched	What I Smelled or Tasted
Where: University Drive in State College When: Saturday noon	girls in red suits and yellow hats yellow heat lamp long French fries ketchup squirted on rolls chocolate shake filling a cup white onion rings orange squares of cheese	hamburgers sizzling "Junior Whopper to go!" slam of refrigerator door ice cubes clinking together	soft rolls crisp hot potatoes cold wet cup sticky ketchup hard counter- top	fish frying sweet cola smoky oil onions

Notice how the writer draws upon those numerous impressions to convey his portrait of the place:

On Saturday at noon I visited Burger King. As I stood at the counter I saw girls in red suits and yellow hats. One girl squirted ketchup on a soft roll. After that another girl put a sizzling hamburger and white onion rings on the roll. I heard a man's voice yell, "Junior Whopper to go!" Then I heard the refrigerator slam. Ice cubes clinked together in a cup, and a man in a tie handed it to me. When I held the cup it felt cold and wet. When I tasted the cola it was very sweet. I could smell onions and fish frying in smoky oil. Finally, one girl put a bag of long French fries on the hard counter top. When I touched them they felt crisp and hot. Burger King is sure a busy place!

This is really a simple narration (again one could argue "description") in which a sequence of events comes clear. You see how the writer relied upon the table of senses he prepared in order to tell his story of a visit to a fast-food restaurant. The words "I saw," "I heard," "I could smell" help present the sensory images in a clear, straightforward way. Words like *as, after, then, when, finally* move the events along. Notice that the writer's story is limited in time. Detail must be intense and drawn in sharp original images. The writer offers his subjective judgment in the last sentence; it has controlled his selection of detail from the first. A more advanced writer might have incorporated the word *busy* into the first sentence in order to focus the quality of the succeeding details.

In the following two paragraphs by eleven-year-olds, see how the opinion expressed in the opening sentence limits and focuses the narrative; and see how the time named so close to the beginning of each selection immediately sets the reader in the moment. In the second piece the writer takes us into the next day, but until then her story covers a brief span of time.

One of the scariest people I know is the dentist. On a breezy cool day in September, I had my first visit with him. Boy! was I scared. My dentist lives a block away from me so I was there in two minutes. The second I walked through the silver squeaky door, I felt chills running up and down my spine. Then, I heard the loud humming sound of the shiny drill. I wanted to scamper out the door, but I was too scared to move. As my turn came and I approached the chair, my shoes crackled loudly on the smooth tile floor. My dentist, Dr. S. K. Amazon, appeared before my eyes. He was middle-sized and was dressed in a white outfit. He had very little left of his black hair. He took me to the big blue and white chair, and I sat down. I guess he knew I was frightened. He said "Relax, I'm just going to look at your teeth." When I went home he gave me a prize. I was very happy. Those fears have left me now, but I'll never forget that day.

On a sunny summer day in July, I went to Palisades Amusement Park for I was determined to go on an exciting ride. When we got there, the first thing I did was to race to the huge gray roller coaster. I was very anxious to go on, but still very frightened. As I plopped down into the rusty brown seat, the humming of the motor scared me half to death! Then, suddenly, the six cars went flashing away up the bumpy hill. When we sped down, I was so scared that I yelled out "Stop the car," but nobody heard me. As we kept on going, I got over my fear and started to look around. I saw the red ferris wheel turning round and round and heard the children screaming in back of me.

Finally the roller coaster stopped. As I got off, my mother ran to me and said, "Were you scared?"

I told her, "In that rusty old car all alone, what do you think?" She didn't say anything. We went on a few more rides and then returned home in our light blue car. The next day I told my mother that I would never go on such an awful ride alone ever again!

Here is one of a thirteen-year-old's embarrassing moments before a class.

A terribly embarrassing moment came when my best friend, Elizabeth, gave me an April Fools' Day gift in front of the whole class. The old gray room was dead silent when I opened the door with the brass broken door knob, and I drifted into the class late that hot summer afternoon. Everybody was staring at me as I shuffled in. My first impression was that tall, erect Mr. Smith, my social studies teacher, was going to give me truck loads of trouble! I hesitated as I tiptoed softly to my seat as the brown wooden floor creaked under me. I sat down and my friend Elizabeth pranced to the front of the room and called me up there. I practically tripped up to the front, red faced and puzzled. She handed me the gift and told me it was for getting the lowest marks all term in that class. The class roared at that. I opened the gift with trembling hands and as I opened the lid, out jumped a giant green bullfrog!! I screamed, I yelled, I shrieked! Boy, was I scared. Again the class burst out laughing with a roar. I slipped into my chair quietly trying to go by unnoticed. But, no such luck. Everybody was still laughing just as hard as ever. I'll never forget that day for the rest of my life!

A fifteen-year-old with a striking command of language brings a moment on a Brooklyn street to life:

The most pleasant memory of my youth in Bedford-Stuyvesant in Brooklyn is the scene of the watermelon man and his crew when he drove into our neighborhood on a summer Saturday. His horse would turn first onto Tompkins Avenue. Straining under the weight of many green-striped melons, the horse chewed on its leather bit and heaved the wagon forward slowly, each step an effort. The straw hat it wore shaded its sad brown eyes. Its coat, a dirty brown and white, rippled with the stress of animal work, like waves slapping some muddy shore. Patched leather straps that served as reins ran over its hide and flicked at lazy green flies; the insects buzzed in the air or hovered over the shining sample of melon, its pits winking in the sun like a thousand brown eyes. The driver and his friends too are unforgettable. The hands that held the reins were calloused and coarse, yet these overly large hands with square dirty nails held the reins with an almost regal gesture. The veins and muscles in the hands and arms of this kingly watermelon man looked like the ropes on an old homemade swing. He wore a dirty vest, a torn undershirt, and melon-splattered jeans, emblems of his trade. Suddenly, his sons and nephews in the back of the wagon laughed and grinned and started the chant, "Melon, melon, watermelon." The watermelon man, his gray hair moist with sweat, his wide mouth showing a perfect set of teeth, now took up the melody. Red bandanas and gaudy handkerchiefs waving in slight breezes, these fine men sang and hummed the chant.

Finally, a transaction began. A woman from a brownstone window across the street called, "Hey, them melons fresh?"

"Yes, ma'am," cried the figures in the wagon.

"Well bring me up one," she snapped from above. "No, not you ugly. You, yeah, the cute one."

"Anything else you wants 'sides a melon, honey?" replied the "cute" one, winking at his companions in the wagon who heckled and howled at this.

"Just a melon!" screamed the hoarse voice of a man from the same window above.

I, standing in front of Jack's Candy Store on the corner of Madison Street, must have snapped that scene firmly in my mind, for I still can hear the cry of the watermelon man as it struts and dances in my ears: "Melon, melon, watermelon. Git de fresh watermelon. Melon. Melon."

Here, unedited, is a narrative from an inexperienced college writer:

> The day I caught a king Cod fish, out by Montauk Point, I will never forget the moment I experienced that spring day out on the ocean. One bright and clear blue morning, my family and I drove to the end of the Island, to do some of the fishing that

was going on out in the Island. On the way to the Island, my family and I were talking about the different kinds of fish that were running at that time. My father said, "Cod, Flounders, and Flukes". So I said, "Let's go fishing for Cod fish". My family agreed to go Cod fishing, and we did. At six AM. we sped into the fishing dock area, and my father looked over the situation, and decided to go fishing on a large brown boat, the Mary II. When a fog horn honked at six thirty the boat pulled out, and went for a cruies of eighteen mile ride into the ocean. Then at eight o'clock the boat arrived at the fishing grounds, and Captain Kallous looked over the side and shouted in a deep voice, "All lines down." The person next to me caught a fifteen pounder which fought on the wooden deck. It smacked its white tail from side to side. Shortly after, I got hit with a bite. The pole started to bend, and I could feel the the weight of the cod fish in the pole. It took me about twenty minutes to reel up a fighting cod fish from the choppy blue water. As I was reeling up the fish, it was man versus the elements. It takes a specal skill to reel up a large cod fish, because as the fish is hooked he will tend to pull down. As the fish is pulling down, you do not reel up, because the fishing line will have an excess of tension, and the line will break. By the line breaking you will lose your rig and the main thing, the fish. So I reel up a thirty five pounder, and I entered the fish into the pool. It took first place, and I won twenty six dollars and changes for the largest fish caught that day on the Mary II.

I thought you'd want to see this as it is, because, despite its mistakes, it's a wonderful narrative—the same young man who wrote the weak piece on women's liberation (see page 95) wrote this one after studying in a writing program like the one I'm suggesting here. What an improvement this paper is over the other! Here the writer has shared a meaningful experience and can begin to explore and to meet the social requirements of language, convinced that he has something worthwhile to communicate. It's unfortunate that at twenty this young man is just *starting* to learn skills that can be studied and developed from a very early age.

Read samples to your child of what other children write before he or she starts a narrative. This helps the youngster understand what is wanted. You might help the child make up a list of things to aim for. In such a list pinpoint several of the key elements of narration. Here's a model for the child to use; adapt it to suit your son or daughter.

Writing Down Your Story: What to Shoot For
1. Tell your story clearly with one event following the other in order.
2. Tell when the story takes place as soon as possible. Name the month or season. Tell the time of day (morning or afternoon).
3. Show the people in your story. Tell how they move and what they do.
4. Describe what they are wearing. Use color words and touch words.
5. Tell one sound you heard. Tell one smell you remember.
6. Use someone's exact words.

Playing with Dialogue

As one feature of the faithful presentation of a narrative and/or descriptive moment, the writer must rely upon spoken conversation, upon dialogue between the figures who people the event. The formal requirements of quotations—such as, where the quotation marks go and where you put *he said*—sometimes mystify the child. However, if you are patient in answering those questions you will reinforce instruction your child has received in school and will give the young writer added options for expanding detail. (In the Appendix, I've explained a simple way of teaching your child how to use quotation marks.)

There are a number of approaches to teaching the child how to write quotations. One asks the child to select a simple comic strip from the newspapers and to paste it on top of a sheet of lined paper. The youngster copies the dialogue from the balloons above the characters' heads, using *He said* or *Archie said* or *Nancy answered* before or after the spoken words. Another activity has the child pretend that two familiar objects at home are having a brief conversation. Here's an example:

Mr. Scoop said, "Ice cream, I'm coming to get you!"
"No you're not! I'm too hard," replied Ice cream.
"Well, how will David have his dessert?" Mr. Scoop asked.

"All right," Ice cream said. "He's been good all week. I'll
soften up."

Such writing leads to opportunities for further development,
perhaps a little play-acting between you and the child in which
you each read and act out the conversation. Children love
acting; encourage your child, alone or with friends, to write a
brief original play about some holiday or special topic studied
at school. Last summer, youngsters of six, seven, and eight
had a grand time putting on their own Fourth-of-July Pageant
in King's Park, New York. Youngsters don't have to memorize
their lines exactly, but writing and performing a play is a fine
way for children to combine the fun of acting with a practical
writing activity.

Point out to your child that the use of a quote will add lively
detail to a narrative. As the child learns to use quotations, suggest that he or she write a narrative that relies heavily upon
dialogue. It might be between two people talking to each other.
You can suggest to older children that the characters be portrayed in some form of *conflict*. In the sample below, the dialogue carries the excitement of the narrative moment and the
details are sparse but effective:

> The gloom of the gray, misty day poured into the bedroom
> shared by my sister and me, casting shadows into the corners.
> Clothes lay spread in a misshapen mass upon the two identical
> twin beds, sorted into two piles on each cover.
> "Wait a minute. That's mine," shouted Susan accusingly, as I
> threw a tartan plaid skirt onto the woolen clothes pile on my bed.
> "It is not," I countered. "You gave it to me last year when you
> went away to school."
> "Well, I want it back. Now!" she demanded, her brown eyes
> bulging with anger.
> Sue lurched forward almost falling over the battered black
> trunk, filled with her clothes, which stood in the middle of the
> room. I backed toward the doorway swiftly side-stepping her
> three pieces of matching red luggage still unpacked.
> "Leave me alone or I'm going to tell Ma," I threatened weakly.
> "You have enough clothes. Why do you want this skirt?"
> The overhead light illuminated my sister's mouth, tight and
> drawn, as she moved closer and closer. "Because it's mine," she
> answered simply.
> Leaping forward suddenly, Susan snatched the now-crumpled
> skirt from my grasp. "It's my skirt and I'm going to keep it . . . it's
> my skirt," she repeated haughtily.
> Eyes blazing, I shouted angrily as I slammed the door, "I
> never liked that skirt anyway!"

A Short Story: Fiction for Thirteen-Year-Olds

The short story combines the narrative skill rooted in reports of sensory experience and the creative act of thinking through an original story. It is a challenging activity for the developing writer, and can be handled by the child who can report faithfully moments in his or her own life.

Be sure to explore *dilemma* and *conflict* when guiding the child in writing a short story; define the terms and discuss them. Good short stories usually have a dilemma where a character thinks through one side of a problem, then the other, finally making a choice whose consequences the writer explores. The dilemma should be important and meaningful, one rooted in the choices people need to make in their lives. If you're thinking that thirteen-year-olds have no sense of dilemma, you'd be surprised. Even more than older children, the thirteen-year-old has a keen notion of predicament. Perhaps the conflicting loyalties for parent and friend, for obedience and exploration, for remaining a child and growing up are particularly keen at this age and the pressures the child must deal with foster insights that are deep and passionate. When I teach short-story writing to eighth or ninth graders, we discuss *dilemma* and *predicament* and give examples of situations in which a person would suffer through a choice. We talk about what might go through a person's mind as he or she considers each side of the decision. Then I ask everyone to write down a dilemma on an index card that I will collect the next day. After I take the cards, I read each one aloud and the youngsters weigh the choices. Here are some typical suggestions that came to me over the years:

- A girl of thirteen wants to smoke. Actually she's not sure she wants to but all her friends do and they are pressuring her. Her father died of lung cancer just last year and she is frightened. There's a Valentine's Day dance this weekend and she knows she'll be tempted there.
- A boy, whose family is poor, wants to give a Christmas present to his little brother. The boy decides that he will steal a baseball glove from Woolworth's. But the manager is someone who helped him out of trouble once. How will he do it?
- A boy has a dog he loves but the dog has attacked two local children who teased him and has bitten them badly. The boy's father says the dog must be put away and the boy must take the animal to the ASPCA. Will he do it?
- A girl who always gets good grades did not study for a science test because her parents had a fight that night. As she sits in her class the teacher leaves the room. The girl has a chance to cheat.

> Although she has never cheated before, her grades are important to her. Will she do it?

Although these are not exceptionally original dilemmas, the discussions that follow always show that such situations are common in the life of a young teen-ager and arouse intense feelings. Once the writer finds a meaningful situation to lay at the heart of a story, I would urge him or her to set down the events straightforwardly, using rigorous sensory language. "The Sabbath Breakers" is a marvelous story from a ninth grader in my writing class. It won first prize in a contest sponsored by the New York City Board of Education in the mid-sixties.

> Mr. Goodman's eyes traced the faded blue pattern on his tallis, folded neatly beside him. It was the same tallis he had worn at his Bar Mitzvah, fifty-one years ago, and it was the same shawl that he would be buried in. His parents had been immigrants from Poland and for sixty years, ever since he was four, he had gone to synagogue on Saturday. The prayers ran through his mind as he remembered the sonorous voice of the rabbi on the first Sabbath he had gone to *shul*. Vaguely, he recalled his mother and older sisters, heads covered as they sat on the other side of the temple in the women's section. Images of his father, rocking in rhythm to the hum of voices as he prayed, flitted through his mind. The strange, awe-inspiring sound echoed in his ears as it had years ago. Mr. Goodman smoothed the fringes on his tallis as he recollected old men reciting the mystical words by heart. A sudden stabbing pain in his hand brought him back to the present. He wondered "Why should I go to *shul*? God's never done anything for me. No family, nothing to do, and this arthritis . . ." He winced as another pain streaked up his arm.
>
> "Never mind *shul*. I'm going to paint my fence. Holed up in that old store all week, I want to get out. Fresh air and the sunshine will do my arthritis some good. That's settled."
>
> Fifteen minutes later Mr. Goodman was shuffling down the walk, swinging a can of paint. The old man reached his fence, and carefully set down his pail. With gnarled hands he popped open the can of paint. His white hair softly sank to his forehead and the enormous blue-plaid shirt he wore filled with the warm breeze. Dipping the brush into the paint he argued, "I pay my dues to the *shul*. He won't mind if I paint on the Sabbath. Besides, look at the cracks in the fence. Another week and it might split. I have to do it now." He resolutely slid the brush down the picket fence. Deftly, his shaking hand caught a bead of paint before it could drip down the plank.
>
> The sun rose higher in the sky and the wiry old man painted on. His scuffed slippers were dotted with paint and the white

boards glistened in the sun. People, strolling home from synagogue in groups, gossiped about the events of the week and
stared at Mr. Goodman. The rabbi, swathed in a black coat,
strode boldly down the street, very conscious of being the most
respected man in the neighborhood. Mr. Goodman hastily turned
his back to hide from the rabbi's piercing eyes. He busily swept
the stickly bristles up and down the pickets as he reminded himself, "It's a free country, I'm not gambling, just painting a fence."

Slowly all his neighbors drifted into their homes. Mr. Goodman continued painting. Only four planks were still bare. Across
the dusty street stood an audience of two boys. They leaned
against a streetlamp and solemnly observed every move Mr.
Goodman made. The old man was very conscious of the four eyes
staring at his back, but tried to ignore them. The boys whispered
to each other. One muttered angrily, "He's no Jew. Painting on
Saturday. Why wasn't he in *shul?* Does he think he's someone
great? God should punish him."

The little one squeaked in agreement, "He's no Jew. He's got
nerve. He should be punished."

The fat one took a step forward and his second chin quivered
as he screamed, "Old man, God will punish you! Just wait!"

Mr. Goodman shuddered but did not turn.

"Hey you!"

The fat one stooped and grasping a large rock, shrieked,
"Nazi!" He took aim and threw with rage.

Blood splattered the glistening white fence and Mr. Goodman
fell with a thud.

The pious boys ran to tell of God's punishment.

In this story the main character resolves his dilemma early
on, and the writer drives home the consequences of that dilemma with ironic pungency. You see how the principles of
narration and sensory language help the story: Instead of flashing back to earlier events the writer tells us details by letting
her protagonist have a dialogue in his mind. The vitality in this
piece of fiction comes from the young writer's perception of the
sharpness of the physical world.

Your sons and daughters often spill over with excitement at
moments of story-telling, of story listening and sharing. You
are still working in Tolstoy's domain when helping the child to
unlock experience from memory, and to convey that experience
to others through sensory language. A child can write a narrative more easily if his oral tale falls on responsive ears, so you
must listen and laugh and question and commend and exchange
tales. Then help focus the child's event, and explore it's sensory
qualities.

11

Adventures in Make-Believe

What holds more promise than a child's imagination? In wonderful leaps the young mind wanders and connects, dreams and invents, projects and uncovers. Surrounded by a world of fiction —television, fairy tales, movies—the youngster absorbs models for imagined stories early into language experience. This delight in fancy is a sea of possibilities for developing writing skills.

The imagined episode about which the child chooses to write depends upon concrete sensory detail, which provides the dimension of reality that helps the reader to suspend disbelief. In familiar fairy tales, glimmers of color, bursts of sound, flashes of hot and cold, sweet smells and rank, snatch readers into the make-believe world. The same realistic touches should appear in a child's imaginative writing.

Descriptive skills of place, object, and person move down new roads with these activities. The narrative skill the child has worked to develop will apply here too. Will the pretend story unravel through a clear progression of scenes? Will the writer identify time and place? Will the sequence of events advance the story clearly and logically? An imaginative tale intensively perceives a *single moment* in sensory language and offers depth and quality of action. Thus, the child can write make-believe while practicing important language skills that you have been encouraging all along.

Riddles and Games on Paper

I've taken a delicious model for two-sentence riddles that children can write from the delightful nonsense in Jane Sarnoff and Reynolds Ruffins' *I Know! A Riddle Book* (New York: Scribner's, 1977). Here is a book that offers lively illustrations and silly riddles in easy sentences. For example:

> Do fish perspire?
> Sure, that's what makes the sea salty.

Eight-year-olds can write their own silly riddles. This makes great practice since the child can focus ideas in two simple sentences. In them you have the chance to establish basic notions of correctness and completeness. You can look for end marks and capital letters and can encourage the use of some lively action or other sensory detail. To focus the child's thinking, you can suggest ideas for riddles on general topics, such as animals, fruits, machines, or weather. Here are some riddles to share:

- How does the snow fall?
  It falls when it's pushed.

- Does a horse laugh?
  Nay, it does not!

- When is the sky clumsy?
  It's clumsy when the rain drops.

- How does an oak grow bigger?
  It opens another branch.

- Why do cows chew grass standing up?
  Grass cannot sit down.

Most of these riddles demonstrate a youngster's ability to play with words. Though that seems a sophisticated skill, I'm always impressed at how well children pick up on multiple meanings and how they are amused when they apply a meaning that does not suit the context. (Don't insist on the *double entendre!*)

One writer wrote this silly riddle, quite different from the last one:

- Why do cows chew grass standing up?
  There would be no room at the dinner table for the rest of us.

Supervise the writing of riddles carefully, because the writer may be tempted to offer an *incomplete* sentence as a response to the opening question. (See Appendix B, pages 230 to 231.) An unguided child might easily write this as the third riddle I mentioned:

> When is the sky clumsy?
> When the rain drops.

The word group *when the rain drops* is only a piece of a sentence; and that's exactly the kind of sentence fragment I find with alarming frequency on the papers of inexperienced writers. You can see why the writer wrote what he did: In his mind the connection between thoughts is clear, and he is depending upon the reader to relate back to the previous sentence. Conventions of edited American English, however, demand that written sentences express complete thoughts: Take the opening question away from the riddle and you have something that does not make grammatical sense: *when the rain drops*. The word *when* tells the reader to expect something else that's going on at the same time as or as a result of what follows it. Unless the writer supplies that information *to the sentence,* it does not express a complete thought.

If the youngster writes the riddle with only a piece of a sentence as the second statement, cover up the first one. Ask the child to read the words aloud to you. See if he thinks it makes sense that way. Talk about the idea of completeness, about a sentence needing to say a whole thought between the capital letter and the period. If the child cannot understand even after you talk, rewrite the sentence piece so it's complete.

Another thing to watch for in these riddles is the correct use of *it's* and *its;* explained more fully on pages 232 to 233. Deceptively simple words, these appear often as errors even on papers by college students. Riddle writing often calls for these words, so you should be able to explain that *it's* means *it is* and that *its* is used in all other cases.

For the two-sentence riddle game you might use the following with your child:

- Why does a dog bark?
- Why does the floor squeak?
- Does a cat read?
- Will the bus be early?
- Can a tree be late?
- Does a shoe talk?
- When does a nose run?
- When does the sun rise?
- Does darkness fall?
- Do dogs laugh?

For children of six or older you can excite their fancy by
asking for riddles in which the child pretends to be some object.
The youngster must give a clue about himself *as* the object
without telling *what* he is. Suggest that the child use words
for colors, actions, sounds, smells, and comparisons in the
riddle. Read these with the child as examples:

> *I have a white plastic body with my name on it. You must take off
> my white hat to use me. When you squeeze me I stick out my white
> tongue. I smell minty. What am I?*

> *I am tall. In the winter I am skinny and naked and shake in the
> wind. In the spring I wear green. In the summer I wear yellow.
> What am I?*

> *I am long and yellow. I have an orange top and a black pointy
> tip. Children always bite me. I know how to write. What am I?*

A child could make a wonderful drawing to follow up any
of these riddles!

Visits with Make-Believe

A parent can stimulate imaginative writing about visits to or
with characters in fairy land, in favorite stories, or on TV shows
by drawing upon the child's familiarity with fictional characters. Here the youngster brings the character into the home or
joins the character on one of his or her adventures. The paragraphs below were written by young children using physical
details to represent reality despite the imaginative framework:

> Goldilocks sits on the furry white rug in my living room. She
> has curly blond hair and blue eyes. She sits on the floor because
> she does not want Daddy's chair to break! I ask her if she wants
> some sweet hot chocolate. She says "No. I would like some oat-
> meal." I want to play outside, but she says she is afraid of the
> bears.

> I played in Toftrees Woods with Little Red Riding Hood yester-
> day. We picked buttercups in the warm sunshine. We smelled
> grass. We heard many sparrows chirping in the blue sky. Sud-
> denly I saw a wolf leaning against an oak tree. I said to Red,
> "Sh! Follow me." On tiptoes we sneaked out of the forest.

> I visited Sesame Street yesterday. I brought one dirty sneaker
> for Oscar to eat. He crunched it with his teeth. "More! More!"
> he yelled. He rolled his big brown eyes. I pushed him back into
> his home in the garbage can.

I was sitting on the couch and Peter Pan was sitting on my new yellow chair with orange spots. He was wearing a green hat, a green jacket-shirt, green pants, and green shoes. He has dark brown eyes. I said to Peter Pan, "I wish I could grow up with you in Never-Never Land." Peter Pan said, "You forgot that I am not going to grow up." He moved his lips over his teeth. Then he flew out the window.

I visited Sesame Street yesterday. I saw Big Bird and he was all yellow. I asked him to play ball with me. "Sure," he yelled. He caught the ball with his orange beak. But the ball fell out with a boom because it is slippery.

Ask your child questions before the youngster writes in order to draw out details: "You saw Peter Pan?" "What was he wearing?" "Where did he sit?" "What did you say to him?" "What did his face look like?" Make up a list of pointers for the child to mention in the visit to make-believe:

Writing About a Make-Believe Visit

1. Tell where you are. Show what you see around you.
2. Tell what your visitor looks like and what he or she is wearing.
3. Use a word to tell sound.
4. Use words to show color.
5. Show lively actions.
6. Tell what you and your visitor say to each other.

Help the more mature writer expand an episode from a book, during which the child puts himself squarely into a scene. Here is a thirteen-year-old's exuberant (if somewhat over-described!) tale of Marc Antony's oration:

I, a lowly Roman commoner, stand amongst crowds of grumbling plebians as they irascibly huddle about in the Forum. My ragged clothes cling closely to my body as people lunge toward the pulpit. The sound of children bellowing and women screeching echo through my ears. My robe which drapes loosely about my body flaps sprightly in brisk breezes. My shoes are worn and battered. And as my feet stand weary, I feel them touch the trodden earth. My neighbors mumble quietly as they slouch over, facing the roaring crowds. Frantic women chatter noisily, flinging their filthy arms into the air. Pushing and jostling halt. Whimpering, growling, shrieking and murmuring: all cease. Antony marches toward the bare and lonely pulpit to deliver his eulogy for Caesar. He stands erect upon the platform. His red robe swoops over his brawny shoulders and flowingly drapes about his body. Brown leather sandals are tied about his calloused knees.

His rapid brown eyes gaze about the silent crowd. "Friends, Romans, countrymen, lend me your ears; I come to bury Caesar, not to praise him," starts Antony with a hoarse voice. As I sway my torso to the side, I give great heed to what is said. As I scan the crowds of people, I realize that they too are swayed by Antony's speech and wish revenge on Caesar's body. Tears trickle down the flushed faces as some bend their heads in a silent prayer to ask for forgiveness. Yes, vengeance is fluttering in the air.

Ask a child who has a special interest in science, art, or mathematics to write about a pretend visit with some great figure in the field that excites the youngster. In the following piece, a thirteen-year-old has read a biography of Gregor Mendel and has studied about heredity in science class. She pretends she is a newspaper reporter and interviews the great scientist, setting the scene in time and place.

On a blustery day in 1857, I arrived at the Modern School in Austria to interview Mr. Gregor Mendel, discoverer of the laws of heredity, for the *Daily Post,* the local newspaper. Anxiously, I scurried up to the oak door of his quarters and meekly took the brass door knocker in my hand and knocked three times. Quickly Mr. Mendel, his merry blue eyes twinkling, opened the door and softly murmured, "Please, do come in."

As I entered the small room, I noticed a high riser bed covered with a blue bedspread, a mahogany dresser, and a desk overflowing with notes, among other things. I situated myself in a plush purple chair and viewed Mr. Mendel. He wore a navy blue suit and a blue striped tie. His gray hair appeared to be receding, his eyes were kind and soft, and he sported horn-rimmed glasses. "Mr. Mendel," I queried, "What made you so interested in heredity?"

He stroked his long chin thoughtfully. "Well, I have been interested in the field ever since I was a child. The laws of life and the mystery of an ordinary garden pea constantly racked my brain. To satisfy my curiosity I have begun research and I have come up with a theory. I am now in the process of collecting data on my peas. Would you like to see them?"

With much excitement, I replied, "Oh, yes, sir. I would like to very much." He rose slowly and motioned to a huge door. The room contained thousands of crystal-clear test tubes and millions of peas. Hanging on the white walls were many charts containing scribbled data.

Mr. Mendel's short round face beamed with pride. "These," he remarked, "are the F_2, or second filial, generation. As you can see there are both green and yellow peas in the pod in the ratio of three to one."

He went on and on with explanations, and after many hours the time arrived for me to leave. I gratefully babbled, "Thank you, Mr. Mendel. It has been very informative and exciting. Thank you again. Good-bye." That ended a wonderful afternoon for me and brought a good story to the *Daily Post*.

Another exciting leap into imagination asks the child to pretend his way into a photograph or a painting. Use a famous art reproduction, such as "Christina's World" by Andrew Wyeth, one of the Rockwell paintings, a lively scene by Degas or Renoir. Ask the child to imagine that he is part of the painting and to write what he would see, hear, feel, and smell if he joined the scene. A photograph from a book or magazine or one from your home collection serves well here, too. You might ask the child to look at a snapshot of some family member and to write a tale about the person. The child can draw upon bits and pieces of family stories told about relatives who lived in times past. This short tale was written by a ten-year-old about his great grandfather who was born in Italy:

Since the time my great grandfather was a little boy he lived in Italy and loved it there. One fine day when the sky was blue my great grandfather went to the market for his mother. Lovely things were at the market: toys, food, everything you can think of. But my great grandfather had just enough money to buy bread. As my great grandfather was walking, he saw a man with a silver knife in his hand. He told my great grandfather he could have the knife for the money he had in his hand. So he gave the man the money, which was two shiny coins, and started for home. When his mother saw him with the knife and not the bread, she took the knife and didn't let him go to the market again.

This simple, lively narrative framework can serve to build important language skills. A parent would say, "I love the colors *blue* and *silver.* Can you use a more specific word than *toys* or *food,* though? Can you use a better word than *walking* to show action? Can you add a sentence to tell what the man Grandpa met looks like?" Because there is confusion about the way the child uses the word *he* here, you have a ripe opportunity to talk about pronouns, and how they must always clearly refer the reader back to someone or something. It's a good idea to remind the child that sometimes it's better to repeat a word instead of using a pronoun which might be confusing.

Animals on Parade

The intense interest a child of any age shows toward animals builds another treasure house of writing activities. This interest in pets leads easily to straightforward and real narratives of moments with animals, such as this one:

It has been almost seven years since the first breezy March afternoon that we took our dog home from the kennel to live with us, yet it seems like only yesterday. Excitement bubbled up inside of me as we rushed into the modern building, and the sounds of pitiful yelping reached my ears. It didn't take long before a soft, fuzzy, sable ball of fur leaped into my awaiting arms. Carefully, I parted his soft white hairs of what I imagined to be a face, and a small, pink, moist tongue emerged gingerly to lick my arm. His warm, friendly, brown eyes stared up at my face while I felt his long tail, with the beginnings of what would someday be a great mass of fur, glide slowly back and forth with a swishing sound. Carefully, I placed him down on the floor and immediately he scurried after some withered leaves somehow left on the floor. They crunched under King's small, snowy white paw, but they got no mercy from him! Soon he tired of this game, and he quietly snuggled up against my leg and fell asleep. It didn't take long for me to realize that I was hopelessly in love with the little ball of fur, and with a happy nod of my head and a smile I watched my father pay the man.

But it is the fanciful excursion into animal land—where dogs talk, chickens carry pocketbooks, and cats sip coffee—that sets a child's fancy racing. There are limitless possibilities for writing!

Children delight in Aesop's fables. Perhaps you and your son or daughter can take a short trip to the library and read some of these together. Then the child can try to write an original animal fable, complete with moral. Here is an eleven-year-old's tale of a fox and chickens:

There once was a red fox who loved to eat chickens. He did not have enough money to buy them. So every night he would sneak into the dark barn and steal a chicken. He always had more than enough chickens for many days, but he still snatched one every night. Farmer Brown bought a big black dog to guard the chickens. One night the dog hid behind a maple tree and waited for the fox to come to steal a chicken. When the greedy fox sneaked toward the barn, the dog growled, "I've got you now!" and jumped on the fox and ate him. The moral of this story is to be satisfied with what you have.

Do you remember Rudyard Kipling's *Just So Stories?* Children love writing their own "just-so" tales in which the writer reveals the secret of some animal's behavior or physical appearance. Your youngster might want to explain

- why flies fly
- how the giraffe got a long neck
- how the monkey got a long tail
- why the lion has a mane
- why the tiger has stripes
- why the elephant has a long nose
- why dogs bark
- why cats lick their fur
- how the canary got a beautiful voice
- how the kangaroo got his pouch

For seven- and eight-year-olds you can give the opening and closing sentences of the tale and can ask the child to tell an original narrative using clear sensory detail. For example, you might offer these:

> You may not know that elephants once had noses just like you and me. _____
> _____
> _____
> _____
> _____
> _____
> _____
>
> And that's why the elephant has a long trunk.

or:

> Dogs once talked like people. _____
> _____
> _____
> _____
> _____
>
> And that's why dogs bark.

Here are some to read and discuss as models:

> You may not know that elephants once had noses just like you and me. But elephants were always butting in to other peo-

ple's business. One day a large gray elephant tried to listen in on
a conversation. Two tigers sat in their living room drinking hot
chocolate and chatting. One tiger said, "My, there's a draft in
here." She stood up and slammed the door shut. But the elephant's nose was stuck! Did it hurt! He tried pulling his nose out
by backing away. He pulled and tugged and pulled some more.
Finally his nose came loose, but it was badly stretched. It looked
like an ugly gray snake. And that's why the elephant has a long
trunk.

Once Joe Turtle was taking a walk over to Clem Rabbit's briar
patch. Clem was pasting a new set of thorns on the thorn bushes.
He always changed thorns every spring. Joe told Clem that he
thought there was a fish in the paste pot. Clem said to look
again. Joe looked very hard and then, ploof! He fell in. The
paste dried on his back. And that is why all turtles since Joe's
time have had hard green crusts or shells on their backs.

Your child shouldn't limit to animal tales his or her excursions into fantasy. Suggest that the youngster expand upon
other ideas such as:

- why leaves turn yellow
- why the grass is green
- how the ocean got waves
- why roses smell
- how the sea got salty
- where thunder began
- how the stars got bright
- why mountains are tall
- how glue got sticky
- why the wind whistles

Here's a fine example of a child's myth on thunder:

One day a giant up in the sky was moving the furniture in his
house. He just couldn't make up his mind where to put the furniture. He started to throw the furniture around the house with a
loud banging noise. He began to get raging mad. Lightning
spurted in green streaks out of his eyes. He threw more furniture
around the house and heaved some out the window. Crash! came
the thunder. The furniture he threw out the window fell on the
white clouds and made the clouds break. Then it rained.

"I Am a Pizza": Personification and Delight
When I explained personification in Chapter 5, I pointed out
that it was a good way for the child to add liveliness to his writ-

ing. By giving human qualities to nonhuman beings a writer can tease out an image with figurative language:

> The car sputtered and coughed along Mitchell Avenue.
> Leaves whispered secrets to the cold, unfriendly ground.

Sputtered, coughed, whispered, unfriendly: These words name human acts or qualities but here they're used for inanimate objects to enliven and clarify the picture.

I've already mentioned the personification-riddle game in which the youngster tells what it's like to be some object. Now, ask your child to pretend that he or she is an object or animal who can speak. Ask the youngster to write a more extended piece about a brief moment in his life as that object. You might suggest:

- a moment in the life of a Ping-Pong ball
- my breakfast cereal speaks
- what it's like to be a door knob
- I am a period
- a ball goes bouncing along
- a vacuum cleaner's life
- the sink speaks out
- the troubles of a toothbrush
- a record's racket
- the ketchup bottle talks

Discuss some pointers the child should consider when writing:

- tell what your make-believe name is
- tell where you are
- show what you look like
- tell a sound that you make
- tell sounds that you hear
- tell what you see around you—colors, actions, people
- tell what somebody says

These samples by writers of different ages show the enchantment and humor of "Pretend-You-Are" writing:

I am Karen's doll Bessie. I live on top of a white dresser in Karen's bedroom. I have short brown hair, brown eyes, and red cheeks. Sometimes I drink make-believe tea from little cups at Karen's tea party. I always wear my pink party dress. When

Karen lifts me I feel warm and I squeak, "Mama, mama, mama."
At night I sleep on Karen's cool soft pillow.

Plop! There I go again sliding down that shiny metal pole onto
the black wheel of Sheri's stereo record player. Ow, how that
needle hurts when it digs into those first few grooves! Why must
she always play me time and time again? There she goes. I can
see her pearly white teeth, and I have a feeling she's going to
sing along. I don't think I can stand to hear her shrill voice in
song, but it could be worse; she could get her girlfriends to join
in! "Monday, Monday, so good to me . . ." she starts screaming
when those first few words blast out of me. Take my advice and
hold your ears if you don't want your eardrum to puncture. My
sister "Never On A Sunday" feels bad since all she does is lie on
her flip side, underneath "Please, Please Me." She complains,
but boy would I like to change places with her. She tells me that
once I'm not in the "Top Ten" anymore, I'll have plenty of time
to sit back and join the other old folks. Oh, my three minutes
and two seconds are up, but she's not letting me off that easy.
There I go again, and let me tell you that a record's racket isn't
as easy as it seems.

Thump! Here I am in Angelo's calloused hands ready for a
dunking into a can of bloody tomato sauce in the Avenue T
Pizzeria. Why does my floppy, powdery dough have to be attacked by lumpy herbs? Yes, the life of a pizza can be frustrating.
There is an enormous crowd tarrying to thrust their fangs into
my luscious body. First I'm pounded, tickled, and then
s-t-r-e-t-c-h-e-d to three times my size. A flying saucer ride
around Angelo's head follows, with prayers that his butter-
fingers don't release me. Spicy, fiery sauce drowns my nose, as
tickly cheese crumbles over me. My trip to the Sahara desert
begins as Angelo shoves me into Maestro's 550 degree oven. My
flat skin rises to an auburn bubble as I'm swirled around the
scorched wall of the oven. Bing! I'm done. "One slice!" Vivian
yells above the mob. Begging and pleading not to amputate my
eight slices, I feel Angelo swish the knife, breaking my cheesy
heart in two. Gulp! Vivian drools over my tantalizing flavor
and aroma. In vain, I hope for crumbs to be left, so I can rebake
as another slize of pizza in Angelo's Avenue T Pizzeria.

Flash! Flash! Flash! My life as a glittering green and orange
neon sign may not be exciting, but it is a lot of fun. Many people
hurry past me on a wintry night with their heads bent and their
collars up as they battle their way up Avenue U. Some stop and
come into Enrico's Kosher Delicatessen where I live. It is a cozy
little restaurant with candles melting in wine bottles which are

on top of gaily covered tables. At five o'clock, when Enrico turns me on, I feel proud to be a part of the shimmering sea of light that dances over Avenue U's slush-filled streets. This morning a man named Maxie came and polished my fluorescent tubes; it tickled as he picked up the worn brush and gently passed the bristles over the "O" in Enrico's. After he had finished, he carefully poured the soapy water from the bucket into the streets and picked up his tools and packed them in the trunk of an old Oldsmobile. Maxie is a kindly old man with sparkling gray eyes and a patch of silvery hair; the back of his faded blue uniform loudly proclaims in black letters—Maxie's Window Washing and Sign Cleaning Service. Sitting here behind the sparkling plate glass window, I get the chance to notice many things. There's Mrs. Rosen's daughter, Paula, playing hop scotch on a thin chalk outline which barely stretches against the cracked gray cement. As she jumps, her blond ponytail bounces up and down, and her gray-and-red jacket streams out behind her. Oh, oh, she'd better be careful! Billy, her mischievous, red-haired brother, creeps up behind her with a cracked pea shooter tightly grasped in his mitten. Just in time, their mother sticks her head out the window. She calls, "Billy, Paula, come in for dinner!" Whirling around and seeing her brother's grin, Paula gives him a hard kick in his shins and me a sly wink. Now I'm alone again. I wish my brother Charlie were here, but a mean little boy, with hard black eyes and a good pitching arm, threw a snowball at his face. He was sent to the hospital for repairs, but now his face will always be scarred by a long, twisting crack. Sometimes I wish I could be human and roar through New York's jungle of glass office buildings. But, my own life has its rewards too; it was just yesterday that my flashing light saved a little boy from stepping in front of a car whose headlights were turned off. The life of a neon sign is fun and rewarding; why don't you try it sometime? Flash! Flash! Flash!

On Your Own in Fantasyland

You are more familiar than the teacher with your youngster's sense of make-believe. Invent writing games to excite your child's pretend world. When holiday seasons approach, ask the child to assume the identity of a familiar object and to write about his feelings: a Christmas tree, a *menorah,* a Thanksgiving turkey, a holiday candle, or a pumpkin. These make wonderful identities for tales of fantasy. When the child buys or makes a gift for a member of the family, let the child pretend he is the gift and ask him to write about himself. Make a cassette, in the youngster's voice, of the story that the child has written; give it to Mommy, Daddy, or Sister along with the gift. Encourage the youngster to write fairy tales of his own design. Some children love to write continuations of familiar stories, legends, or fairy tales: "Snow White's Family," "When the Little Engine Couldn't," "Goldilocks, Part II." And the "tall tale" is another exercise in delight; it's the kind of dizzy silliness children adore in romps through make-believe.

12

A Child's Message
Through the Mails

If the whimsy and joy of traveling through make-believe add wings to the child's writing, a message mailed and answered can also set his or her skills and interests soaring. First help the youngster see how the post office works. Look at the process through the youngster's eyes: a trek through the snow to a blue metal box; a pull on a squeaky handle; a flip of the wrist; a letter diving into darkness. Then the enchantment happens: a phone call ("Yes, I can come") or a note in response ("Thank you for your letter. . . ."). Why, some man or woman actually brought that message to Sacramento or Phoenix, Martha's Vineyard or Brooklyn!

Using the Mails
In Chapter 2, I showed how little notes to members of the family were a painless writing practice for the child. The notes that a child leaves on the refrigerator door or bathroom mirror for Mommy and Daddy have their own reinforcement in the immediate response of a smile or nod. Letters and post cards bring responses *in writing*. Watch your daughter's eyes when she watches for the letter carrier stepping up the path; see your son's electric grin when Mr. Bloom pauses in his rapid sorting of letters at the tin maze of mail boxes in your lobby and says, "Here's one for you, David!"

Use the mails! So much of the child's school letter-writing activities is hopelessly unfulfilled: Term after term your child painfully writes letters to fit the school's demands. The teacher examines the class' letters, then the children take their letters home and throw them into the trash bag. Letters need envelopes! They need stamps! They need mail boxes, postal clerks, and letter carriers!

It's incredible how many teachers have eliminated the only step that justifies so much letter-writing practice to the child— mailing the letter! Of course, letter-writing is a good activity for building skills and a short easy-to-grade exercise, often no more than five or six sentences. The child establishes good patterns of social behavior by sending and receiving invitations, thank-you's, and mannerly requests for help. Even the *form* of the letter is a strong approach to correctness: A period must go there; a capital must go here; a comma must *not* go there. Red pen in hand, the teacher can quickly check off a child's indiscretions.

You can diminish the terrors of such an approach for your child. Point out the requirements of the letter form, but explain that they are conventions that people expect, and that these conventions simplify the reader's task. Demand form only when the child intends to *mail* the letter! Then, you have his attention and interest, because his message is worth laboring over— someone will receive it, read what the child has written, and probably write back to him.

Creative Letter-Writing

Think of the last letter you enjoyed receiving. What made it a pleasure to read? Perhaps it was something you would want to read again in the quiet of the living room after the children are asleep, or you might want to quote a word here and there to your spouse. Aside from the joy of hearing news from far away, and from sharing the experiences of men and women you love but cannot often see, you respond to the words that mirror an image of the writer's personality. That sounds just like Suzy, you might think. "Isn't that just what Mom would say," you murmur. "Why, that's something only Michael could write."

Messages reflect a child's personality, become documents of his or her perception, and serve in the youngster's program of creative growth in writing. I define creative letters as messages written in the child's own language that convey necessary information to people in his or her real world.

"Come to my Party"

A letter of invitation is a good message to begin with. For your child's next party, set aside a few afternoons so the birthday girl or boy can write original invitations to the guests. Depending on the youngster's age, help out as much as necessary. Don't insist on too much writing at once, especially for very young children. Talk about the message you need to send, and encourage the child to write a brief note that will highlight all the important information guests need to know. Make a list with the youngster to remind him of what to include:

What We Need to Tell in the Invitation
- What time the party will start
- What day the party will take place
- Where the party will be
- What kind of party it will be
- One special thing about the party

Work on scrap paper to plan the simple message, reminding the child that he'll have to write the same note for each guest. You don't want to overtax the youngster, so help out significantly if your child gets too tired. In at least a few of the cases, however, the child should follow through on the whole process: Writing the message, folding the letter, addressing and stamping the envelope, and, finally, mailing the finished invitation.

Here is the message for one birthday invitation a parent and child prepared:

Please come to my house for my
birthday party
on Sunday, March
2, at one o'clock.
We'll have chocolate
cake with whipped
cream, and my daddy will
show cartoons.

The little detail of what the guest might expect reveals the child's special delight at this party and is perfectly fitting to include in the message.

Once the message has been composed, the child should make a final draft. The youngster will use the final version as a model to copy as he writes out all the other invitations. If you want to, you can write in the return address and the opening sentence, then have the child print in the message. Point out the information the return address gives. Name and explain words a writer might use instead of *Love* (*Sincerely, Fondly, Your friend*) before he or she signs the message. Here's a model to present:

> 9899 Cricklewood Drive
> Boalsburg, Pennsylvania 16801
> December 8, 1977

Dear Susan,

   Please come to my house for my birthday party on Sunday, March 2, at one o'clock. We'll have chocolate cake with whipped cream, and my daddy will show cartoons.

> Love,
> Audrey

You might also take the time to explain RSVP, if your planning requires responses to the invitations. Many parents expedite replies by offering a phone number, but it's better to ask for written responses, so the child can anticipate receiving return notes.

   I've printed, below, a reference form for writing the friendly letter (the correspondence we're considering here is called a *friendly letter;* I'll discuss the more official *business letter* in a while). In the sample, I've pointed out trouble spots, places children often make errors when following the format. Because I think it's unnecessary, I've omitted the terminology used for the various parts. Notice the labels and the spacing for clarity. There are wide borders; and spaces are left after the address, the greeting, the end of the message, and before the signature. This model is a good reference tool for older children; they can keep it available as they write. You can use it as a model to consult when making concrete suggestions to your child about the need for correctness in written responses. Know your own child; never bear down on right and wrong to the extent that his or her creative efforts flicker and die, and never push the very young too early to obey these conventions of letter-writing.

   When it's time to address the letter, be sure you have selected an envelope that's large enough for the young child's sprawling print. Addressing the envelope must be done carefully, because without clearly written words and numbers the letter may go astray; but with the parent's supervision even a six-year-old should be able to write clearly enough.

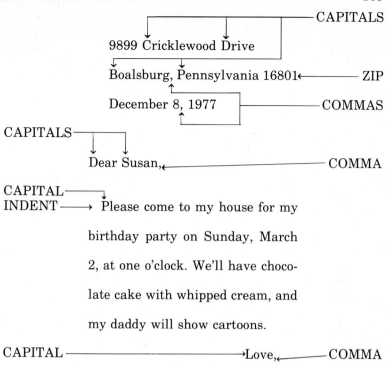

Here's a model envelope that will guide you as you help your daughter or son with the party invitations.

Some parents draw wide horizontal lines on the envelope for youngsters to write on. That's a good idea: the lines hold the child's print to reasonable size. If you're wondering about abbreviations and when to use them, sticklers still insist that all words, including *Street, Avenue,* and even the name of the state, be fully written out, but the Post Office Department says that two-letter abbreviations for state names (*PA* for Pennsylvania, *CA* for California, and so forth), accompanied with zip codes, speed up the mails. Make your own choice; but use the official abbreviations listed in the zip code directory at your local post office if you decide on them.

A trip to the post office during the letter-writing project may hook your child on mail forever! Watching those enormous canvas crates squeaking down an aisle, eyeing a clerk stuffing mail into pigeon holes, and standing in line and paying for stamps add an exciting dimension to the child's letter-writing experience.

Let's Write Letters
There are numerous opportunities for using letters in a realistic context. Here are a few:

• *The Homemade Postal or Greeting Card.*   With unlined index cards that are roughly equivalent to post cards in size, the child uses scissors, paste, crayon and paint to become a card designer. On one side of the card the youngster can draw a picture and add a written-in word or two. Or an original photograph or a picture cut from a magazine can be pasted onto one side of an index card and then can be protected from rough handling in the mails by painting over it with a thin coat of lacquer or some clear nailpolish. *Voilà!* You have an original picture post card. On the reverse side the child draws a line down the middle and puts a brief message on the left side, and the address and stamp on the right. To make a homemade greeting card, the youngster should cut a thin piece of cardboard a little less than double envelope size; folded over, the cardboard forms a greeting card upon which the child can draw a picture on front and can copy a message inside. Who knows, maybe Mr. Hallmark started this way!

• *Thank-you's.*   Etiquette demands a note in response to a gift, and parents who are concerned with their children's growth in writing skills should start using this kind of letter for good practice early. A present from Grandma, a gift from

Mommy or Daddy, toys from the neighboring children at birthday party time all provide realistic impetus for letter-writing. In fact, thank-you's to guests round out a party project. A child's sense of order responds to the completed cycle. Encourage your youngster to use language that shows his or her unique personality in all these friendly letters. The child can show the gift-giver his appreciation of the toy or game by mentioning some special joy it has brought. Don't be elaborate; if there are many notes to write, use the same message, except perhaps for the last sentence.

The freshness of a child's perceptions speaks out in these messages:

Thank you for your gift.
I love Sindy's brown hair
and her soft pink skin.
Will you come to play with
me and her soon?

I love the softball you
gave me for my birthday.
Dad and I tossed it around
in the grass at Sunset Park.
But we had to snatch it away
from little Tommy. He likes
to sit on it!

How did you know that calcu-
lator was what I wanted? I
like the way the numbers
flash in red on the little
screen. Thank you for helping
my arithmetic.

Thank you for the
money for my birthday.
I am going to buy a
pair of white boots
and bubble gum. Please
visit us soon.

The tone of these will warm the giver for having chosen the gift so well. Your youngster learns an important social obligation and at the same time practices writing.

• Letters, Notes, Cards to Shut-ins. Your youngster should send brief notes to classmates or relatives who are ill at home or in the hospital. It's letter-writing for a *reason,* sent to people the child can cheer with a message.

• *Fan Mail.*   Most of the television programs for children, such as, *Romper Room, Captain Kangaroo,* and *Sesame Street,* encourage children to send in mail to the characters. Often the actors simply request drawings, but you can urge the youngster to write a brief message to his favorite star. Often the stars respond, and the child has a letter to cherish. As the young writer grows up, encourage him to write to his favorite stars or heroes: You'll be amazed how many take their fan mail seriously. Years ago a twelve-year-old in one of my classes wrote to John Steinbeck and delighted the class when she read aloud his handwritten note of response.

• *Letters to Far-away Friends and Pen Pals.*   If you have a cousin or friend who has recently moved out of state, or if you and your family have been uprooted because of a job change, or if an older sister has gone off to college, try to encourage your child to send letters every week to those who are far away. Here is a letter to a child who recently moved to State College, Pennsylvania, from a nine-year-old California friend back home.

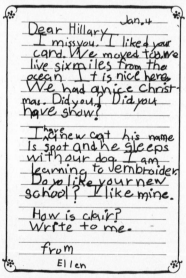

Ellen mentions specific details about her new move, and asks questions about activities and family members, inviting a letter in response. Hillary's mother says the breezy style of the letter is very much like the child herself. I can't tell whether or not her parent helped Ellen compose the note, but I know how I would have helped if she'd asked my advice. I wouldn't tell her what to say or what questions to ask, but I might say, "What a wonderful letter. You've told Hillary such good things and you've asked fine questions. Why don't you add a sentence that shows what our lovely beach looks like, maybe tell a sound of the ocean or give a picture of the sea." Or, "I think Hillary would love to know a little more about Spot. Why don't you tell her what he looks like and one funny thing he did last week." Or, "Tell your friend what you are embroidering." Thus, I might coax out sentence groups like these:

- I have a new cat. He is brown with big white circles on his paws and back. His name is Spot and he sleeps with our dog. Yesterday he knocked over Mom's coffee cup. When it crashed to the floor, he jumped into my arms!

- We live six miles from the ocean. The water is blue and warm and we see sailboats.

- I am learning to embroider. Now I am making pink-and-green roses on the border of a pillow case.

In my concern for correctness I'd ask Ellen about using a capital *S* in Spot's name. I'd suggest she read the second paragraph aloud slowly so she could hear her voice drop after the word *cat*. I'd ask how she should show that one sentence is over and another about to begin. I'd discuss the letter format: the absence of her return address, the small letter in *from* (I might suggest possibilities for other closings), the placement of her signature to the left, the abbreviation of *January*. Her age and temperament would determine my pursuit of these matters; I would not want to overwhelm the child. Knowing that the letter will travel thousands of miles to sit at a friend's breakfast table excites any child and encourages concern for correct expression.

If you're lucky enough to have friends or relatives in another country, try to find a correspondent about the same age as your child. Help start pen-pal communications that will assure frequent letters and provide an opportunity for you to influence your youngster's writing growth. As the child grows older, she'll be less likely to want you reading her letters! If you can't find a pen pal on your own, help the child write a letter to Washington, D.C. to the embassy of some country where he'd like to have a correspondent. Or, write the American Junior Red Cross in Washington for the names of pen pals. You might ask around your own neighborhood for likely correspondents for your son or daughter—children who live in other cities here in North America or in Africa, Europe, or Asia.

Business Letters for Home-Bred Dynamos

Everyone likes something for nothing and children are not exceptions! Innumerable public and private institutions stand ready to send pamphlets, booklets, photographs, and free samples to anyone who writes asking for them. This is precious motivation for your boy or girl to write business letters.

The business letter is like the friendly letter in regard to matters of courtesy, clarity, and correctness. The differences are in tone and purpose. The letter to a company or agency is straightforward and more formal. This does *not* mean one uses Dreadful Big Words, such as *heretofore, forthwith, pursuant to your letter,* and so on, that often appear in letters we adults must suffer through. Business letters explain, demand, apologize, and inform; all these goals are action-oriented. Someone is being asked to fill a need the writer has.

The conventions of the business letter are much stricter than those of the friendly letter. In the sample below I've labeled the parts of a business letter so you can point them out to your child. The letter makes its point and supplies critical information quickly; a busy respondent can act easily and decisively to fill the writer's request.

		1550 Winthrop Street
	a.	Brooklyn, New York 11203
		January 7, 19__

b.

    Information Office

c.

    Williamsburg, Virginia 23185

d.

e.   Gentlemen:

f.

       My family and I are planning a vacation this year during my Easter school vacation, April 3 to 10. We would like to know more about Williamsburg.

g.

       Will you please send me information about hotel rates, restaurants, and sightseeing? I would also like to have a map of the city. Any other information you can send would be helpful, too.

h.

i.   Yours truly,

j.

k.   *[Signature]*

l.   Richard Siskind

m.

a.   *Child's address.* Note these trouble spots:
1.   Capitals for name of street, word *street* or *avenue* cap-italized as well.
2.   Capitals for city, state, month of year.
3.   Comma between city and state, between date and year, and no place else!
4.   No abbreviations.
b.   *Space* between child's address and next part.
c.   *Address of people the child is writing to*
1.   Capitals for name of office or company, for city and state
2.   Name of person—if you know it—goes first in this address with *Mr., Mrs., Miss,* or *Ms.*
d.   *Space* between business address and next part.
e.   *Greeting*
1.   If you know the person's name, say *Dear Mrs. Santini* or *Dear Mr. Davis.* Otherwise, *Gentlemen* or *Dear Madam* or *Dear Sir* is fine, if you're not addressing one person in particular. Since the reader is just as likely to be a woman as a man, however, you might want to address the company in the greeting: *Dear Information Office* or *Dear McGraw-Hill Book Company.* Notice the capitals.
2.   A colon follows the greeting.
f.   *Space* between greeting and rest of letter.
g.   *Letter* itself. Brief, clear, courteous, important information included, to the point, correct.
h.   *Space*
i.   *Closing.* Watch these trouble spots children often miss:
1.   Capital letter only for the first word in the closing. Other choices: *Yours very truly, Respectfully yours.* Less formal choices are *Sincerely* or *Sincerely yours.*
2.   Comma after the closing
j.   *Space* here.
k.   *Child's signature*
l.   *Child's name* printed clearly (if the letter is typed, this will be typed, of course).
m.   *Margins.* Notice the spacing—wide borders, clear layout—for easy reading.

The business envelope follows the same conventions as the envelope for the friendly letter. You'll want to take some time explaining how to fold the letter into thirds horizontally. A standard sheet of stationery for business letters is 8½-by-11 inches, unlined, but you may have to rule lines to aid the young child to print clearly.

You may be wondering who will answer a letter from a child.

Which companies might you suggest to your sons and daughters as likely correspondents? Let me say that, increasingly, businesses recognize that answered letters develop good will. Children usually live in a house with a mother and a father who are consumers; and, as he grows, each child is a potential consumer with his own funds to spend. Public relations offices in the private sector, business, and industry exist to disseminate information about their organization, their products, and their concerns. Below I suggest some possible recipients of your child's business letter, but the list of free things to write for could fill the rest of this book. (In fact, a book you might want to buy for sources is: *1001 Valuable Things You Can Get Free* by Mort Weisinger—New York: Bantam Books.) To avoid disappointment—companies go out of business; letters get lost; poor public relations departments ignore requests—I suggest you encourage your youngster to send off three or four letters to different corporations. Discuss with your child the possibility that a company might not answer, so your youngster is not too disappointed if he or she receives no replies at first.

All right, here are more than two dozen ideas for business letters, which children from six to nineteen might consider:

- Write to the chamber of commerce of your town or city—any town or city—and ask for information about vacationing, historic landmarks, and places of interest.
- Write to a publisher to ask for a catalog of children's books.
- Ask for a book about how to care for your animal from the company that makes the pet food you use.
- Write to your local Internal Revenue Service for a social security application or to your local motor vehicle office for an application for a learner's permit.
- Write to your local savings bank for an application for a passbook savings account.
- Write to the local board of education for a list of summer activities for children.
- Write for a free catalog of roses from Jackson and Perkins Co., Rose Lane, Medford, Oregon 97501.
- Write for a catalog of toys from

Gabriel Industries, Inc.
200 Fifth Avenue
New York, NY 10010

Fisher-Price Toys
East Aurora, New York 14052

The Ertl Company
Dyersville, Iowa 52040

- Write for free recipe books to

California Raisin Advisory Board
Fresno, California 93755

Campbell's Soup
Box 494
Maple Plain, Minnesota 55348

Rice Council of America
Box 22800
Houston, Texas 77027

California Almond Growers Exchange
P.O. Box 1768
Sacramento, California 95808

Fleischmann's Yeast Co.
P.O. Box 509
Madison Square Station
New York, New York 10010

Betty Crocker
Minneapolis, Minnesota 55460

Morton Salt Company
Chicago, Illinois 60606

- Write for pamphlets on baby care and feeding from Gerber Products Company, Fremont, MI 49412.
- Write for a free color brochure of greeting cards to UNICEF Greeting Cards, 331 East 38th Street, New York, N.Y. 10016.
- Write for a catalog on planting and farming, consumer affairs, historic sites, or health care from the Superintendent of Documents, Government Printing Office, Washington, D.C. 20402.
- Write for a book about rubber to B. F. Goodrich, 500 South Main Street, Akron, Ohio 44318.
- Ask for a list of their free publications from John Hancock Mutual Life Insurance Company, 200 Berkeley Street, Boston, Massachusetts 02117.
- Write for hints for good picture taking from Eastman Kodak, Rochester, New York 14603.
- Write for material on nuclear power plant safety to Edison Electric Institute, 90 Park Avenue, New York, N.Y. 10016.
- Write for information about the girl scouts to Girl Scouts of the USA, 830 Third Avenue, New York, N.Y. 10022.
- Write for a booklet about artificial food additives (*Today's Food and Additives*) to Miss Peggy Kohl, V.P., Consumer Affairs, General Foods Consumer Center, White Plains, New York 10625.

With all those built-in excitements about letter-writing encourage your child to pick an idea and to get started first thing tomorrow!

13

Words in Focus:

Creative Definitions for the Young Writer

A large vocabulary increases the child's potential as a writer. I'd like to describe some challenging games and activities designed to advance a child's use of the language.

What Does It Mean? How Does It Feel?
One of the exciting—and often troublesome—features of words is that they arouse both intellectual *and* emotional responses. It's comfortable but not correct to believe that for every word there is simply one (or even only several) definitions stored in a dictionary. Words evoke a range of feelings and associations that no dictionary definition can accurately suggest.

The exact definition of a word is called its *denotation*. When your child copies the meaning of *night* from a dictionary, his definition draws upon what the word *denotes*. The *connotation* of a word is its suggested meaning, the thoughts and feelings (in language) aroused by the word. If when the child thinks of *night* he feels *fear* or *comfort* or *quiet* or *warmth,* those words are what night *connotes* for him. The connotative meanings for words are no less legitimate than the denotative ones: These dual conditions of meaning act together, enriching language possibilities for everybody. However, you can see why it's important to keep clearly in mind these different qualities that belong to words. Otherwise it's possible to substitute associated feelings, definitions, and ideas for actual meanings. A good example of this idea is the word *shark*. The dictionary tells us a shark is any of numerous, chiefly marine, fishes with a skeleton of cartilage and tough skin covered with small toothlike scales. But is that what leaps into mind when most people hear the word shark? The associations of *shark* are overpowering: fear, blood, massive jaws biting limbs off innocent bathers, terror as a gray, wing-like fin races through the waves. Peter Benchley, the author of the book *Jaws,* knew he could rely upon our connotative responses to sharks; in some respects he developed his story through connotations that, as you may have learned, are not really accurate. Very few sharks are interested in humans for a Sunday dinner! Yet we will continue to shudder, cringe, and despise this maligned creature of the sea —the *shark!*

When you worked on word meanings using the dictionary and the thesaurus (in Chapter 7), you worked with denotative meanings. When you encouraged definitions in images (the associations the child makes for words like *red*, for example), you highlighted the connotative.

To understand better these characteristics of word meaning, children of nine and ten can play together in a variation on the old parlor game of word association. You're not interested in instant associations, however. Rather, you are going to ask the child to think about what a word means and what it suggests to him. On a sheet of paper folded into three columns have the youngster write down a word that you provide in the first column. In column two, ask for a definition of the word; and in column three request words or images suggested by the word. You might encourage the child to use the dictionary for practice, but don't ask him to copy the word's meaning. Your aim is to help the child distinguish the *definition* from his *feelings* about the word. Here are some examples:

Word	*Meaning*	*Suggestions and Feelings*
summer	warm time of year from June 21 to September 20	fun at the beach cherry ices heat no school roses and lilacs water sprinklers
alone	not with other people	lonely friendless sad my dark bedroom

Stimulate the awareness of a word's *shades of meaning*—the differences between what words denote and what they suggest (frequently based upon how they are used)—by looking up the words that the dictionary says are similar in meaning but which arouse different feelings and attitudes. Look at these:

bad	evil
heavy	fat
bright	vivid
cry	sob
big	enormous
tasty	delicious
weak	helpless
active	restless
tall	lanky
tired	exhausted
intelligent	brilliant
dry	parched
car	jalopy
doctor	physician
thin	slender
little	petite

Heavy and *fat* mean pretty much the same, but *fat* is a more negative word when it is used to describe a person. When you list and discuss these words, ask your child to write sentences for each one after he understands the meanings by checking the definitions in a dictionary. The child's age and level of comprehension determine which words to examine.

Another exercise that helps the child appreciate the variety and economy of words plays with words that have multiple definitions. In *The American Heritage Dictionary dark* has more than ten meanings; *dead* has fifteen, *horn* eleven, *light* more than *forty* depending on whether it's a verb, a noun, or an adjective. There are many such simple words with various definitions: *lift, mind, moral, bad, bat, limit, fast, blink, civil, class,* and *drop* are just a few other examples. Look at some of these words with your son or daughter; discuss the various definitions; and ask the child to practice by making up a sentence for as many words as possible. Each sentence should demonstrate a different meaning. Here are some sentences written for the word *dark:*

It was dark at six o'clock.
Mother wore a dark brown hat.
I am not allowed to go out in the dark.

Sally's idea kept me in the dark.
He had a dark reason for sneaking into the house.
The Dark Ages is a period of history.

Work with a dictionary that suits the child's level of ability, and try to excite the youngster's delight in how words sound, in what strange and interesting words mean, where they come from and how their meanings came about, and in how to use them. Try working on some of these:

fiddle-faddle	unicorn
muscovado	papyrus
porringer	polonaise
pop-in-jay	loon
lemming	dromedary
dandelion	bonsai
crazy quilt	aqueduct
boomerang	Amazon
longhorn	zeppelin
zircon	porcupine fish

Suggest that your child *make* an original dictionary. The child's age will determine the scope and intent of this home-made word book; but here is an activity that children of most age groups enjoy. For younger children you can combine the verbal and the visual: The child writes a word on top of an un-lined page and then draws a picture beneath it (or cuts one out of a magazine and glues the picture on) to illustrate the word's meaning. Supply a binder and dividers marked with alphabet tabs; make twenty-six sections and insert lots of loose-leaf paper. When the youngster finishes writing and illustrating each word, have him insert the page in the correct section. This is also a wonderful opportunity for the child to practice alphabetizing. Make sure each new entry goes in the correct place. The words the younger child selects for illustration will be essentially concrete objects like *ball, oak, lilac, airplane, pen, refrigerator,* and words suggesting clear actions like *skip, drip,* and *fly.*

As the youngster grows older, propose a variation. For each word, the child will write a brief definition to go with the illustration. A sentence should appear beneath each drawing, using the word in a statement about the illustration. Older children who choose not to illustrate words should be encouraged to prepare a private dictionary of new words they hear or read. Using a looseleaf binder, they would use a sheet of paper for each letter and might rule or fold the paper into three columns: one for the word, another for its definition (in the child's *own* language, even if he looks the explanation up in the dictionary), a third for a sentence that uses the word correctly. Some parents encourage a fourth column that indicates the pronunciation of the word. Part of a typical page in this kind of home dictionary might look like this:

Word	*Meaning*	*Sentence*
brawny	strong and having muscles	I saw his brawny arms.
biped	animal with two feet	Humans are bipeds.
bleat	cry of an animal like a sheep or goat	The lamb bleated for its mother.

For a new word to join a child's vocabulary it must be practiced in a variety of contexts: The word must be read, spoken correctly, written, and used in a sentence to demonstrate understanding. The private dictionary provides opportunities for the youngster to practice those stages in small doses, as the words crop up in the child's experience. Encourage your youngster to read through his or her dictionary once or twice a week in order to refresh acquaintanceship with new-found vocabulary.

This homemade dictionary advances skills on important fronts: As a writer the child expands his resources for expressing his own ideas with precision; as a reader, he expands his resources for understanding ideas expressed in writing by others; as a speaker with an increased supply of words, the youngster will advance his capabilities with oral language.

Writing Clear Definitions

Despite practice with words and the dictionary, your child may not always be able to put the knowledge he has about a word into a coherent statement. That's true for everyone. Remember those occasions when your son or daughter asked you the meaning of some word you knew but were helpless to put into language. Recall the humorous episode in a *Candid Camera* television segment in which men and women tried to define *scruples*. Twisting, squirming, and stammering accompanied their incredible statements. (One man said the word meant a kind of meat, and that you ate scruples with spaghetti.)

It is important to master the skill of constructing a solid definition if the child is to be a success as a writer. Beginning with

the basic exercises in grade school that ask a child to define
words from a list supplied by the teacher to the complex activity
of telling the class the meaning of a concept in history, mathematics, or science to the rigors of writing a report, memo, or
letter on the job, the ability to state, succinctly and clearly,
the definition of a key term is essential.

There are four critical parts to a good definition of any word,
and if you familiarize the child with those parts, you can establish a pattern from which he or she can construct accurate definitions for other words.

A good definition:

- Names the word or term (sometimes in more than one word) that
  will be defined.
- Uses the word *is, are, was,* or *were.*
- Tells what general group of things or ideas the word belongs to.
- Names the special qualities that make the word different from
  other things in that group.

For example:

If you use this definition, with its arrows, as a model, explain
the various parts. Help your child understand that establishing
the general group to which a word belongs does not sufficiently
establish the meaning of the word. Not every plot of ground
is a garden. What other plots of ground can the child name or
describe? Here are some other samples to look at:

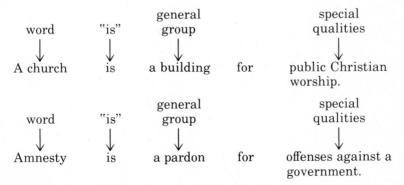

For children who are just learning this skill, you might want to try a different visual approach. With colored chalk, pencil, or crayon draw four rectangular boxes of different sizes and colors on a page. Each one must correspond to a feature of the definition. Write the feature over the box. The page should look something like this:

The child fills in the boxes with their correct parts; if you have colored pencils, the youngster can write the words in the same color as he has drawn the box.

Another way to present this is to make a grid, in which you list the various parts of several definitions in ruled columns.

word	"is"	general group	special qualities
A silkworm	is	a caterpillar	that spins a fine thread to make a cocoon
A handbook	is	a manual	of information on a special subject
A nail	is	a pointed piece of metal	hammered into wood or other material as a fastener
A pogonip	is	a dense fog	of ice particles
A bracelet	is	a band or chain	worn around the wrist for decoration

Caution the young writer about definitions: First, he must avoid using the word itself or a form of it in the meaning he offers. If he wrote "*Division* is to *divide* something" he wouldn't be helping someone who didn't know the meaning of the word. Second, he should avoid definitions that use negatives. "Sadness is not being happy" is a weak definition; "Sadness is a feeling of sorrow or depression" is much more accurate. (Some words, such as *widow,* have negative qualities as their specific characteristics—in those cases negatives are all right.) Finally, remember that it is not grammatically correct to use *when* or *where* after the word *is*. The child must write "A closet is an enclosed place for storing clothing, food, or tools," not "A closet is where you store. . . ."

Here is a list of words you might want to try for good one-sentence definitions; but you'll have more fun if you and your child come up with words based on your own interests:

- summer
- ink
- prejudice
- Buddhism
- union
- calculator
- Goth
- drizzle
- evaporation
- isobar
- tide
- fear
- diary
- matzo
- penguin
- rayon

When the teacher asks your child to write extended definitions of objects, institutions, or concepts, he or she will have to work closely with a dictionary, encyclopedia, or other source books or magazines. You have already laid the foundation for these writing assignments by helping your child learn about word definitions.

When your youngster asks how to expand the definition of one sentence to a fuller effort, point out the kinds of questions he or she might ask about the object being defined:

- What size is it?
- What does it look like?
- What shape does it have?
- What color is it?
- What might the object remind us of?
- Does the thing look like anything else?
- What materials contribute to the object?
- What is the object used for?
- How is the object made?

Here is a brief definition of rayon which was built from significant features the writer discovered after thinking about some of those questions:

Rayon is a manmade fiber produced from cellulose and used to weave fabrics. Chemicals dissolve the cellulose (wood pulp or short cotton fibers) which machines then force through tiny holes. The dissolved material, hardened in warm air or liquid, forms filaments which may be either twisted into threads or cut and spun. Spun filaments of rayon may look like wool, linen, or cotton. Because yarns with new features are developed all the time, rayon now has a variety of uses: it appears in automobile tires, in grease-proof cellophane sheets, in sponge rubber as a substitute for cellulose, and in special glass that cannot be shattered.

Definitions like this one clarify the nature of words and expand the child's facility with language.

Personal Meanings, Personal Words

When I wrote of the denotative and connotative meanings of words, I stressed the glorious variety those qualities give to the language. I want to close this discussion of creative definitions by celebrating those private, personal, and associative attachments people make to words and ideas.

Here is a definition rich in sensory diction and highly personal in the response it arouses:

> *Green:* a row of unripened tomatoes sitting on the kitchen table; the dirty old blotter on my desk filled with doodles in pencil and red ink; wool velvet carpet in the living room; hundreds of pickles floating in the barrel at Mike's Delicatessen on our corner; the large, round, sparkling eyes of my cousin Elizabeth; ivy clinging to the side wall of the quaint old schoolhouse on Mill Road in Brooklyn; diced scallions peering out of a container of cream cheese, small clumps of lettuce, and a handful of olives all at Sunday breakfast; a slippery trail of seaweed stretching at the water line along Brighton Beach at low tide; a statue of a smiling Buddha sitting on the roof of the Ho Sai Kai Restaurant on sunny Pitkin Avenue.

This is the work of an eighteen-year-old who is an advanced writer: There are riches of original detail and of sharply drawn, specific images in the descriptions. Here you have proof that a good writing exercise goes beyond age limits. The child who listed sensory images in response to the word *red* (see page 45), though many years younger and less practiced than the writer who defined green, used the same skill, drawing upon her own powers of observation and linguistic resources. For another definition by an older child reread the paragraph on *rain* on page 55.

When I face a group of inexperienced writers whose word power is undeveloped, I turn to a visual technique which I find opens up the exploration of words and meanings. I ask the youngsters to select a word that is rich in definitions—either a concrete word such as *summer* or *Thanksgiving* or an abstract term such as *fear* or *love*. The child then makes a collage that visually represents the meaning of the word to him without using written language. It's easy to see how interesting conceptions are and how connotations are varied and resourceful. It's also difficult for someone else to guess the word the creator of the collage had in mind. This is especially true of abstract words. One person's series of representations for *love* or *loneliness* varies widely from another's; even representations for concrete terms like *spring* or *school* are hard for an observer to crystallize in the same word the artist had in mind. This shows how inadequate visual means often are in conveying precise information; despite their problems in communicating ideas accurately, words are often more exact than pictures in saying what is meant.

Word exploration has a number of possibilities for other visual reinforcements. A young child exploring concept words (*love, tenderness, anger*) can illustrate the word with a drawing or a series of drawings. You might suggest the child cut photos from a magazine and mount them to illustrate the word he is exploring. These visual exercises interact nicely with the verbal skills you are trying to advance.

As a final experiment in personalized meanings, I suggest you ask your young writer to select some word that can be defined through his or her own experience in a single point of time. It should be an experience that helped the writer to understand the real meaning of some important word. Language users constantly seek new meanings and applications for words they already know. You could all look up *ghetto,* for example, and think you understood its meaning. (*The American Heritage Dictionary* says "A slum section of an American city occupied predominantly by members of a minority group who live there because of social or economic pressure"); but it's not until you experience ghetto life that you can really see the fullest implications of the word. Someone who experiences a ghetto for a short time (as does the writer below), although his understanding of the word has been advanced, still has a weaker sense of what *ghetto* means than does the child raised in an urban slum. Furthermore, a child who seeks out the meaning of *ghetto* in books beyond the dictionary will ripen his conception, but his vision will still lack the personal, indelible meaning that only experience can assure. Youngsters perceive language as a living, vital entity when they write definitions that grow from experience.

The two samples below rely upon descriptive and narrative skills, but each writer's redefinition of a word stretches his knowledge of language beyond the limits that would bind it.

I learned what *ghetto* meant after my first drive down Washington Street in Brooklyn one December morning. A dozen empty buildings in one side of the street had broken windows and large black smears from a fire. I saw boarded-up doors, overturned garbage pails, and clumps of newspapers along the sidewalk. Three black children without coats played with the stuffing of an abandoned couch on an empty lot. A scraggly mutt stretched out on the corner. Everything looked so old and depressing and worn out. No dictionary ever gives that idea in its definition.

On a crisp October afternoon right in the middle of Manhattan, I learned an important lesson in *tolerance* from men who disagreed with my ideas and beliefs. Rather than watch the national election float by me, I decided to show my political beliefs by campaigning for George McGovern for President. Receiving a bulky supply of blue and white McGovern posters and borrowing a heavy stapler from my friend, I started to erect my paper peace monument on the lampposts along Fifth Avenue. The day grew dark and colder as the posters in my hand grew fewer. The sky turned gray as midtown traffic, like a huge snake, slipped tiredly down Fifth Avenue. Rush-hour crowds hurriedly fled down the steps into the BMT subway. When I reached the intersection of Forty-Eighth Street and Fifth Avenue, I viewed uneasily a group of street diggers busy packing their muddy shovels, picks, and drills. Crossing Fifth Avenue to put up the last of my signs, I watched several workers in their yellow hats calmly rip down one of my posters. Obviously biased against my political beliefs, one of them turned and angrily stared across the avenue at me. He had broad shoulders, a rough face, and deepset eyes that flashed the hate he felt. Suddenly, he screamed above the din of the traffic, "Why don't you faggots go back to Russia where you belong?" Anger boiled up inside me. Throwing the remaining posters to the ground, I started to cross the street, cursing under my breath, but the trucks and cars held me back. The peaceful face of George McGovern on a poster suddenly blew by me, swept up in the wind. Then it occurred to me! Wasn't this stupid. Here I was, ready to fight for my "peace" candidate! In a sense, I was worse than that ignorant man across the street. As I thought about why I was out campaigning, my anger died down. Picking up the remaining posters, I continued up Fifth Avenue, leaving the worker, his fists tightly clenched, on the other side. As I trudged on, my hands in my pocket, I thought about the incident that had occurred and was at peace with both myself and everybody else. I couldn't help feeling grateful to that worker. He had taught me, in one succinct moment, the meaning and importance of tolerance, and I saw in it an important feature of world peace.

Here are some words to offer the young writer for extended definitions. Use the more abstract ones with mature children:

- hope
- joy
- friend
- old age
- success
- teacher
- courage
- money
- hero
- a child
- American
- fun
- happiness
- fear
- sports

14

Language Singing:

The Child As Poet

In recent years, agencies like the National Endowment for the Arts have worked along with state and local art councils to sponsor artists in the schools: Children learn firsthand from men and women with creative skills. One of the most exciting of these projects is the Poet-in-the-Classroom Program where poets work in residence alongside young children in school settings. Through poetry workshops, individual writing, group and collaborative poetry, youngsters in many parts of the country experience the thrills and delights of constructing their own poems. Under the wings of these poets the child's efforts grow closer to the spirit of poetic experience than anything the schools have done in the past. Children love poetry; they delight in rhythms and sounds, in sharp visual images, in the emancipation of spirit through language. Kenneth Koch's impressive book *Wishes, Lies, and Dreams* (New York: Chelsea House, 1970) is a source of great inspiration for those who love to see children feeling the force of language through poetry. Read Koch's book; he's an exceptional teacher who describes countless ideas for involving kids in writing poems, and offers wonderful examples of their work.

Your child's library should include a shelf of poetry books, which you can read aloud together. The sound of the human voice breathes excitement into written language.

In this chapter I'd like to point out some activities that will delight the waiting poets in your family. I'd also like to share ideas about what to stress when the child writes a poem, and to mention some techniques poets use when they write.

Talk-to-Me's and Word Whackies

No one can deny the hypnotic delight in rhyming language. In fact, most people when they think of poetry think only of rhyme. Recall those poems you learned along with the nursery rhymes: "Hiawatha," "The Highwayman," "Evangeline," and, perhaps, some from Robert Louis Stevenson's *A Child's Garden of Verses*. Reading specialists use rhyme to teach reading skills, and rhyming plays an important part in a child's use and recognition of word families.

Children respond to rhyming; they sway and bounce as they savor the melody of a poem that trips along. In the exploration of language, rhyme tickles the young child; and there is the chance to make those sallies with words permanent in *writing* poetry.

A good, simple way to involve young children with rhyming is to play with couplets, two lines that rhyme at the end of each:

I take a drink
from the kitchen sink.

Somebody sat
on my red hat.

I like to talk
when I take a walk.

Some parents will leave out the last word or two of the second line of a couplet they write so very young children can add the rhyme themselves before they try to compose their own couplets. Practice for three-line rhymes in similar ways:

Into the sky
I saw a kite fly
Waving his tail good-by.

There's a maple tree
Would you like to see
How it stands beside the house with me?

Rhyming works best when the subject of the poem is not serious. Encourage the child to write silly rhymes that play

with words in improbable situations. Lovely couplets appear
when children write "If I Were" rhyming poems:

> *If I were a brown cow*
> *Would I know how?*
>
> *If I were a table*
> *Would I be able?*
>
> *If I were a pen*
> *What then?*
>
> *If I were green*
> *I'd be mean, I'd be mean.*
>
> *If I were a cloud*
> *How could I talk loud?*

Another way to involve the child in little rhymes is by encouraging him to write "Talk-to-Me's." In a Talk-to-Me rhyme,
the child speaks to some inanimate object:

> *Ice cream, ice cream, take my hand*
> *We'll play in never-melting land.*
>
> *I like you white refrigerator.*
> *Do I get my apple now or later?*
>
> *Faucet, faucet, your tears are dripping.*
> *Is it from your daddy's whipping?*

Older children might try a game of Word Whackies. These
rhymes have two or three lines, too, but they repeat a particular
sound made by letter combinations in words. The results are
delightfully ridiculous, as in this rhyme which uses the *h* and
m sounds.

> *Ho, ho, ho, I have a happy heart*
> *I helped a hippopotamus*
> *To make his motor start.*

Here are some others:

> *Fo, fo, fo, I'm funny, freddy Frog*
> *I fight with flies and frankfurters*
> *Then flip into the fog.*
>
> *A tree told me on the telephone*
> *"Take me to a taxicab and help me home."*

When children have trouble selecting words that rhyme, you can build rhyming word groups in lists for the youngster to use as he writes. Guide him as he composes, seeing that he rhymes at the end of each pair of lines. Encourage the child to suggest his own words too. These are some examples:

shoe	hat	try	still	away
blue	cat	fly	frill	hooray
new	fat	why	will	delay
true	bat	by	bill	array
do	rat	cry	hill	today

Parent and child can prepare groups of words with repeating sounds as well.

chill	snake	over	light
cheap	snoop	open	lazy
Charlie	sneeze	ox	lettuce
chime	snarl	olive	leaping
chair	snap	orange	loon

After the two of you prepare the lists, make sentences using the words with similar sounds, adding words where you need them:

An orange ox opened olives over a lake.

Come up with a silly line to complete the couplet in rhyme:

When he finds all the pits, goodness sake!

By combining a rhyming exercise with sensory language, you'll be helping the child work as a poet. An excellent activity suggested by Don Wolfe uses one of Christina Rossetti's poems, "What is Pink?" to build from. Here are the first few lines:

What is pink? A rose is pink
By the fountain's brink.

What is red? A poppy's red
In its barley bed.

What is blue? The sky is blue
Where the clouds float through.

Using this delightful model, ask the child to ask his own question, starting with a color:

What is gray?

Then, the child must think of something he remembers that has the color. He repeats the color word at the end of the line:

Smoke is gray.

In the next line, the child expands upon the idea he just expressed, offers details of setting, action, or place, and rhymes with the color word at the end of the line:

As it curls away.

Thus, the three lines look like:

What is gray?
Smoke is gray
As it curls away.

You need not confine the child to color—sound, smell, taste, action, and touch work equally well.

What is loud?
My cat was loud
When she meowed.

What is dry?
My garden is dry
In hot July.

You can also get the child to enjoy this as an exercise in metaphor, selecting an abstract term for concrete definition:

What is hope?
A puppy is hope
On a long, long rope.

What is sorrow?
A dream is sorrow
When it ends before tomorrow.

These little games in rhyming and writing improve the young child's facility with words and his pleasure in them.

What's Wrong with Jingling?

But rhyme is not poetry!

In a recent essay, William Slaughter of the University of North Florida in Jacksonville, an author and a poet in the National Endowment for the Arts Poetry in the Schools Program, named a number of ways to get children to write poetry. The first point he insists upon is that children must be helped to overcome the notion of poetry as rhyming. Yes. *Overcome* it.

Does that shock you? If you've seen *any* poems written in school by children, you've no doubt noted the jingling:

> *Nice turkey roasted well*
> *Pilgrims and Indians got along swell*
> *Thankful for good things past*
> *A day to celebrate at last!*

> *In the summer I go to the beach*
> *There I like to eat a peach*
> *In the sun I bake and bake*
> *And after that I have a milkshake.*

Mr. Slaughter is not a lone voice. Another poet-in-the-schools in New Jersey tells of a school being rhyme-crazy, the children starved in self-expression. I agree that children must be moved away from rhyming in poetry.

First, rhyme can trivialize the quality of the thought and experience a poem attempts to convey. There are many definitions of poetry, but to me a poem is the honest communication of experience compressed in intense, concise, and electric language. If a child is groping for words to rhyme with others, and feels compelled to rhyme in order to make his or her poem, the young poet is forcing experience into prescribed language rather than using language to report experience. The youngster who wrote about the beach strained to rhyme that word, struggled to stretch out what she wanted to say so that *peach* wound up at the end of the next line. Unless rhyme is used with great skill, it detracts from the meaning of the poem itself. Coupled with a strong rhythm, rhyme bounces along, so the reader crosses the range just to get over the mountains, without any thought to the meaning of the journey. Keep in mind that the selection of words, the way the poet places them in a line, the sounds made by letter combinations, the stresses required by pronunciation and meaning, and the pattern of sound and word are much more important in the poet's rhythmic skill than rhyming. Finally, the schools overteach "rhyming poems."

Poems in the classrooms frequently mean nothing other than rhyming. Selections read aloud by the teacher, white sheets of children's writing tacked to bulletin boards, original poems filling school newspapers and magazines are products carved in rhyme. A group of thirteen-year-old boys squirms at the prospect of poetry because of the "silliness" of rhyme and because of the preconceived notion that love and flowers and gush define the poetic experience.

This is not to say that rhyme is evil, ineffective, worthless: Rhyme has the power to rivet a child's attention to a tale, to stick ideas in the mind. But if you believe that a poem is the intensification of experience through the language of sense imagery, then you see that rhyme has a subsidiary role. Don Wolfe calls rhyme "an almost magic adjunct to the poet's art . . . a subordinate theme to his music, not the stream of its melody."

The young girl of eight who wrote about her summer day on the beach (see page 191) obscured real experience by forcing rhyme, by pouring honest perception-like water into paper bags. Without depending upon rhyme but with a feeling for the flexibility of language, and a sense of the possibilities of poetry to express emotion, she might have written

> *In the summer*
> *I go to Jones Beach,*
> *Eat a peach*
> *In the sun.*
> *I bake and bake and bake*
> *Dreaming of milkshakes.*

There is a change in thought here, and though this poem lacks instant sensory appeal, it is quite an improvement over the previous effort. The rhyme still remains, but it does not stick out; it works *for* the ideas. The writer forces the reader to take in the words "Eat a peach in the sun" by the way she lays out the lines and by the way she has shifted some parts, so that he barely notices that *peach* rhymes with *beach* directly above it. The use of *Jones* not only adds specificity but also changes the stress on the line, again calling attention away from the rhyme. Notice how the repetition of *bake* creates its own rhythm, how *milkshakes* really misses as a rhyme yet maintains some music through the *-ake* sound.

Look at the two versions of the poem side-by-side to see how they speak about similar experience, one using language to advance ideas, the other trapped by rhymed language which weakens the thought the writer intends:

In the summer I go to the beach	*In the summer*
There I like to eat a peach	*I go to Jones Beach*
In the sun I bake and bake	*Eat a peach*
And after that I have a milkshake.	*In the sun.*
	I bake and bake and bake
	Dreaming of milkshakes.

If the child's poem uses rhyme at all, it should serve the total intent of the writing. Notice that the rhyme in the following poem effectively serves the purpose of freedom and delight in love, yet doesn't overpower the other rhythmic qualities. The teen-age poet repeats words and sounds of letters, varies the length of the poem's lines, shifts usual word order in the sixth line, and breaks rhythm by commas in the last line.

The grass is green
The grass is high
The sun is yellow in the sky

The air is fresh
The air is sweet
My fingertips the cool breeze meet

The flowers nod
The flowers stand
My love, the spring, now holds my hand

It won't be easy convincing children of six to nine that rhymed poetry has fewer virtues than unrhymed—the sing-song is appealing to them as an end in itself. The best way to establish the value of unrhymed poems is to read them aloud to the child at home, or at least to select those whose rhyme does not intrude. Poets like Langston Hughes, Rachel Field, Frances Frost, Vachel Lindsay, Robert Frost, and Walter de la Mare have written poems that avoid rhyme, and which children will enjoy.

Language Singing, Sharp and Clear
In attempts to move children along in their writing skills, your main goal has been to tease out gently the kind of concrete language that will impress upon a reader the full sensory impact of the child's responses to daily life. Poetry requires an even more intense expression of the experience than prose.

Poets choose words with even more care than other writers, each word making an essential contribution to the poem's meaning. In prose the writer can lead up to and lay the ground-work for later elements, but poetry is streamlined and every word counts. The words must convey exactly the meaning the poet wants and must also contribute to the rhythmic effect he's trying to achieve. The writer of poetry must be much briefer than the prose writer; this means the poet must compress ideas and observations into as few words as possible.

When you encourage the child to write poetry at home, any subject is fair game. You must mine the same kinds of things you mined before: the gold of sensory diction, precise action, and figurative language. The use of simile, metaphor, and personifi-cation brings an added dimension of imagination to the poem and delights writer and reader alike.

You're not interested in rhyme, but in the sound of words together, the way the voice moves in rhythm as it reads the lines aloud. Offer these guidelines to the young poet:

- Use a word picture in every line.
- Use color, sound, smell, touch, and taste.
- Try to show an action on every line.
- Make a comparison.
- Don't use words that sound harsh together, so read your poem aloud to hear how it sounds.
- Don't use rhyme.

These aren't rules; use them loosely depending upon the boy or girl's age and interest. An eight- or nine-year-old can look at and understand those pointers and can incorporate many of them into his or her writing as the poem takes shape. For other children, use the guidelines to ask constructive questions: "Why don't you use a color in this line?" "Why don't you use a word that gives a better picture of action than *is* or *walk?*" "Are the words in this line easy to say together?" Rhythmic language is a hard goal for a child to achieve. Along with an attention to the sounds of the words themselves, you can suggest repetition of words, even whole thoughts, in order to achieve rhythm.

Start your home poetry writing right away with activities that practice the use of the senses, encouraging the child to spread the words out in varying lines on the page. Pick a sense and suggest a poem that focuses upon it. A color, for example, makes a good starting point. In the following selection from *Indiana Writes,* a journal of children's writings, notice how

Patricia McGraw starts with a color and then calls into play the
other senses:

> *If I could touch dark blue,*
> *it would be soft like a pussy cat*
> *or like silk or a baby's hands.*
>
> *If I could taste dark blue,*
> *it would taste good and sweet,*
> *sugary like cinnamon,*
> *or maybe like bacon.*
>
> *If I could smell dark blue*
> *it would smell strong*
> *like skunk or like a hot iron.*
>
> *If I could hear dark blue*
> *it would sound like running water,*
> *running mad*
> *or like rain in the night,*
> *or quiet like falling stars.*

And nine-year-old Mike Davis, writing in the same journal,
takes red and in three comparisons calls up taste, sound and
sight.

> *Red is sweet*
> *like an apple*
> *red is loud*
> *like blood*
> *red is quiet*
> *like the sea*
> *at night*
> *when the tide*
> *is going out.*

Use a familiar sound as a starting point and help develop a
poem that uses simile as this eight-year-old does:

> *My heart beats like a bat in a baseball game*
> *And like the thumping of the rain*
> *And like a tornado whirling a rock at a house.*

Give the child the opening part of a line, perhaps:

> *"My shoes squeak like . . ."*
> *"My voice sounds like . . ."*
> *"My clock ticks like . . ."*
> *"Our car coughs like . . ."*

Another good approach to sense poetry is to take a word and
to ask for five lines, each giving a picture of that word in terms
of a different sensory appeal, as this ten-year-old does:

> *Smiles taste like candy*
> *Smiles smell like cherries*
> *Smiles sound like laughter*
> *Smiles feel like lips*
> *Smiles look like cracks*

or

> *Hair smells like rosebuds*
> *Hair looks like grass*
> *Hair sounds like whispers*
> *Hair tastes like leaves*
> *Hair feels like feathers*

Here are some words to give you ideas for sense poems of this
type: *hands, books, a ball, a daisy* (any flower), *the wind,* a
table or chair, a *pencil or crayon,* a *banana.*

The child's natural world is a perfect source for ideas.
Wherever possible, offer guidelines urging the child to look
at a single moment in time as he gives his sensory impressions
of nature. In the school children's poems below notice how the
simple use of comparison joins with sharp and original images.
The repetition of words contributes to the rhythm:

> *How loud the wind yawns,*
> *Roaring so hard as it whizzes by*
> *Weird sounds in my ears*
>
> *The drooping branches of my maple*
> *Hang low:*
> *The bitter cold of winter*
> *Makes them helpless old men.*
>
> *Smoky*
> *Smoky-gray*
> *Like a fire when leaves blow in*
> *And billow away;*
> *Leaving behind them*
> *Smoky*
> *Smoky-gray*
> *Like a book I once read*
> *And stored away;*

A memory that is
Smoky
Smoky-gray
Like an early fog
On a morning in May
Before the sun clears the web of
Smoky
Smoky-gray
And all the thoughts
In my mind today
Are
Smoky.

The snow melts like syrup
Falling off pancake hill
The flowers bloom like
Ribbons opening

When it rains an angel is crying.
Tears pour like a stream.
Falling gently from her cheeks.
Blessing the world below.
When it rains an angel is crying.
Her tears cool the summer heat.
Making us cool and restful.
Relaxing in our sleep.

Today I saw a leaf
So crisp
So dark
So brown
Yes, I saw my first leaf of the day
Upon this solid gold morning.
Its veins, swollen,
As if it labored hard
Upon this golden morning.
I had to leave this treasure
For there was much of the morning
*   left, so*
I quickly let the leaf glide to the
*   ground*
And I strolled away,
Still wondering.

The sky is very blue and the
*   clouds are very mean—*
And when you touch the clouds the
*   rain begins to pour—*

And when it drops on me
My hair begins to cry.
The rain has a gray color
And always bends my roses.

A whispering rain
Gently cracking a mirror pond.
Water cries autumn.

Blue sea
with empty harbors,
the sun's rays
carving ripples
into the water.
A child with
a sun-burnt face,
shielding his eyes
against the glare.
A lazy breeze
brushing over the sand,
leaving the waves
of unspoken words
and quiet thoughts.

The wind snaps its whiplike tongue and a billowy cloud of
*   white sand leaps up and marches over the*
*   barren beachhead.*
The wind shouts a command, and murky blue waters churn
*   into a frenzied mass of white foam.*
Furious, the wind wrenches an oak from the ground and
*   hurls it, howling, "I am King, and no force on*
*   earth can resist me."*

Snow!
Snowballs, snowflakes, snowmen.
Scattered round the world like a blanket.
Good snow.
Bad snow.
Little snow
Dark snow
Light snow
Doing things, each different
Twirling, swirling, swaying with the wind.
Then sun:
The enemy,
The feared
No more big, little, bad, dark, light,
Twirling, swirling snow.

But do not worry
It will snow again
Very soon

Fall:
The dead leaves,
Red, yellow and brown,
Rustling
As the breeze winds through the yard,
Swirling
In the driveway
Skipping
On the sidewalk.

Fall:
Winter's coming,
The cold wind blowing raindrops
Like frozen steel daggers in my back.
The sky,
Gray and dark with thunderclouds
Pouring down hail,
Like a child throwing pebbles at an ant,
Forcing it into the ground.

Fall:
Back to school,
Yellow crossing guards
Sloshing through puddles near clogged up sewers.
The line in the candy store
Waiting for new binders and paper.
Friendships renewed,
New faces,
In the fall.

The following list of subjects for nature poems might give your youngster some ideas.

- the lake in the rain
- thunder at night
- a rose at dawn
- a sparrow on the roof
- the sea in winter
- a frozen lake
- ducks in the sky
- clouds rolling on
- trees in the wind
- summer grass
- bees
- spiders

- fall leaves
- snow
- spring breezes
- the daisy
- dandelions
- climbing ivy
- a brown mouse
- seagulls
- alley cat
- stray dog
- blue jay
- sunrise
- sunset
- river bank

In a poem, personification has extraordinary possibilities. Discourage rhyming and look for clear images, strong and appropriate rhythms, and words that roll easily from the tongue. In these pretend-you're-something poems encourage a bit of nonsense and make-believe:

> *I am a bee*
> *I buzz the roses on the ground*
> *I buzz the grass, I buzz the lamp*
> *I buzz your window sill*
> *But don't say I'm busy.*
> *I'm buzzy.*

> *I am Arthur's bed*
> *I wear a white sheet*
> *And a white pillow hat*
> *I smell like fall*
> *When he crawls into me late at night*
> *I groan a little*
> *Then I play him a song on my springs*
> *Until he sleeps*

Recommend an appeal to one of the senses or a lively action in each line of the personification poem. The subjects suggested on page 157 work fine here, too.

A variation on the personification poem is one in which the child and some nonhuman object have a conversation. Look at these two poems by nine-year-olds from *Indiana Writers*. The first, a talk with a beaver, is by Darrin McGowan; the second, a talk with a turtle, is by Karen Sue Evans.

Why are you cutting down trees?
Because I do not like fingers.
Why do you have such a long tail?
So I can play Ping-Pong over spider's webs.
Why do you have short paws?
I fell in a river and they shrunk.

Turtle, where did you come from?
The water and my mother.
Why do you have a hard back?
To protect myself.
Why do you go slow?
Because I have short legs.
When your head and legs go in you look
like a flying saucer.
Turtle you are always green.
In the dark just me and you.

There are many possibilities for early experimentation with poems. The whole world of experience lays topics at your child's feet: glittering moments of pleasure and love; sudden bouts with pain; an emotion at once alive, real, and understandable; the objects that pass before the youngster's eyes during a day.

Shapes and Rhythms for the Poet's Song

One of the reasons I suggest moving away from rhyme is that poems rely upon other qualities of language to play their music. The marriage of rhythm and image is the hallmark of poetry.

Many poems insist upon an exact form: lines must have so many syllables, so many stresses, and must be grouped in a certain way. Rhymes must appear in prescribed places. Poems with these exact and specific rules for composition based upon rhythmic qualities help children develop their powers as writers.

The Japanese *haiku* gives even an eight-year-old the opportunity to measure and to use the rhythmic qualities of words. Haiku is a three-line poem that offers an observation upon one moment in nature, usually relating to a season of the year. It has strict requirements in form: the first and third lines must have five syllables each; the second line, seven. Look at these haikus written by children; count the stresses; and note the succinct statement, the rhythmic flow, the use of image, and the absence of rhyme.

Fields of blue meadow
A lone star twinkling above
A thousand wishes

The snow falls slowly
On the cold and lonely fields
A flower withers

A little bird perched
On a tree stripped of its leaves
Whistled death's sad tune.

A gusty wind blows
Trees quiver; leaves toss and shake
Stillness. A white dove.

The day is silent
Birds and flowers are asleep
Come and wake them up.

First read the haikus aloud to the child. Count the syllables, and write numbers beside each line or put check marks or X's so the child can count the syllables at the end of the line. Treat this like a puzzle: Can your child write one line about a tree? a flower? the wind? The line must have only five syllables all together? Help out with words and ideas wherever necessary. (Remember the old trick of holding your hand beneath your chin and saying the words; when your chin drops you have a syllable. This is not entirely accurate, but it's good enough for counting syllables in haiku.) You might want to offer the first line of a haiku, asking the child to complete the rest. Try some of these as starters:

Winter whips the trees

_____ _____ _____ _____ _____ _____ _____

_____ _____ _____ _____ _____

A red summer sun

_____ _____ _____ _____ _____ _____ _____

_____ _____ _____ _____ _____

When autumn leaves dance

_____ _____ _____ _____ _____ _____ _____

_____ _____ _____ _____ _____

A bud in spring said

_____ _____ _____ _____ _____ _____ _____

_____ _____ _____ _____ _____

Another poem with precise requirements in form is the *cinquain,* a five-line poem, each line with a required syllable count as I've shown below:

There are a number of variations on these. Some people simplify the syllable counting by asking children to write cinquain according to word count. Line one has one word, line two has two words, line three has three words, line four has four words, and line five has one. Others make arbitrary word requirements for each line, believing any five-line poem with varied word count is a cinquain.

> *A lake*
> *Beside an oak,*
> *A sad and silver face*
> *That cries with yellow, yellow leaves.*
> *Autumn.*

> *Cat*
> *Black cat*
> *Yellow beady eyes*
> *Slowly moves the grass*
> *Cat*

> *Endless thread*
> *from a giant spool,*
> *winding over the face of the earth*
> *twisting, turning, connecting—*
> *highways.*

Consider the *limerick,* and you move into wonderful choices for humor and imagination. The strong rhyme and rhythm interact to build the silliness children love. Read Edward Lear's limericks and enjoy the complete abandon with which he treats reality. A limerick form has five lines of bouncing rhythm; the first, second, and fifth rhyme with each other, and the third and fourth rhyme with each other. A limerick often starts with "There once was a . . ." or "Said a . . . ."

Said a lovely young apple up high
"I don't like being pretty and spry
When old farmer McGee
Smiles brightly at me
I just know he thinks only of pie!"

There once was a boy from New York
Who tried writing a poem with a fork
He flew into a rage
When he punctured the page
Then erased his mistake with some chalk.

A "pure" limerick requires a specific stress pattern and a specific number of those patterns per line, but don't be rigid about requirements with your child. Make dashes to show where the words would appear on the lines. Or start the youngster off with a line and/or two pairs of rhyme. Or arrange rhyming words in groups before the child starts writing. You might lay the poem out this way:

——— ——— ——— ——— ——— ——— ——— ———
——— ——— ——— ——— ——— ——— ——— ———
——— ——— ——— ——— ——— ———
——— ——— ——— ——— ——— ———
——— ——— ——— ——— ——— ——— ——— ———

Then go back and fill in the last words on the line with any of the sets you made, leaving rhymes for lines two and three blank for flexibility:

——— ——— ——— ——— ——— ——— ——— ——— *tree*
——— ——— ——— ——— ——— ——— ——— ——— *me*
——— ——— ——— ——— ——— ———
——— ——— ——— ——— ——— ———
——— ——— ——— ——— ——— ——— ——— ——— *see*

Why Poetry?
Poetry demands exact expression of observation and idea, awareness of sound and rhythm in word combinations, and the use of language in a variety of contexts. These qualities are important for all kinds of writing. Poetry has the added dimension of delight and sweetness; it stays in the mind with ease and pleases the spirit. Something happens to a person when he writes a poem. He feels he is on the verge of creation, on the

highest, almost transcendent, level of consciousness, groping with a searing intensity for language that will clarify meaning. For children the experience is magical, too. One young writer says

> *In poetry*
> *the sky's the limit—*
> *we can be free!*

15

A Report for School

During a recent college class I taught, a young woman stood in front of the room to deliver an oral report she had volunteered to present. She leaned against the gray metal desk, holding photocopies of pages from the *Encyclopaedia Britannica* in her hands. As she tried to read those pages aloud—for the first time, it seemed to me—she stammered over the words. Trapped by her own inability to understand the sentences, she couldn't convey her meaning to the class. Later that week, she turned in her paper. It was an exact copy of the *Britannica* article, filled with complicated language and structures. This wasn't an ignorant or incapable student; she had a quickness of mind and a ready intelligence, despite a record of failures and disappointments in school. I've seen sixth graders, eleven- and twelve-year-olds, prepare reports of strength and quality, and I'm certain that poor study skills limited that young woman's abilities and kept her from achieving. She'd learned nothing about gathering information, digesting it, and arranging it in a clear form.

The school teacher does not spare the child reports: An endless stream of science and book reports, reports on faraway people and places, reports on animals and fish and natural resources, on outer space and inner earth wends through the child's homework assignments each week. However, I've seen little to suggest that children learn how to prepare reports in school, how to gather and record information in a meaningful way. I'm sure you have stood over a child who is in tears, desperately asking for help.

"The teacher says to write a report on helicopters. I don't know what to do!" he or she may say.

How do you help?

Some parents help too much; they do the child's work—collect the data, put it together, even write the report for the child to copy over.

Parents shouldn't do their children's assignments. But you will want to help your son or daughter understand how to write a report for school. A child works on a report *outside* the classroom—at home or in the library. The teacher sees only the finished product; but *you* share the labor of creation as the project moves toward completion. So it's a good idea for you to begin to understand the kinds of skills the child has to develop.

A Project in Stages

Report in its most simple definition is a prepared piece of writing on a particular subject. A child writes using information beyond or supplemental to his own range of experiences.

Research and study play key roles in a report, and these are enormous concepts for a child; they must be broken down. The youngster must understand the various stages through which he must move in order to write his or her report. To do this *you* should clarify your own understanding of the components of research and study so you can help your son or daughter.

These are the steps through which a report writer must move:

• *Understanding the Assigned Topic or Finding a Topic to Report On.* Frequently, the language of the assignment is not clear, or if it is, the writer may not understand what the goals are. Often an assignment is open-ended, the child required to define his own area of interest or to select a book to read and to write about.

• *Limiting the Topic.* An assignment may be too broad for a report. For example, "Write a report on the Eskimos" are instructions that would frustrate a child's attempts. There are *shelves* of books in the library on the general topic "Eskimos"!

• *Finding Information on the Topic.*   What sources can the child find for material on the topic? Which materials serve better than others?

• *Gathering, Grouping, and Digesting Information.*   Children must learn how to collect data simply and effectively and how to restate the information in their own words. Even nine-year-olds can learn the rudiments of note-taking and simple outlining.

• *Writing the Report in a Clear, Interesting, and Orderly Way.*   The final presentation must offer the facts in a manner that involves readers and holds their attention as it informs.

The parent's role is to direct and to guide the youngster's progress without doing the child's work. You shouldn't serve as ghost writer or editor for your youngster, but should aim to help him or her develop self-sufficiency in the written activity.

Let's consider these five parts in the process of writing reports for school:

"What Do I Do?": First Questions First

The problem of finding a reasonable subject for investigation has two faces: Your son or daughter may come to you with a set of instructions that somehow escapes understanding. Your role is to help the child see what the assignment means. Ask, "What do you think Mrs. Coleman wants in this report?" Often the teacher uses part of the day's school instruction as the basis of an assignment. The teacher assigns a report assuming the students will recall their classwork and will elaborate on the day's instruction in their writing. Get the child to talk about the work that preceded the homework assignment. Was it a lesson from one of the books the class uses? Was it a poem the children worked on together? Was it an assembly program everyone watched, or a walk in the neighborhood during recess, or a television show the class looked at together? Encourage talk and ask questions that probe the topic. You can often get youngsters to clear up on their own complications about the assignment. Do not hesitate to suggest a phone call to another child in the class or a brief conversation with the teacher early the next morning.

Sometimes the language of the assignment is not clear—this is especially true as the child advances through the grades. This may stem from poorly worded instructions that are too vague or too complicated for the youngster to grasp. The child or the teacher may not understand the meaning of key question words like *analyze, contrast,* and *describe.* These words are often used by teachers to state assignments.

Word	What it means
analyze	break a subject down into parts
compare	show how things are alike
contrast	show how things are different
define	give the exact meaning of something, showing how it's different from other things like it
describe	show what something looks like
explain	tell why or how something happened
illustrate	give examples to support an idea
prove	give factual reasons to show something is true
summarize	give the main points about something

It's possible that one misunderstood word can push the child off track, so be sure that he or she understands the wording of the assignment before work on the report begins.

Most teachers will state a general idea on which they want the child to report, but occasionally the youngster has a free choice. This is especially true for book reports. Frequently, "Your book reports are due in three weeks" is expected to lead the child to a meaningful project. Knowing your son's or daughter's interests and strengths as well as you do has its advantages: You can help steer the child toward clear goals. "So you have a book report. Remember how you wanted to know about children who lived in big cities? Let's go to the library to find a book about a girl who lives in New York." Or, "You love kittens. Let's find a book about them. You'd write a wonderful report about a book on kittens!"

Such direction rescues the child from disappointment and turns him or her to productive activity.

Shaving the Topic Down
Related to, and often the cause of, the child's confusion is an inability to limit the subject of a report. In my experience,

teachers do not suggest adequate topics for children to investigate and they don't provide sufficient guidance to help the child come up with an original topic for the assignment.

A youngster who announces, "I have to make a report on helicopters," needs your advice. First check with your son or daughter about the *exact* nature of the assignment—perhaps the teacher did offer a very clear and specific topic; perhaps the child copied the instructions into a notebook or can retrieve a ditto sheet from his bookbag. Read the instructions together. Ask, "What do you think your teacher means? What would she like you to find out?"

Often the topic stands alone: "helicopters." Then you must help the child find a more limited target. Achieve this by phrasing questions that turn his or her attention to a specific feature of the subject, one that is reasonable in scope and interest. Approaches vary from report to report, but I think it's best to try to state a question with a *how* or a *why*. A question will fire the child's interest with a challenge and at the same time give a focus to the report itself. You might use one of the words whose meanings I discussed on page 209 in a question or a statement.

"Helicopters. There's so much you could report about helicopters. Why don't you try to find out how helicopters fly? You might try to find out how they are made or why they are used by police or how they are different from other kinds of flying machines." I've by no means exhausted the *how* or *why* possibilities even for helicopters, but I think you get the point. If the child must write about Eskimos, pose these questions to direct the activity:

> How do Eskimos live?
> How do Eskimos get their food?
> Why do Eskimos live in igloos?
> How is an igloo built?
> How do Eskimos make clothing?
> What are the four Eskimo groups?
> How does an Eskimo child spend his or her day?
> Describe an Eskimo's house.
> What is the Eskimos' religion?
> What kind of clothing do Eskimos wear?

Other good questions might ask *when, where, what kind of* along with the other possibilities I've mentioned. A simple answer to one of these questions might not qualify as a "report" in the teacher's eyes, but one answer leads to other questions which the child can explore through several resources. Or he or she can answer three or four questions and relate them in some way to serve as the girders for a well-built report.

There *is* a risk that a teacher who assigns "Eskimos" as a report really wants a comprehensive treatment. But I believe that a child who clearly defines the aspect he'll treat in a topic will earn rewards not blame and will have performed a reasonable task. You have to help the child find a narrow focus within the broad topic.

One approach you might take with older children (eleven and up) asks the youngster to slice smaller and smaller pieces from a general topic. Suppose the teacher names *education* as the topic for a report. Children *must* limit so broad an idea for any productive exploration. The youngster learns to narrow the field by moving through stages as described on the chart below. Children prefer *general* topics for investigation because they find comfort in the broadest possible subjects and think there's more freedom in such an approach. Some psychologists have tried to show that thinking first begins on levels of abstraction and that generalizing is a much more basic quality of thought in young children than was once believed. However, cherishing the general is a trap for a writer. If he doesn't limit a subject, his writing becomes vague and insubstantial because there's too much ground to cover and he cannot offer enough detail to support all his statements. The treatment becomes superficial.

Too General	Still Broad	Less Broad	Narrow: Good Report Topics
Education	Education in Russia	How arithmetic is taught in Russia	Elementary school arithmetic in Russia
Examinations	High school examinations	High school essay examinations	The value of essay exams in high school
Teachers	Elementary school teachers	Kindergarten teachers	How kindergarten teachers are trained
Teaching	New ways of teaching	New ways of teaching children	New ways of teaching biology to children

Your Friends: The Encyclopedia and Other Source Books

There's no more valuable and no more misused tool than the encyclopedia. A world of information lies between the covers of its volumes and usually they are easily available in the library or in the child's own house. There are many encyclopedias for different age levels, so that even a child of seven or eight may mine the gold and diamonds from these books.

Since the encyclopedia is the first and most complete source for the child who writes a report, you should know about encyclopedias for children, so that you can encourage your son or daughter to use the one that suits his or her needs. Among the most popular for young children (four to eight or ten years) are *Childcraft, My First Golden Encyclopedia, Compton's Precyclopedia,* and *Child Horizons;* for children from seven to twelve or fourteen are the *New Book of Knowledge, Brittanica Junior,* and *Golden Book Encyclopedia;* for children from nine to eighteen are *Compton's Encyclopedia, World Book Encyclopedia,* and *Encyclopedia International.* If you want a comprehensive comparative discussion of encyclopedias on all levels, I urge you to examine Kenneth Kister's *Encyclopedia Buying Guide* (New York: R. R. Bowker, 1966). Mr. Kister has strong opinions about encyclopedias, but his reports are so complete that you'll be able to make your own judgments.

Selecting an encyclopedia that looks as if it suits your youngster, examine together information under topics that might interest the child. Then, using *how, why,* or some other good question word, frame a question the child might answer by reading the encyclopedia entry. For instance, if you're investigating *mouse,* ask, "How did mice come to America?" or "Where are mice usually found?" or "Why don't wild mice live longer than three months?"

When the child begins to use the encyclopedia, he is usually hunting for an answer to a specific question. Once he finds the response, reinforce the skills built earlier. Ask for a whole sentence that repeats part of the question. Suggest the youngster tell you, in his own words, about the information he has uncovered. Thus, you might read sentences like these:

Mice came to America in English, French, and Spanish ships which arrived here in the 1500s.

Mice are found in most parts of the world. They live in mountains, fields, swamps, and deserts.

Wild mice do not live longer than three months because they have so many enemies like hawks, owls, and rats.

I said, earlier, that the encyclopedia is a misused tool. First, because children have little training in how to use the book, they will often copy a complete entry word for word. Second, because the youngster can gather so many blossoms from an encyclopedia, he rarely ventures into other parts of the garden —the vast reserves of source books in a library.

Word-for-word reporting is a runaway problem much ignored by the teacher. A child looks up his topic; turns to the correct page; copies what is before him; submits what he has copied to the teacher; and receives a check of approval. These questions of ethics aside, such practices defeat the whole purpose of the report, which is to teach the child something that he can then convey in his own written language to someone else. The child rarely interacts with what he reads when he copies a full page of encyclopedia material.

A parent should train the child to take notes on readings— nothing elaborate, just a few words in a list on a page; perhaps, a few phrases that the child will group, later, into a meaningful whole as he draws upon information he's gathered from more than one source.

Data collected in note or list form should be a common sight to your son or daughter. At school the events of a day are listed on the chalkboard; on the bulletin board may be a chart of weather conditions for a given month or season; the science class writes down daily observations about a celery stalk that the teacher puts in a glass of red ink and water on the window ledge.

At home establish situations in which your child keeps records of information. A supermarket list is data collection at its simplest level—it stimulates some action. You can also ask the youngster to record weather observations, seasonal changes, varied activities on the street as the day moves on. All of those should be based upon what the child sees out the kitchen window. If you've followed my advice about preparing sense charts, you've encouraged even more practice in record-ing data, and you are even anticipating the skill of *grouping* which I'll discuss with you in a little while.

I'll point out some real examples so that you can have a clearer picture of the goals the child should try to achieve: In response to a report on *hibernation,* a ten-year-old turns to that section in an encyclopedia and reads the page there. First, he might talk with you about the report, and you'll help him limit his subject. Perhaps he or she can report on why animals hiber-nate. Maybe the child will explore the differences in hiberna-tion of warm-blooded and cold-blooded animals. He might want to explain why small animals hibernate. Or, he may simply explain what hibernation is and how animals do it.

Once there's a clear purpose to the report, the child is ready to take notes. (This is not *always* the order: In some cases children who don't know what they will report on will need to take extensive notes *before* they establish a topic; the notes serve as a way to define the broadest possibilities of the subject which the child will narrow down.) The simplest approach demands thinking beforehand in order to determine some limited topic in advance of gathering material.

Here is part of the entry on hibernation that appears in *The New Book of Knowledge* (New York: Grolier, 1974), pages 121 to 122:

HIBERNATION

Many animals pass the winter in a state known as winter sleep, or **hibernation**. This helps them to live through the difficult period of the year in the cooler parts of the world.

In other regions the intense heat and dryness of the summer can be dangerous to life. Here some creatures, such as certain frogs and fish, seal themselves in mud and suspend all activity until the season is over. This is known as **estivation**. ("Estivation" comes from a Latin word that means "having to do with summer." "Hibernation" comes from a Latin word meaning "to winter.")

Hibernation and estivation both serve as means of avoiding death because of lack of food or water during part of the year. Hibernating animals, however, are more familiar to us. The best known are the woodchucks, ground squirrels, dormice, hedgehogs, hamsters, and the small common bats.

A hibernating animal does more than just go to sleep. A true hibernator falls into a state of apparent death during the winter months and comes to life again in the spring. A good example is the dormouse, a tree-climbing, squirrel-like mouse that is common in Europe and Asia. By early autumn the animal becomes very fat. Then it builds its winter nest. It lays up a store of food. And it retires to

sleep, curling itself up with its forepaws against its cheeks and its tail wrapped around its head and back. The sleep may last for 6 months, with breathing so slow that it is hardly noticeable. The creature becomes so cold and stiff that it can be rolled about like a ball. When it wakes again, in the spring, most of its fat has disappeared.

The woodchucks (groundhogs) and marmots of North America behave much like the dormice. Both of them become loaded with fat before retiring. And this fat forms their only support for life until spring comes. Their close relatives, the gophers and the true ground squirrels, are also hibernators. But before hibernating, these animals lay up large stores of roots, seeds, and berries for occasional feasts during the winter. (The true squirrels do not hibernate but simply store food in hiding places for winter use.) A good hibernator, therefore, does three things. It stores up as much food as possible, either as body fat or as actual stored food. It finds or makes a suitable winter shelter. And it goes into a long and very deep sleep, during which its body becomes cold and usually stiff. In the case of the ground squirrel, the body temperature drops from about 98 degrees Fahrenheit to a few degrees above freezing; the heartbeat

The child who looks at the full selection wants to explain what hibernation is. Here are the notes she prepares:

Notes on Hibernation
The New Book of Knowledge. Vol. 6
pages 121 to 122

1. Hiber. is winter sleep for many animals
2. Helps animals live through cold weather

3. Hiber. comes fr. Latin word "to winter"
4. Some hib. animals are woodchucks, ground squirrels, dormice, hedgehogs, hamsters, small bats
5. Hib. like death in winter. Anim. comes to life in spring
6. Anim. who hibernates stores up food as fat or actual stored food like roots and nuts
7. Finds or builds winter shelter
8. Goes into long deep sleep. Body gets very stiff and cold. Squirrel's body temperature drops from 98° F to a little above freeze.
9. If anim. wakes too fast it may die

slows from 400 beats to 10 a minute; the rate of breathing slows from 200 to 2 or 3 times a minute.

If the hibernating animal is awakened too fast, it may die—which shows how close to a living death the state of hibernation really is.

• WHY ANIMALS HIBERNATE

In regions where winters are severe, some animals migrate while others hibernate. Migrating animals travel far enough to find food and warmth, and they return in the spring when conditions become favorable again. That is what most birds do, since they can fly long distances without difficulty. But except for certain bats, the small, hairy mammals cannot migrate over long distances. They must by some means survive the winter conditions right where they are. Hibernation is a way of doing this.

In these regions the question of food is more important than the outside temperature. Birds and mammals, with their covering of feathers or hair, can usually keep warm if they get enough food. Hibernation or migration is necessary if the food supply fails. Birds migrate because the winter kills their food supply—not because they cannot keep warm in a cold climate. Certain mammals hibernate when their food supply fails.

• PARTIAL HIBERNATION

Some creatures appear to hibernate but do not really do so. The bear is an example particularly the American grizzly and black bears. The male bears prowl through the woods and find food throughout the winter. The female bear retires to her den in the autumn, with her young already starting to grow inside her body. She then goes to sleep. Yet her body temperature drops only a few degrees. The young are born early in the new year and are able to get milk and warmth from the mother, who is at least half awake at that time. All winter long she lives on her own fat. She wastes no energy on unnecessary activity. And she is easily awakened and warms up quickly. The long sleep of the female bear is a kind of hibernation, for it serves very much the same purpose. Yet it is not true hibernation, which leaves the body cold and rigid.

• BODY TEMPERATURE

Scientists have been puzzling over the nature of true hibernation for a long time. They have been trying to understand what takes place to make the body seem so lifeless. Actually, it is in a state of coma from which it can be awakened. How is this coma brought about and how is it ended? As yet, scientists do not know.

This sample can serve as a good model to show your child. Notice the differences between the printed selection and the child's notes. When you offer guidelines to your son or daughter, point out:

- Use a separate index card or sheet of paper for each source (this makes it easier to group information later on).
- Write the name of the source on top of the card.
- Write clearly.

- Write down the pages on which the information appears in case you have to check back.
- Abbreviate wherever you need to. However, make sure you understand what you're writing.
- Copy information accurately.

If you've been encouraging the child to use his own language in taking notes, don't worry about explaining the use of quotation marks when he copies down someone's exact words. Later on, when he turns to sources other than the encyclopedia, you'll have to mention the importance of giving credit to someone else's ideas when he uses them in a report. Techniques of quoting, paraphrasing, and mentioning sources (in footnotes or bibliography) are beyond the purpose of this chapter, which is to provide a basic model for you to influence the youngster's preparation of an effective report.

Many elementary school teachers will be content with reports based upon a single source, and for younger children I have no objection to that approach. Still, if the encyclopedia prevents the child from looking beyond it and into other resources, it defeats its purpose. I use the encyclopedia as a starting point: It's where *I* go for an overview of something I need to research. It outlines the broadest possible dimensions of the problem; in it I find a subject that I will investigate further in other books and in periodicals.

Ten-year-olds can see the encyclopedia in the same light. On a topic like *hibernation* a youngster who looks in the subject card catalog in the library will find named a number of interesting books that can expand the quantity and quality of the information the child has already gathered from the encyclopedia. Show the child how to use the card catalog. If it poses too difficult a problem to the youngster, don't worry. Librarians are trained to help children use the tools of research. Don't be embarrassed to ask librarians for help. That's one of the things they get paid to do. Bother them—if they're good, they'll love it!

Getting Things in Order
Once you have helped the child find and check a variety of sources and he or she has gathered sufficient information in notes, help the youngster organize material with some methods of grouping.

Some writers use an outline, which is a formal way of putting information into groups so that the writer has a guide for organization. But at this stage leave the intricate elements of outlining to classroom instruction. Encourage the child to group information even if it's just an informal clustering of details. Any outlining technique is supposed to make the writer's task easy, so don't stress letters and Roman numerals.

When the youngster made sense charts he or she put details into predetermined groups headed with words like *sounds, colors* and *actions, smells.* Now you're going to help the child look at details and group *them* in some orderly way.

Remember those shopping lists? Once you itemize the food you need, show the youngster how much easier it will be to fill the cart if the food is listed in related groups. That way you can gather up items placed near each other on the shelves, and you won't have to run from aisle five for soaps to aisle three for canned string beans and back to aisle five for bleach. Give a heading to each group; base it upon the signs above the supermarket aisles. Below on the left is a shopping list; to the right is the same list reorganized so that items are grouped together.

milk	*Dairy*
canned mushrooms	milk
M & M's	butter
laundry detergent	American cheese
potato chips	sour cream
1 lb. tomatoes	*Fresh fruits and vegetables*
1 doz. oranges	1 lb. tomatoes
frozen peas	1 doz. oranges
chicken	1 head lettuce
1 lb. chopped meat	2 lb. apples
paper towels	*Canned vegetables*
canned peas	mushrooms
frozen spinach	peas
butter	tomatoes
napkins	*Frozen vegetables*
American cheese	peas
2 lb. apples	spinach
Milky Ways	*Meat*
sour cream	chicken
1 head lettuce	1 lb. chopped meat
canned tomatoes	salami
hand soap	*Candy and chips*
salami	M & M's
	potato chips
	Milky Ways
	Soap and paper goods
	laundry detergent
	paper towels
	napkins
	hand soap

Using simple, recognizable items like these helps the child to organize materials so that the relationships between items in groups are clear. The reason for the groupings is important and should be readily apparent. There are lots of other lists that you and your child can make: You can organize lists of Christmas gifts and chores to be done around the house. Or provide a batch of photographs or magazine pictures and ask the child to group the items in some way—all children, all adult women, all adult men, all appliances. If, after practice, the child can establish his own groups, you've done a good job!

These easy activities are not much different from the techniques a youngster must employ when he or she tries to relate bits of information for a report.

After this, by guiding practice in simple outlining, a parent teaches the child a skill rarely developed in the classroom. Below is a more formal outline for a report on hibernation. Notice the Roman numbers: Each of them will provide the main topic of a single paragraph. The subheadings (A, B, C) will serve as reminders that each topic should have supporting details. Each item is a full sentence.

Outline: What is Hibernation

I. Hibernation is winter sleep.
  A. Hibernation comes from Latin for "to winter."
  B. Hibernation helps animals live through cold weather.
  C. Some hibernating animals are woodchucks, ground squirrels, dormice, hedgehogs, hamsters, and bats.
II. Animals do many things to hibernate.
  A. They store up food within bodies as fat.
  B. They store up roots and nuts for special winter feasts.
  C. They build or find winter shelter.
  D. Animals fall into a long deep sleep.
  E. The body may grow stiff and cold, like the squirrel's.
  F. Animals can die if they wake too fast.

Enter the Finished Product
With the outline in hand you can see how a report like the one below developed. A ten-year-old can easily prepare it. Notice that the writer did not follow the outline slavishly. He returned to his notes for more information in order to expand the paragraph. And see how the clearly limited topic was supported with solid details.

Hibernation is a winter sleep. The word comes from a Latin word meaning "to winter." Hibernation helps animals live through the cold weather. Some hibernating animals are wood-chucks, ground squirrels, dormice, hedgehogs, hamsters, and bats.

Before hibernating, animals must store up food as fat within their bodies. For special winter feasts they hide roots and nuts. Also, they must build or find a good winter shelter to protect them in the cold. Some animals use caves. Others dig holes in the ground. Finally, hibernating animals fall into a long deep sleep. Their bodies grow stiff and cold. For example, the ground squirrel's temperature drops from 98° F. to just above freezing. If you see a hibernating animal, don't wake him too fast! He might die.

The procedures I've discussed here will serve, with some modifications, for most kinds of report writing. Older children will select topics that they can expand with more details: A thirteen- or fourteen-year-old would research more fully the nature of hibernation, would explain more completely the chemical and physical changes the animal undergoes, and would offer a view of an animal that first awakens from winter sleep. All these details would be gathered from several sources, outlined, and then written up in a longer report.

In a science report, a child might be asked to identify some problem and to plan some method of determining an answer to it. He'd have to explain his experiment step by step in writing and to draw conclusions from it. He might need to read what others have suggested about the problem. The child must practice objectivity in the science report. His emotional responses to a problem have no place in such an essay.

The book report is perhaps the most frequently assigned report in school. The teacher usually supplies the youngster with a list of general areas to cover in a one-page overview. You might observe these as requirements for a child's report on a fictional book:

I.   Name and author
II. Setting (where the action of the book takes place)
III. Characters (the main people in the book)
IV. Plot (a summary of the main events)
V.   Opinion (what you think of the book)

Under each heading the child puts down a few sentences. I imagine that there are some positive qualities in such kinds of reports: The youngster does learn something about the features of books and the language used to describe them, and if there's any need to refresh the memory about a book, it's easy to check back over such neatly devised responses. Besides, such outline-form reports are very easy to grade! Nonetheless, report writing can be a much more imaginative challenge than this.

There is merit in straightforward reporting, whether it takes the form of an outlined book or two or three paragraphs on hibernation, but a child's creative abilities should be stimulated, even in report writing. A young writer in the elementary grades who works with a body of collected data can interact boldly with the materials. The child can tap his or her own inventiveness for a written report.

If your son or daughter has an open-ended assignment, which, despite a required topic, makes no specific demands about format, why not suggest one of the following ways of writing up the report?

• *Personification.* Let the child pretend he's an animal and write about himself as the animal. The youngster must use accurate information that he or she has discovered by researching. Here's one example, reported by Don Wolfe:

> My name is Joey. I'm a canary about five and a half inches long. My head is oval shaped, and I have black beady eyes. My tongue is long and thin, like a snake's tongue. Most of my feathers are yellow, but when I was young my feathers were gray. I like seeds and cold water. I eat seeds all the time, but now and then I get the yolk of an egg, a carrot, a tiny piece of lettuce, and other vegetables. I love chocolates, but my mistress says they are not good for me. I hop about on my feet and fly with my wings. I do not fly so well as other birds do. Because I am a male, I have a beautiful singing voice, but my wife does not. I don't want to brag, but we canaries are very intelligent in recognizing certain people. I flutter and make an ugly noise at people I don't like, but I wouldn't dream of fluttering at my wife.

• *Pretend You Are Some Person.* The young child should write as if he or she were one of the main characters in a book or some historical figure. The youngster's report will discuss key features of his or her life.

• *Write About a Moment.* For a child's book of fiction or biography or autobiography, write about one single moment that is important in the hero's life. Fill in the moment with details.

• *Pick a Meaningful Quote.* This is an especially interesting activity for older children. As the child reads, he should jot down page numbers on which interesting, challenging, beautiful, annoying, or unusual statements are made by the author of the book. The child then looks back over all the statements and selects one or two key quotations. After copying down the author's statement, the child writes an original paragraph explaining why he made that selection. I find the most interesting responses come when children explain from their own lives some experience that relates to a statement in the book.

• *Be a News Reporter.* Let the child pretend he's a cub reporter for a local newspaper in order to interview a person. Or, he can write a news report about some key event he's been asked to investigate.

• *Make Up a Character.* The youngster can invent some character, then narrate major events in the life of the historical or fictional character the child chooses to report on. That delightful children's book *Ben and Me* is an excellent example. In it a mouse who is a companion to Benjamin Franklin writes about his adventures with the famous statesman-inventor.

• *Write a Play or Dialogue.* The youngster writes a play based on an important scene in a book the child is reading. Or, the child can write a play or a dialogue on some moment in history, some discovery or invention.

• *Describe a Moment with a Character.* In this writing activity the child pretends he visits some famous character (see pages 150 to 151).

• *Make a Bookcover.* The child combines writing and illustration. Drawing, painting, or cutting and pasting, the youngster reproduces one scene from a story on a sheet of colored paper that is folded like a book jacket. Then, he or she writes a summary of that scene, and copies it onto lined paper which is pasted onto the front and back flaps of the book jacket.

• *Who Am I?* Without naming the character of a biography or autobiography, the boy or girl writes ten sentences (or brief groups of sentences) that point up highlights in the life of the person. The child ends the report with the question "Who Am I?"

Using Your Will Power

Reread Chapter 6, so that you keep your role as helper for school writing in perspective. You must remember that *you* are not the student. I know how tempting it is to give answers, lay out plans, find materials, summarize research, and write the report for the young man or woman you so love. But it won't help the child—he or she must learn how to do all those things. You are a facilitator, one who frees a task from obstacles, one who makes things easier. Establish a warm home setting that encourages your child to write—but *don't do the child's work!*

16

An Afterword for Too-Busy Parents

In a school district in Central Pennsylvania a high school English chairman described the effect of recent cutbacks in his department. Local citizens would not approve higher taxes: The superintendent insisted upon across-the-board cutbacks. The English staff dropped to eight teachers for fourteen hundred students! Figure it out: one teacher for every one hundred seventy-five children. Given the usual five-class teaching load, that's thirty-five in a class.

How much writing will be going on in those classrooms? Developing writers *must* write several hundred words at least once a week, preferably each day. What kind of job can even a specialist in writing do in such circumstances?

In 1968, I left my high school teaching job as an instructor in English: I'd taught five classes a day, and each had more than thirty students. Things have not come very far since then! National organizations have not convinced school officials that the special responsibilities of teachers of writing demand smaller classes and lower child-to-teacher ratios. Unless teachers in elementary schools have reasonable numbers of children to work with, writing skills will suffer. When administrators try to convince the public that statistics show class size has no relation to how well children learn, insist upon seeing the tests that "prove" this position. I'll bet those tests don't ask children to write!

I'm not hopeful that the schools can do what they should to help children develop as writers, in spite of the sudden and far-reaching interest in the skill. Even the college, which once assured close attention to writing, now asks instructors to teach three or even four sections of composition, with as many as thirty students in a class.

All this is to answer your question "Who can find the time to do all this?"

My reply is: "If not you, then who?"

I've given you lots of ideas. You're ready to start things going, so don't put it off! What you do in your home will reward you with delightful proof that any child *can* write.

Appendix A

One Hundred Ideas
for Writing at Home

This is a list of specific writing activities for your youngster. They follow the topics of this book. Some ideas are more appropriate for older children, so use your good judgment.

1. Make a list of your favorite toys.
2. Make a shopping list.
3. Make a list of school supplies.
4. Make a list of people you'll invite to a birthday party.
5. Make a list of clothing you want to buy.
6. Write a note for your father or mother asking permission to do something.
7. Write a note to the mailman.
8. Make a holiday greeting card and write a message inside.
9. Make a sign for your room door.
10. Write an absence note for the teacher's records.
11. Draw a picture of someone in your family doing something and write a sentence under it explaining what he or she is doing.
12. Describe your kitchen at breakfast.
13. Describe your living room at night.
14. Describe your bedroom in the morning.
15. Describe your classroom as it looks early in the morning.
16. Describe the sounds of the schoolyard at three o'clock.
17. Describe a room in the library.
18. Describe the supermarket on a Saturday afternoon.
19. Describe a sports stadium during a game.

20. Describe a visit to a farm or a zoo.
21. Describe a moment at the beach or at a river bank or at a pool.
22. Tell about one moment on a train ride.
23. Describe the sights and sounds on the school bus on a rainy Monday morning.
24. Describe a busy street in your town during shopping hours.
25. Describe a moment on a car ride.
26. Tell about a visit to McDonald's or Burger King or some other fast food place.
27. Describe your mother when she's angry.
28. Describe a relative from a color photograph.
29. Describe a dream you had.
30. Describe dad (or mother) relaxing.
31. Describe dad (or mother) working.
32. Tell about one adventurous moment on your bicycle.
33. Tell about a time you felt proud of your brother or sister.
34. Describe a dinner you remember.
35. Describe your pet at a single moment.
36. Describe the sounds you like (or do not like) when you're lying in bed and waiting to fall asleep.
37. Describe your brother (or sister) playing.
38. Describe your sister (or brother) eating.
39. Look at a famous painting and describe what you see.
40. Describe an exciting moment in a game or sport you played.
41. Describe your street in the winter (summer, fall, or spring).
42. Write about a moment in your park or playground.
43. Write about an embarrassing moment.
44. Write about a job you hate to do.
45. Write about a funny moment.
46. Write about a moment in which you felt happy.
47. Write about a moment in which you felt proud.
48. Write about a moment in which you felt sad.
49. Write about a moment in which you felt frightened.
50. Write about a time you got lost.
51. Write about a moment when you were disappointed.
52. Write about a time you helped someone.
53. Write about a time you had an argument with a friend.
54. Write about a time someone helped you.
55. Write about a moment in church or synagogue.
56. Describe a department store at a moment during Christmas shopping.
57. Write about how to make your favorite sandwich.
58. Write about a time you cleaned up your room.
59. Describe your favorite meal.

60. Describe one of your friends.
61. Write about a moment you got in trouble.
62. Look in the mirror in the morning and describe what you see.
63. Describe your favorite toy.
64. Write about a moment in an airplane.
65. Pretend you are a refrigerator.
66. Pretend you are a washing machine.
67. Pretend you are your mirror.
68. Pretend you are the family car.
69. Pretend you are your bed.
70. Pretend you are one of your own toys.
71. Pretend you are a pencil.
72. Pretend you are a farm animal.
73. Pretend you are Mommy or Daddy scolding you.
74. Pretend you are your dog, cat, canary, or goldfish.
75. Pretend you are the grass talking to the wind.
76. Pretend you are a bumble bee speaking to a rose.
77. Pretend you are a fairy tale character (Hansel, Gretel, Little Red Riding Hood) and write about one adventurous moment in your life.
78. Write a letter to a sick friend.
79. Write a letter to an author you like.
80. Write a letter to your favorite television or recording star.
81. Write a letter to the editor of your local newspaper.
82. Write a letter to invite a friend to your house for a party.
83. Write a thank-you note to someone who sent you a gift.
84. Write a post card to a friend when you are on vacation with your family.
85. Write a letter to your teacher to invite her to lunch.
86. Define *happiness*.
87. Define *fear*.
88. Write your definition of *friend*.
89. What is an American?
90. What is poverty?
91. What is courage?
92. Write a poem about fall.
93. Write a poem about a moment at the beach.
94. Write a poem about a moment you felt lonely.
95. Write a poem about a silly moment.
96. Write a poem about a tree or a bush on your street.
97. Write a poem about happiness.
98. Pretend you are a character in your favorite book. Write about an adventure.
99. Describe an exciting moment in a biography you read.
100. Read about some famous person in history; pretend you are a reporter who interviews the person; write up your interview for the newspaper.

Appendix B
A Parent's Primer on Correctness

This appendix is *not* going to teach you everything you ever wanted to know about grammar but were afraid to ask! At your local stationery stores, magazine stands, and bookshops there are lots of books designed to help adults improve their own skills in writing and grammar. Your son or daughter's language arts book from school can serve as a good resource for you about writing.

What I want to do here is to give you an overview of the basics, the main points of correctness, in clear, simple language so that you can:

- recognize serious problems your child may be having in correct language use when he writes at home.
- help the child understand an error he makes in writing under your direction.
- help the child understand an error the teacher has pointed out on his school writing.

In trying to achieve these goals, I've left out a great deal. For example, I omitted a discussion of agreement of subject and verb because it's too tricky to reduce to a brief discussion. I've also not mentioned commas which, though necessary for clarity, are not worth bothering about in these basic recommendations, in the light of other serious problems children have in writing. You have more important work to do!

Sentence Completeness

It's hard to name the exact qualities that make a group of words a sentence because there are so many different kinds of sentences and because there are so many exceptions to the definitions grammarians offer.

Some say a sentence is a word group that has a subject and a verb and expresses a complete thought.

Others say that a sentence is a group of words that name some subject and tell something about that subject.

Whatever definition you use, the point is that you've got to help develop a sense of sentence completeness for the child.

Help children test for sentences that make sense:

- make sure that all sentences begin with capital letters.
- make sure that all sentences end with periods, question marks, or exclamation points.
- remind children to read sentences aloud slowly, listening to their own voices. Wherever the voice stops and drops use a period.
- after the child writes several consecutive sentences, insist he make a conscious effort to look for complete ideas in his own writing. If he's having trouble seeing how one sentence should stand apart from the sentence before or after it, have him read his sentences from the last to the first. That will help him keep ideas separate.

You want to keep a lookout for two major types of sentence errors.

1. Run-together sentences. In this major error (also called *run-on, fused sentence, comma fault,* and *comma splice*) the child fails to separate sentences correctly.

Sometimes there's no punctuation:

I ate quickly then I rushed to school.

Sometimes there's a comma between the two sentences.

I ate quickly, then I rushed to school.

Sentence sense tells you (and your voice as you read aloud slowly helps, too) that one idea ends after *quickly.* In order to keep the two ideas separate the writer needs a period between them:

I ate quickly. Then I rushed to school.

The comma, though it signals a minor pause, is not a strong enough mark of punctuation to stand alone between sentences. Some writers might choose a semicolon to keep the ideas apart (no capital after it!):

> I ate quickly; then I rushed to school.

Semicolons are helpful in joining sentences that are very closely related to each other in meaning.

A child may sometimes correct run-together sentences effectively by combining them with connecting words (notice the comma; here it works along with the connector):

> I ate quickly, *and* then I rushed to school. (Other connectors that work in this way, given the sense of the new sentence, are *but, or, nor,* and *for.*)

> *After* I ate quickly, then I rushed to school. (Other connectors that work in this way, given the sense of the sentence, are *although, since, because, besides, when, while,* and many more.)

2. *Sentence pieces.* Beginning writers frequently use word groups that are incomplete; they do not qualify as sentences. These word groups, called *fragments,* usually belong to full sentences that go before or come after the fragment. Sometimes these groups need to have more words added in order to make sense as full sentences. Fragments need the parent's patient attention because they are one of the major errors on the papers of inexperienced writers. Look at some examples below; then I'll suggest some ways you can help the child find incomplete sentences on his own. The words in boldface in the left group of words are fragments. On the right, italics point out the complete sentence which was formed from the fragment.

I	II
1. A dog played with a rubber ball. He rushed after it. **Over the curb and into the street.**	A dog played with a rubber ball. *He rushed after it over the curb and into the street.*
2. Everywhere I can hear the wind's howl. **Rushing noisily through the trees.** It scares me!	*Everywhere I can hear the wind's howl rushing noisily through the trees.* It scares me.

or

3. One afternoon I stood at the freezer in the A & P. **When an empty cart shot down the aisle.** I knew a little child was to blame.

Everywhere I can hear the wind's howl. *Rushing noisily through the trees, it scares me.*

One afternoon I stood at the freezer in the A & P. *When an empty cart shot down the aisle, I knew a little child was to blame.* (The fragment could be attached to the first sentence, "One afternoon . . .")

4. In the street I saw my cousin Steve. **Who really looked ridiculous.** He was wearing his Halloween ghost costume.

In the street I saw my cousin Steve who really looked ridiculous. He was wearing his Halloween ghost costume.

5. He cannot tie his shoe. **Unless someone helps him.** He will probably leave his laces open.

He cannot tie his shoe unless someone helps him. He will probably leave his laces open. (The fragment might be attached to the sentence after it.)

Help the child learn to find sentence pieces in his own writing. There's no sure-fire method—fragments keep cropping up straight through writing I examine in college classes—but some things work:

- Have the child walk away from his writing for a while, and then come back and read aloud what he's written.
- As he reads, encourage the child to stop for a long breath after each sentence he's written. Train him to ask, "Does this sentence make sense?"
- Encourage the child to read his sentences from the last one to the first one. This helps him see whether or not each makes sense, whether or not each names some subject and gives some information about that subject.

One Hundred Words Most Often Misspelled

As you consider these and keep on your guard for them in your child's writing, remember the pointers I mentioned in Chapter 7 for learning them.

accommodate	all right	apparent
achievement	among	arguing
acquire	amount	argument
across	annually	article

beautiful   mere   professor
become   necessary   profession
believe   ninety   pursue
benefited   noble   quiet
breathe   occasion   receive
category   occur   recommend
chief   occurred   referring
coming   occurring   repetition
conscious   occurrence   rhythm
definitely   opinion   sacrifice
dependent   opportunity   safety
description   paid   sense
disastrous   parallel   separate
effect   particular   separation
embarrass   performance   similar
exaggerate   personal   studying
existence   personnel   succeed
expense   possession   succession
experience   possible   surprise
explanation   practical   than
fascinate   precede   then
height   prejudice   thorough
heroes   preferred   transferred
huge   prepare   unnecessary
interest   principal   villain
involve   principle   woman
led   privilege   write
lose   probably   writing
losing   proceed
marriage   procedure

Words Often Confused

Some words resist a child's ability to remember how to spell
them because they are easy to confuse with other words. I've
grouped five sets of the most troublesome of those words together in ways that you might present them to a child. Notice
how the sentence example makes the use clear. It's helpful to
have the youngster look at one set of words at a time, so that
he sees the difference clearly. You might want to check that
the child understands by speaking sentences that contain the
two or three words under consideration. The youngster must
then write the sentence down. For example, if you're checking
on the correct use of *too, to, two,* you might read a sentence like
this:

The *two* of us want *to* go to the movies *too*.

too, two, to

two means *2,* the number
    I see *two* boys.
too means *also*
    Kiss me *too.*
too means very
    I am *too* young.
to   use *to* like this
    Go *to* the bank.
    I like *to* swim.

it's   its

it's means it is
    It's Monday.
  (If you can say *it is* you can use it's.)
its   shows ownership by some nonhuman thing
    The cat hurt *its* paw.
  (If you can say *his* or *her* use *its.*)

there, their, they're

there   means *a place;* it means *not here*
    Put it *there.*
there   also works with *is, was, are* or *were*
    There is my Father.
    There were three of us.
their   means ownership or possession
    by more than one person
    They lost *their* tickets.
they're means *they are*
    They're my toys.
    If you can say *they are,*
    you can use they're.)

your   you're

your   means ownership or possession by *you*
    It is *your* book.
you're means you are
    You're right.
    (If you can say *you are,* you can
    write *you're.*)

who's   whose

who's	means who is
	Who's there? (If you can say who is, use who's.)
whose	means possession. It asks, "Who does this belong to?"
	Whose book is that?
whose	may also be used this way
	The man *whose* glasses fell picked them up.

When to Use Capitals

More productive than a lengthy list of rules, clear charts that demonstrate correct use of capitals serve the child best. The chart on page 235 and those on the following pages are from my book, *Creating Compositions.*

Some Punctuation Pointers

• *End Marks.* The period, the question mark, and the exclamation point end sentences and serve as marks that separate one sentence from another.

The period (.) ends a sentence that makes a statement.

> I watched a crow circle above the oaks. It swooped down. Then it landed on a high branch.

The question mark (?) ends a sentence that clearly asks a question.

> Who brought her doll? Did Mary bring Drowsy? Did Carol bring Raggedy Ann?

Some sentences say that a question is being asked but they do not really ask the question themselves. For those, use a period, not a question mark.

> She wondered why he did not call.
> He asked who brought the station wagon.

The exclamation point (!) ends a sentence that shows strong emotion, sharp surprise, a forceful command, or strong emphasis.

> I hate olives!
> I don't believe it!
> Just try making me eat one!

QUICK REFERENCE CHART: WHEN AND WHEN NOT TO CAPITALIZE

Geography

Passaic River
Catskill Mountains
     not
a tall mountain

New York City
     not
our city

Yellowstone National Park
Market Street
     not
a noisy street

Historical Occurrences,
Names and Writings

Tonkin Resolution
Boston Tea Party
Seward's Folly
Fifth Amendment
The Constitution

School Things

LaGuardia Community
College
     not
a new college

Mohawk High School
     not
our old high school

Coleman Junior High School
          not
a junior high school

English, Spanish, French
American history
     not
economics, biology, business

Hint: Languages are always cap-
italized. Other subjects are not,
except when specific courses (usually indicated by numbers) are
meant:

Economics 13.2
History 64

a sophomore in college
the senior class

Buildings and Organizations

Dime Savings Bank
Sears Roebuck and Company
Brookdale Hospital
Pathmark Supermarket

Republican Party
San Francisco Giants
Girl Scouts

The Word "I"

Always capitalize the word I
When *I* saw her, *I* was
delighted.

Days, Months, Seasons,
Celebrations

Monday
April
     not seasons
spring, summer, fall,
autumn, winter
Election Day
Festival of Lights
New Year's Eve

Religion, Race, Nationality

God, Lord
Bible, Genesis
New Testament
bless His Name
the Egyptian gods
Catholicism
the Jewish religion
Protestant beliefs
Negro, Indian
Dutch Reformed Church

Titles
Books, Stories, Shows, Poems

"Oh Captain, My Captain"
Love Story
A Tale of Two Cities
     not
a book by Dickens

The Washington Post
The Ed Sullivan Show
"The Legend of Sleepy
Hollow"

People

President Nixon
Judge Black
Dr. Bracken
He is the president of the
     company.
Mr. Davis, President of the
     company
          or
Mr. Davis, president of the
     company

Harriet Parsons, Ph.D.
          not
a teacher, a lawyer, a
     professor

Hint: If the title takes the place
of a person's name, use a capital.
The Mayor arrived late.
The mayor's job is difficult.

Areas and Directions

Lower East Side
East-West relations
Far East
Midwest
lives in the West
     but not for
          directions
New York is six miles east of
here.
They drove north across the
bridge.

The Family

I get along with Mom.
          or
I get along with mom.
This is Aunt Celia.

No capitals to show
relationship:
That is my sister.
Our uncle is generous.
My aunt is very helpful.

Writing Letters

Opening: Capitals for first
word and any names.
     Dear Mr. Stevenson:
     My dear Miss Trumball:
     Dear Jerry,
Closing: First word only:
     Sincerely yours,
     Yours truly,
     Very truly yours,

No Capitals for Plants,
Animals, Games

daisies	a vicious lion
sycamore tree	baseball
an old oak	football
bananas	swimming
a bluebird	monkeys
six sparrows	apple

• **_Quotation Marks._** There are several tricky things about the correct use of quotation marks.

First, the child must learn to distinguish between the part of the sentence that tells about who's talking and the part of the sentence that gives the words the speaker says.

Next, he must make the distinction between a sentence that tells exactly what a person says and a sentence that merely summarizes what a person says. The first kind requires quotes; for the second they are incorrect:

> Tai shouted, "Sit down quickly!"
> Tai shouted that we should sit down quickly.

Last, you need to demonstrate the different kinds of punctuation required by quotation sentences, depending upon where the part that tells who's talking appears—at the beginning, the end, or somewhere in the middle. The best way I know to show this is to show each separately and to use arrows to point out all the marks to remember.

I. EXACT WORDS AT THE END [Quotation marks]

[Capitalize first spoken word]

My mother shouted, "Don't stay out too late, hear, because the

[Comma]

alarm's going off early and you'd better be able to get up for

[End mark inside: period, question mark, or exclamation point]

work!"

[Quotation marks]

Hint: If the same person speaks another sentence—without being interrupted —right after his first one, DON'T use another quotation mark. Put the last quotation mark after the very _last_ word any one person speaks.

My mother shouted, "Don't stay out too late, hear, because the alarm's going off early and you'd better be able to get up for work. I won't be able to wake you!"

II. EXACT WORDS AT THE BEGINNING

[Quotation marks]

"Don't stay out too late, hear, because the alarm's going off

[Capital letter]   [Quotation marks]   [Small letter]

early and you'd better be able to get up for work," my mother

[Period]   [Comma, question mark, or exclamation point: no period]

shouted.

III. EXACT WORDS BROKEN UP

[Quotation marks]   [Close quotes]   [Small letter]   [Open quotation again]

"Don't stay out too late, hear," my mother shouted, "because

[Capital]   [Comma]   [Comma]   [Small letter (A sentence is *continued.*)]

the alarm's going off early and you'd better be able to get up

for work."

[End mark]   [Close quotes]

- *Apostrophes.* The most difficult of all punctuation marks to master, the apostrophe, has two main uses.

It shows when writers leave letters out of words in contractions.

can't	weren't
don't	hasn't
it's	I've
doesn't	I'll

Apostrophes also show possession or ownership. Look at these examples, so you can help your child understand possession.

a. It is the *car of the man.*
b. It is the *car belonging to the man.*
c. It is the *man's car.*

In sentence *a,* the car belongs to the man. Ownership is shown with the words *of the man.* The car is owned. The man owns it.

In sentence *b,* the car belongs to the man. Ownership is shown with the words *belonging to the man.* The car is owned. The man owns it.

In sentence *c,* the car belongs to the man. Ownership is shown by using an apostrophe s (*'s*) after the word that tells who owns the thing. The car is still being owned. The man still owns it. But in this sentence the owner is named *before* the thing that he owns. The only way to know the owner is through the apostrophe *s.*

It is the man's car.

       [owner]

       [thing owned]

Sentence *a* sounds clumsy and unnatural. You would rarely say or write such a sentence. Sentence *b* is natural but takes too many words to say something very simple.

Sentence *c* is the most convenient and most usual way of indicating ownership. When people speak of *possession* it is usually this form of showing ownership that they mean. Because of the misunderstood apostrophe, this method causes many difficulties.

For possession, two separate ideas are involved.

- Somebody or something is the owner. That word will contain an apostrophe.
- Somebody or something is being "owned." That word usually comes soon after the word with the apostrophe.

Apostrophes *do not* show plural. Plurals are formed by adding *s* or *es* or by some special way (chil*dr*en, *gee*se, alumn*i*). But apostrophes play no part in showing that the writer means more than one thing. A familiar error children make when they first learn the apostrophe is this:

I saw *turkey*'s and *chicken*'s.

The words in italics are both incorrect. When an apostrophe *s* stands at the end of a word it means that the thing the word refers to owns something. What do the turkey and the chicken own? Nothing—at least not according to the meaning of the sentence. Since the writer really wants to show that there is more than one turkey and that there is more than one chicken, the sentence should look like this:

I saw turkeys and chickens.

HOW TO FORM POSSESSIVES: TWO SIMPLE REMINDERS

Reminder I for Possession:

If the word that shows the owner *does not* end in s, add an apostrophe s (*'s*)

girl   The girl's dress ripped.

[apostrophe s   [This is owned by the *girl.*]
added to
girl]

senator   The senator's campaign failed.

[apostrophe s   [This is owned by the senator.]
added to *senator*]

Hint for Reminder I: It does not matter if the word is plural or singular. If the word does not end in s, add an apostrophe s.

This word is plural, → *men*   The men's cars crashed.
even though it does   [apostrophe s   [These are owned
not end in s: added to men]   by the men.]

Reminder II for Possession:

If the word that names the owner *does* end in -s, add only an apostrophe (').

boys   The boys' bicycles broke.

[an apostrophe   [These are owned
added to *boys*]   by the boys.]

governors   The governors' meeting ended when the chairman

[an apostrophe   [This is owned by
added to   the *governors.*]
governors]

      fainted.

Hint for Reminder II: It does not matter if the word is plural or singular. If the word ends in s, add only an apostrophe.

This word is singular: → *Doris*   Doris' trip was canceled.
it ends in s.   [apostrophe   [This is owned
                 added to   by Doris.]
                 Doris]

There are other complications in the correct use of apostrophes to show possession, but they are more advanced skills than those I intend to focus upon here. Your child's grammar book (the upper grades) will point out these special uses of the apostrophe.

Here's a helpful review chart I developed for inexperienced writers who need to stop to think carefully about using apostrophes correctly.

REVIEW: IF YOU THINK A WORD NEEDS AN APOSTROPHE BECAUSE IT SHOWS POSSESSION:

1. See if you can figure out what is being owned.
2. See if the word in which you want to use an apostrophe is the owner of something. Usually, the thing owned appears in the sentence soon after the owner.

   Exceptions: It is David's.
                We ate at Carl's.

   Here the thing owned is not specifically mentioned, but understood.

   David's (book)
   Carl's (house)

3. Sometimes the owner is more than one. Make sure the word shows plural with the right ending.
   a. If the word does not end in *s,* add an apostrophe *s.*
   b. If the word does end in *s,* add an apostrophe.

   Example: a. You want to show that a boy owns books. The word *boy* does not end in *s.* The possessive is shown this way:

   the *boy's* books
           \ [Add apostrophe *s.*]

   b. You want to show that many boys are the owners of books. The word *boys* ends in *s.* The possessive is shown this way:

   the boys' books
           [Add apostrophe after *s.*]

There are more complicated rules than these that many people follow in making possessives. But these I have presented are clear, simple, and acceptable.

Appendix C
Books for
the Home Shelf

1. Children's Word Books

The Cat in the Hat Beginner Book Dictionary, by the Cat himself and P. D. Eastman (New York: Beginner Books, Random House, 1964). Heavily illustrated in full color, this dictionary for beginning readers explains words through simple sentence examples and pictures by Dr. Seuss.

The Charlie Brown Dictionary, compiled by Charles M. Schulz (Cleveland: World Books, 1973). Based on *The Rainbow Dictionary* and recommended for readers in grades kindergarten through three, this picture dictionary is illustrated with over 580 cartoons of the popular "Peanuts" comic series. The 2,400 entries reflect the language that children speak and hear, especially on television.

The Courtis-Watters Illustrated Golden Dictionary for Young Readers, compiled by Stuart A. Courtis and Garnette Watters; consultant on pronunciation, Allen Walker Read (New York: Golden Press, latest edition). Designed for children in grades one through four, this volume defines over 10,000 basic words, including some scientific and geographic entries but none for persons, slang, or foreign terms. Entries contain part of speech, simple pronunciation aids, and sentence examples, and are supplemented by over 3,000 black-and-white drawings, a center section of color illustrations, and an appendix of weights and measures, abbreviations, geographical information, Presidents of the United States, and rules for capitalization.

The Harcourt Brace School Dictionary (New York: Harcourt Brace Jovanovich, 1972). Approximately 50,000 entries, correlated with modern textbooks for readers in grades four through seven. The entries are arranged attractively and include synonyms, usage notes, some etymologies, and sentence examples. Introductions for the reader explain the use of the dictionary and provide exercises. The two-color illustrations include maps and diagrams.

The Home Activity Series (New York: Dell, various editions). Designed "for parents who want to help their children to learn basic educational skills." The series includes workbooks on handwriting, spelling, phonics, and reading readiness, all based on matching, tracing, copying, and pronunciation exercises, with illustrations. Each numbered book is keyed to the needs of a particular age group, and instructions for parents appear at the bottom of pages when appropriate.

Macmillan Dictionary for Children, edited by Christopher G. Morris (New York: Macmillan, 1975). Designed primarily for readers of middle to late elementary grades, the *Macmillan* contains approximately 30,000 words, including some geographic and scientific entries, each identified by its part of speech, placed in a context sentence, and followed by its phonetic pronunciation. An 8-page illustrated introduction instructs the reader in understanding entries, dividing words by syllables, and using the phonetic pronunciation key, which appears on alternate pages. About 1,100 full-color illustrations accompany the text, along with several hundred brief narratives on the etymologies of interesting words. Definitions are simple and precise but not condescending.

The New Golden Dictionary, compiled by Bertha Morris Parker; illustrated by Aurelius Battaglia (New York: Golden, 1972). Recommended for preschool and beginning readers, this picture dictionary defines over 1,200 words, with 880 inflected forms and an additional 450 illustrative examples. Geographic, historical, and biographic names are omitted, and entries do not include pronunciation or part of speech; words are defined in sentence examples and reinforced with full-color illustrations. A parent's guide and a series of dictionary games appear in the appendix.

The Rainbow Dictionary, compiled by Wendell W. Wright (Cleveland: World, 1974). This dated but still respected dictionary for beginning readers contains 2,300 entries based on word-frequency lists and defined in sentence examples from Mother Goose, Robert Louis Stevenson, Lewis Carroll, and others. Written for five- to eight-year-old children, it omits pronunciation, syllabic division, and word forms, along with geographic and scientific terms, but its framed entries, large clear print, and over 1,100

full-color illustrations make it convenient for the young reader
to use without the help of an adult.

The Random House Dictionary of the English Language, school
edition, edited by Stuart Berg Flexner (New York: Random
House, latest edition). Over 47,500 entries, based on word frequency lists for fourth to eighth grade students, include biographical and geographic terms and abbreviations; entries give
phonetic pronunciation, part of speech, and sentence examples.
A substantial introduction for the student, along with a map
section and tables of weights and measures, are especially
useful.

Scott, Foresman Beginning Dictionary (Glenview, Illinois: Scott,
Foresman, latest edition). Over 25,000 entries, containing part of
speech, pronunciation, sentence examples, and synonyms where
possible; includes ethnic, slang, geographical, and scientific
terms. Heavily illustrated with approximately 1,000 photographs, drawings, and art reproductions, this volume also includes an extensive series of self-help lessons on skill topics,
supported with exercises and review tests appropriate to the
needs of students in the middle and late elementary grades.

*The Scribbler's First Copy Book: Practice in Writing the Alphabet and
Numerals* by Joanne Wylie (Racine, Wisconsin: Western, A
Whitman Book, 1974) and *The Scribbler's Second Copy Book:
Combining Alphabet Letters to Form Simple Words* by Joanne
Wylie (Racine, Wisconsin: Western, A Whitman Book, 1974).
The Scribbler's series relies almost exclusively on tracing and
writing, rather than games and coloring activities, to teach
letters and simple words. The *First Copy Book* provides practice
in copying basic shapes, letters (upper and lower case), and
numerals, but does not associate letters and pictures. Beginning
with a review of letters, the *Second Copy Book* teaches the child
to print groups of words—family, color, number, vehicle, clothing,
and furniture—most of which are reinforced with drawings, and
concludes with the copying of simple sentences.

See A Word—Say a Word by Joanne Wylie (Racine, Wisconsin:
Western, Golden Press, 1974). Designed for beginning readers,
this workbook reinforces the recognition of basic words with
illustrated exercises and activities, involving matching, tracing,
copying, and writing. Word-picture games identify names of animals, colors, toys, and household items.

The Sounds and Shapes of Letters by Adelaide Holl and Linda Segel
(Racine, Wisconsin: Western, 1972). Part of the Golden Press
Readiness Workbook series, this book introduces preschool
children to letters, using tracing exercises, simple recognition
games, and numerous pictures to reinforce initial sounds. Activ-

ities include coloring, puzzle-solving, drawing, word pronunciation, and rhyming, with a cut-out picture section for each letter.

Thorndike Barnhart Beginning Dictionary, compiled by E. L. Thorndike and Clarence L. Barnhart (Glenview, Illinois: Scott, Foresman, latest edition). Over 26,000 words, including a limited
number of geographic names and scientific terms, are defined
and placed in context; each entry includes part of speech and
phonetic pronunciation. Approximately 1,300 charts, diagrams,
and black-and-white line drawings supplement the text. Intended
for use in grades three and four, it contains an extensive introduction, explaining the use of the dictionary, alphabetization,
phonics, spelling, and word forms, with two-color illustrations
and review exercises after each section. Etymologies are limited
to words derived from people's names and terms that have under-
gone interesting changes.

Thorndike Barnhart Intermediate Dictionary, compiled by E. L.
Thorndike and Clarence L. Barnhart (Glenview, Illinois: Scott,
Foresman, latest edition). Listing approximately 57,000 words in
a single alphabet, including colloquialisms and biographical,
historical, geographic, and scientific terms, the *Intermediate
Dictionary* is designed for readers in grades five through eight.
Definitions contain sentence examples, parts of speech, and
phonetic pronunciations, and the text is heavily illustrated with
black-and-white line drawings, maps, and diagrams. A comprehensive preface explains the use of entries and provides a helpful
guide to spelling, and several pages of end notes give spelling
and phonics rules. Over 1,800 etymologies appear in the entries.

Thorndike Barnhart Junior Dictionary, compiled by E. L. Thorndike
and Clarence L. Barnhart (Glenview, Illinois: Scott, Foresman,
latest edition). Recommended for the child in late elementary
or junior high school, the *Junior Dictionary* has 44,000 entries,
including colloquialisms, foreign words and phrases in common
use, and biographical, historical, geographic, and scientific terms;
definitions contain sentence examples, parts of speech, and
phonetic pronunciations, with several thousand black-and-white
drawings and charts. A three-part introduction for the reader
explains how to use the dictionary, find meanings, and determine pronunciation, followed by a review of the parts of speech,
a spelling guide, and numbered exercises and questions suitable
for group or independent work. *The Thorndike Barnhart Advanced Junior Dictionary* is similar but contains 30 percent more
entries. The entire Thorndike Barnhart series, frequently revised
and updated, is a high quality student set and a popular choice
in the classroom as well as the home library.

Webster's New Elementary Dictionary (New York: Merriam, 1975).
Written for the late elementary and junior high school student,

this volume contains 32,000 entries, with an introduction for the reader and tables of information.

The Young People's Thesaurus Dictionary, compiled by Harriet Wittels and Joan Greisman (New York: Grosset and Dunlap, 1971). A collection of synonyms and antonyms arranged in a continuous alphabet, this work is designed to accompany (but not replace) a comprehensive dictionary for the child of late elementary or junior high school age. An introduction for the reader explains the advantages and drawbacks of the thesaurus format, including some interesting examples of the variety of sources from which English words derive. Its weakness, common to almost all thesauri, is the failure to discriminate adequately among parts of speech and shades of meaning.

2. Language Skills Books for Parents

Books, Young People, and Reading Guidance by Geneva Hanna Pilgrim and Marianna K. McAllister, 2nd edition (New York: Harper, 1968). Among the somewhat theoretical discussions on the reading interests of junior and senior high school students are several sections useful to parents: Chapters 4 and 5 deal with the social and psychological factors that influence adolescent reading interests, and chapter 6 reviews the basic terms of literary analysis for parents who wish to discuss books with their children. Included is a comprehensive list of sources that evaluate young people's literature.

Children and Books by Zena Sutherland and May Hill Arbuthnot, 5th edition (Glenview, Illinois: Scott, Foresman, 1977). Valuable chiefly for its comprehensive and up-to-date annotation of hundreds of books for young people, *Children and Books* also includes chapters on encouraging responses to literature, on the child's literary interests and needs, and on contemporary issues of interest to parents: censorship, sexism in children's stories, the influence of television on literacy. An annotated list of adult references appears at the end of each chapter.

A Child's Mind: How Children Learn During the Critical Years from Birth to Age Five by Muriel Beadle (Garden City, New York: Doubleday, 1970). Written in concise, conversational prose for parents and educators, *A Child's Mind* surveys and synthesizes research in children's mental development, providing impartial coverage of cognitive theories and suggesting ways to make the home a good learning environment. Especially useful are chapter 13, which explains how children perceive the written word, and chapter 14, on the acquisition of speaking, writing, and vocabulary skills.

Explorations in Children's Writing, edited by Eldonna L. Evertts (Champaign, Illinois: National Council of Teachers of English,

1970). Intended primarily for teachers, this brief collection of essays and transcripts of recorded discussions provides parents with a comprehensive and provocative survey of alternative ways to motivate and appreciate the writing of elementary school children.

Helping Your Child to Read Better by Robert M. Goldenson (New York: Thomas Crowell, 1957). In this informative study for parents seeking to stimulate their child's verbal skills and enrich reading experiences at home, Goldenson suggests games and activities for improving language arts and concludes each chapter with a question-and-answer discussion of the issues. Though the book relies too heavily on anecdotes and hypothetical dialogue, it does provide a wealth of practical information. Several chapters contain reviews of spelling, diction, and sentence correctness.

Home Reference Books in Print by S. Padraig Walsh (New York: Bowker, 1969). This concise, detailed handbook is indispensable for the parent interested in building an adequate home library. Part One evaluates English language dictionaries according to age suitability and size, Part Two rates world atlases in print, and Part Three surveys the numerous subscription books available to homeowners—from encyclopedias to specialized collections on gardening, sports, and religion—with ratings by cost and advice on sales techniques. Each section includes annotations and price information.

The Horn Book Magazine, published six times per year by The Horn Book, Inc., 585 Boylston Street, Boston, MA 02116. In addition to articles of general interest in the field of children's literature, each issue reviews children's books and audio-visual materials and recommends new books by suggested reading level. A yearly index lists reviews by author and title.

How to Help Your Child in Reading, Writing, and Arithmetic by Frieda E. Van Atta (New York: Random House, various editions). This series, published in separate workbooks for grades kindergarten through eight, provides explanations of typical verbal and mathematical skills taught in each grade, with review exercises at the end. Somewhat outdated, it still contains useful information on the terms and standards of English usage. Many of the early grade books are now out of print.

The Language Arts in the Elementary School by Ruth G. Strickland, 3rd edition (Lexington, Mass.: D. C. Heath, 1969). This useful overview, designed primarily for teachers, begins with several chapters on the language development of preschool children and presents writing activities—from dictation of invitations and letters to independent "creative expression"—adaptable to use in the home as well as in the classroom. Chapter 15 is a condensed, intelligent discussion of the value of grammar, usage, syntax, and punctuation (including a review of some basic standards of correctness and the terminology of traditional grammar). Chapter 16 deals with levels of spelling proficiency and the relationship of correct spelling to oral and written English. Other sections help parents understand possible difficulties for the child acquiring language skills.

A Parent's Guide to Children's Reading by Nancy Larrick (Garden City, New York: Doubleday, 1975). A readable and up-to-date discussion for parents of elementary school children. *A Parent's Guide* includes dozens of activities for stimulating the child's reading interests at home and a helpful annotated list of several hundred selected children's books, organized by subject and reading level. Especially valuable are the suggestions for maintaining a home environment conducive to reading and writing.

Poetic Composition through the Grades: A Language Sensitivity Program by Robert A. Wolsch (New York: Teachers College Press, 1970). This handbook for teachers includes several sections of interest to parents seeking to promote language sensitivity. Emphasizing the development of precise, evocative language "for improved ways of stating ideas and feelings," chapters 6 and 7 discuss the relationship of writing to experience, and chapter 10 suggests ways to use words with variety, vitality, and precision.

Rose, Where Did You Get That Red? Teaching Great Poetry to Children by Kenneth Koch (New York: Random House, 1973). Emphasizing written responses, Koch discusses ways to help children understand "mature" poetry by Shakespeare, Blake, Whitman, and others, with suggestions for parents seeking to foster the child's appreciation of poetry in general. Like its predecessor *Wishes, Lies, and Dreams, Rose* includes dozens of student poems, along with some perceptive discussion of how children react to imaginative literature, and why.

When You Are Alone / It Keeps You Capone: An Approach to Creative Writing with Children by Myra Cohn Livingston (New York: Atheneum, 1973). The author, a noted children's poet, explains a number of techniques that help children express emotional responses in writing, striking a balance between unbridled expression and disciplined creative art. Especially useful to parents are Ms. Livingston's recommendations for adult responses to children's poetry. Chapter 16 suggests activities and topics to stimulate interest in writing.

Wishes, Lies, and Dreams: Teaching Children to Write Poetry by Kenneth Koch (New York: Chelsea House, 1970). Believing that "the best way to help children write freely is by encouragement, by examples, and by various other inspiring means," Koch describes the techniques he discovered to help elementary school students write poetry and to grow more sensitive to expressive language. Though designed for teachers, the suggested methods and discussions of children's response to words are valuable for parents as well, and the numerous student poems are delightful and useful stimuli for a child.

You and Your Child's Reading: A Practical Guide for Parents by Charlotte Mergentime (New York: Harcourt, 1963). In this informative and comprehensive handbook, Ms. Mergentime discusses some causes of reading difficulties, outlines ways to aid the child in developing spelling and vocabulary skills, and suggests dozens of activities and games to stimulate reading and writing. Chapter 7 presents a systematic and sensitive program for introducing children to work patterns, syllabication, and prefix/suffix rules, with an explanation of phonics and word building for parents. The reading lists are dated, but the suggested activities, including many nonverbal preludes to writing, are varied, interesting, and valuable.

Index

Abbreviations in addressing envelopes, 166
Abstract words, writing images for, 53–54
Achievement in writing, 5–7
  effect of teacher preparation, 6
Action words, 45, 123
  "Name the Action" game, 41–42
Aesop's fables, 155
Alphabet and word books, 10–11
Alphabetizing, 177
American Heritage Dictionary, 176
Animal stories, imaginative writing, 154–156
Apostrophes ('), 236–240
  forming possessives, 238–240
Assignments, 63–71
  code for ethics for parents, 63–71
  how much help should parents give, 63–71
  understanding, 65, 207
Attitudes toward writing, 6, 60
  developing positive, 12–13, 17, 26, 107

Basics of correct writing, 62
Ben and Me, 221
Benchley, Peter, 175
Book reports, 209, 219–220
  making a book cover, 221
  personification in, 220–221
Books:
  home-made word books, 177–178
  language skills books for parents, 245–248
  My Book of Red Things, 45
  scrap books of word portraits, 121
Brown, James, I., 89
"Build an Image" game, 42–44
Business letters, 170–173
  (*See also* Letter-writing)

Candid Camera, TV program, 178
Capitals and capitalization, 234–235
  at beginning of sentence, 30, 44, 148
  correcting errors in, 74
  titles, 30
Captions of pictures, 25–27, 116
  accent on sentence sense, 27–29
  avoiding incomplete statements, 29–33
  use of complete sentences, 27–29
Careers, effect of lack of writing skills on, 6–7
Chalkboard and chalk, 10
  notes written on, 15
Characters in stories, 150–153
  list of details about, 151
  make-believe visits with, 150–153
Chronology of events, 135–137
Cinquains (five-line poems), 203
City University of New York, courses in
  teaching writing, 5
Clarity and impact, use of comparisons for, 50
Class newspapers, 4
Colleges and universities, 5–7
  English departments, 5

freshman writing courses, 5
students lack writing skills, 5–7, 83
teaching writing courses, 5
Color words, 37, 50. *See also* Sensory language
Columbia Teachers' College, New York, 5
Communications: effect of modern advantages
  on, 6
  nonverbal forms, 6
Comparisons, 50–56
  figurative language, 50–51
  metaphors, 53–54
  personifications, 52–53
  similes, 51
  for solid imagery, 50–56
  use of sensory language, 51
  using *like* or *as,* 51
Composition skills, 3
  goals in schools, 76–81
  college programs, 5
  training in teaching, 5
Concrete sensory detail, 38–39
  for images, 38
Concreteness in choice of words, 37–39
Confidence in ability to write, 2
Connotative meanings of words, 174–175
Conrad, Joseph, 39
Content matter, 2
  written language and, 3–4
Conversation: sentence fragments, 28–29
  use of dialogue, 142–143, 221
Coonfield, Professor, 113–114
Copying final draft, 68–69
Cornell University, writing courses, 5
Correctness of expression, 3, 57–83, 86–107
  age variables, 58
  corrections made after development of ideas,
    61
  creative impulses destroyed by overemphasis
    on, 58–59
  errors and mistakes, 10, 57–59, 62–63
  hysteria of neatness and, 57–59
  letter-writing, 169
  "A Parent's Primer for Correctness," 228–240
  praising child's efforts, 61
  professional writers and, 59–62
  proofreading, 71–74
  punctuation, 58, 229–231
  reacting to errors, 62–63
  rewrites and correction of errors, 61–62
  rough copies, 59–61, 65–67
  sentence completeness, 57–59, 100–107,
    229–231
    run-together sentences, 229–230
    sentence fragments, 28–29, 230–231
  spelling skills, 58, 95–100
    words often confused, 232–234
    words often misspelled, 231–232
  tips and pointers for parents, 65–71
    before writing, 65
    copying over final draft, 68–69

Correctness of expression (cont.):
    graded paper returned, 70
    rough copy, 65–67
Crayons and colored pencils, 10
Creating Compositions (Wiener), 234
Creative writing, 17, 18–23
    autobiography, 20–21
    creative questioning, 21–22
    environment for, 2
    experience and creative expression, 18–23
    letter-writing, 162–166
    pressure valve for child, 32
    sensory language, 21
    writing and photographs, 117
Crossword puzzles, 77
Curriculum in language skills and composi-
    tion, 76–81
    (*See also* Writing programs)
Cut-and-paste fun, 117
    sentence construction, 33–34

Definitions of words *see* Words, definition of
de la Mare, Walter, 193
Denotative meanings of words, 174
Descriptive writing, 108–117
    building and combining sentences, 112
    cameras and crayons, 116–117
    classroom descriptions, 109–110
    definition of words, 184
    describing a room, 112–113, 117
    examples and models, 111–112
    expectations and aims, 111
    first sentences, 115
    focus on sense impressions, 118
    goals, 111
    importance of, 130
    list of sense words, 110–111, 127, 137, 213,
        217
    objectivity and subjectivity, 113–114
    opinions in focus, 112–114
    about a person, 118–130
        one-sentence descriptions, 119
        in photographs, 120–121
    places, 100–117
        choice of, 108–112
        snapshots of special, 108–117
    portraits, 120–127
        in particular time and place, 127–130
    report on anatomy of dogfish, 113–114
    riddles, 119–120
    selecting key details, 112–114
        subjective responses, 114–116
    self-portraits, 121–127
    simple, direct statements, 111
    techniques, 130
    use of dialogue, 142–143
Details, 37–55
    "Build an Image" game, 42–44
    concrete sensory details, 38–39
    creative questioning to elicit, 22
    of daily experiences, 21–22
    descriptive writing, 112–114
    objective writing, 113–114
    quotations and, 22
    selecting key details, 112–114
    sense charts, 110–111, 127, 137, 213, 217
    sensory, 37–55
    statistics, 22
    subjective responses, 114–116
    supporting, 5

Dialogue, use of, 142–143 221
    use of quotation marks, 142–143, 221
Dictionaries, 10–11
    children's editions, 11, 93–95, 241–245
    denotative meanings, 175
    for expanding word power, 92
    home-made word books, 177–178
        illustrations and drawings, 177
        writing definitions, 177
    list of, 93–95, 241–245
    picture dictionaries, 93–94
    practicing dictionary skills, 92–93
    use of, 91–95
    words with multiple meanings, 176
Dilemma and conflict, short-story writing,
    144–146
Dogfish, anatomical description, 113–114
Drawings and writing, 24–36
    avoiding incomplete statements, 29–33
    connecting pictures with words, 25–27
    to develop writing skills, 24–36
    sensory impressions conveyed by, 24–25

Effective writing, 3
    experience and creative expression, 18–23
    speak-listen-write formula, 23, 24–25
    use of mature sentence structures, 100
Eliot, T. S., 61
Embedding activities, 102–103
Encyclopedia Buying Guide (Kister), 212
Encyclopedias: list of, 212
    for preparing reports, 212
    selecting, 212
    taking notes, 212–216
End marks, 234
English courses: literary appreciation, 5
    and programs in teaching writing, 5–6
Environment *see* Home environment
Erasers, 58
*Errors and Expectations: A Guide for the
    Teacher of Basic Writing* (Shaughnessy),
    83
Errors and mistakes, 10
    corrected by child, 61–62
    proofreading for, 71–74
    rewrites and correction of, 61–62
Essays, photo, 33–34
Evaluation by teachers, 2–3
Evans, Karen Sue, 200
Examples and models: descriptive writing,
    111–112
    use of, 43–44
    word portraits, 126–128
Exclamation point (!), 234
Experiences and creative expression, 18–23
    basis of vocabulary building, 83
    daily living, 18
    emotional responses to, 18
    importance of details, 21–22
    questioning by parents, 21–22
    sensory responses, 19–20
    shared by parents and child, 18–23
    storytelling and, 22–23
    talking over, 21–22

Factual writing, 114
Fairy tales, 147
    visits with characters in, 150–153
Family stories, 153
Fan mail, 168

Fantasy tales and myths, 156
Field, Rachel, 193
Figurative language, 50
Finger painting, 33
Flashbacks, 135
Florida State University, 102–103
Fragments, sentences, 28–29, 106, 149, 230–231
Franklin, Benjamin, 102, 221
Frost, Frances, 193
Frost, Robert, 193

Games: "Build an Image" game, 42–44
    to determine guest's seating plan at birthday party, 16
    "free association," 55
    Jigsaw Sentence, 104–106
    language, 95
    "Name the Action," 41–42
    party riddles, 119–120
    recording sense impressions, 110
    rhymes and rhyming, 46, 187–190
    riddles, 49–50, 119–120
        two-sentences, 148–150
    scrap books, 45
    "Sentence Building," 44–49
    sentence-combining ideas, 103
    "Sentence Staircase," 47–48
    spelling problem words, 97
    to stimulate child's sense of make-believe, 159–160
    vocabulary building, 83–84
    "What's the Best Word?" 40–41
    word associations, 175–178
    word opposites, 84
    words with multiple definitions, 176
Grammar, 3–4
    correcting errors, 107
    influence on writing skills, 4, 102
    transformational, 102–103
    See also Composition skills
Greeting cards, making, 166
Grouping information, 216–218
    list-making and, 217–218

Haikus, Japanese, 201–202
Happiness Is (Schulz), 53
High schools: composition skills, 80
    instruction in writing, 4–5, 80
    language skills, 80
Historical reports, 132
Home environment for writing, 2, 222
    materials needed for writing activities, 9–12
    source of creative experiences, 2, 108, 222
Homework assignments, 2
    parent's role, 63–71
    understanding requirements, 65, 207
Hughes, Langston, 193

I Know! A Riddle Book (Sarnoff and Ruffins), 148
Ideas: dealing with thoughts and, 3
    detail observations and, 22
    expression of, 3–4
    one hundred ideas for writing at home, 225–227
    organizational strategies, 3, 82
Illustrated Dictionary for School and Home, 93
Image-building, 37–55

comparisons, 50–56
concrete sensory details, 38–39
definitions, 54–55
"free association" game, 55–56
personification, 52–53
use of sense words, 37–55
Imaginative writing, 20, 147–160
    animal stories, 154–156
    fables with a moral, 154
    family stories, 153
    fantasy tales and myths, 156
    focus on single moment, 147
    games to stimulate, 159–160
    language skills, 153
    models for, 147
    personification and, 156–159
    about photographs or paintings, 153
    "Pretend-You-Are" writing, 157–159
    riddles and games, 148–150, 159–160
    visits with make-believe, 150–153
Implements for writing, 10
Indiana Writes, 194–195, 200
Inductive reasoning, 114
Instruction in writing: composition skills, 76–81
    departmentalized, 4–5
    language skills, 76–81
    teacher's responsibilities, 4–7
Invitations, writing, 163–166
    addressing envelopes, 163–164
    composing message, 163–164
    copying model, 163–164
    responses to, 164
    RSVP, 164
Iowa, University of, 5
It's and its, use of, 149, 233

Japanese haikus, 201–202
Jaws (Benchley), 175
Johnson, Ben, 61
Junior high schools: instruction in writing, 4–5
    language skills, 78–79
    writing exercises and composition skills, 78–79
Just So Stories (Kipling), 155

Keats, John, 61
Kennedy, John F., 73
Kipling, Rudyard, 155
Kister, Kenneth, 212
Koch, Kenneth, 186

Label-makers, 11
Language arts, 17
    basics of correct writing, 62
    writing skills and, 75
Language patterns: fragmentary utterances, 28–29
    use of complete and complex sentences, 27
Language skills: books for parents, 245–248
    comparisons, 50–56
    figurative language, 50
    imaginative writing and, 147–153
    sensory language see Sensory language
Lear, Edward, 203–204
Legal profession, writing skills required, 6–7
Letter-writing, 6, 161–173
    addressing envelopes, 163, 165–166
        use of abbreviations, 166
    business letters, 170–173

Letter-writing (cont.):
  addresses, 171
  conventions, 170–171
  format, 170–171
  list of firms to write to, 172–173
  model of, 170–171
  closings, 171
  conventions, 164, 170–171
  copying model letter, 163–164
  correctness, 169
  creative, 162–166
  envelopes, 165–166
    addressing, 163–164, 171
    fan mail, 168
    folding letter, 163
    format, 162, 169, 170–171
    greeting, 171
    home-made postal or greeting cards, 166
    invitations, 162, 163–166
      responses to, 164
    letters and cards for shut-ins, 167–168
    mailing letter, 161–162
    message, 163
    models
      business letters, 170–171
      copying, 163–164
      friendly letters, 165
      invitations, 163–164
      notes, 14–15, 161
      pen pals, 168–169
      return address, 164
      signature, 171
      stationery for, 9
      thank-you's, 162, 166–167
Library card catalog, use of, 216
Limericks, 203–204
Lindsay, Vachel, 193
Listening without distraction, 62
Lists and list-making, 12–14, 213
  shopping lists, 7, 12, 217
Literary appreciation, 5
Literary magazines, 4
Literature programs, 5
Logic in writing, 3

McGowan, Darrin, 200
McGraw, Patricia, 195
Make-believe, 147–160
  games to stimulate interest in, 159–160
  imaginative writing (*see* Imaginative
    writing)
  visits, 150–153
Marginal comments, 2–3
Meaning of words (*see* Words, meaning of)
Mechanics of writing, 3
Metaphors, 53–54, 194
Miami Dade Junior College, 5
Milton, John, 102
Moments, 131–146
  capturing essence of moment, 4
  definition, 132
  details, 132
  dialogue, 142–143
  in focus, 133–135
  imaginative writing, 147
  narrative writing, 131–135
  report writing, 220
  sense of sequence, 135–137
  sensory language, 137–142
  writing about single moment, 220

Movies, models for imaginative writing, 147

"Name the Action" game, 41–42
Names, proper, 39
Narrative writing, 131–146
  conflict between characters, 143
  definition, 131–133
  dialogue, 142–143
  examples and models, 137–142, 184–185
  importance of correct sequence, 136
  moment in focus, 133–135
  scientific or historical reports, 132
  sensory language, 137–142
  sequence of events, 132, 136
  single narrative moment, 132–133
  short-story writing, 144–146
  suggestions for, 133, 225–227
  table of senses, 110–111, 127, 137–138
  time sequence, 135–137
  writing dialogue, 142–143
National Endowment for the Arts, Poet-in-
  the-Classroom Program, 186, 191
Neatness, over-emphasis on, 58–59
News reporting, 221
Newspapers, class, 4
Nigger of the Narcissus, The (Conrad), 39
Note-taking, 213–216
  encyclopedias and source books, 213–216
  guidelines for, 215–216
  quotations, 216
Notes and note-writing, 14–15, 161
  between parent and child, 15
  to excuse absence from school, 15–16

Objective writing, 113–114
Observations, 22
  turning into language, 43–44
  vocabulary-building and, 83
O'Hare, Frank, 102–103
Ohio State University, 5
1001 Valuable Things You Can Get Free
  (Weisinger), 172
Opinions, 112–114
  expression of, 112
  in focus, 112–114, 128–129
Organizational strategies, 3, 82
  report writing, 216–218
Outlines, 208, 216–218

Parents: avoid doing child's work, 207–208
  children imitate actions of, 8–9
  code of ethics, 63–71
  correcting errors and mistakes, 61–63
  effect of cutbacks in school systems, 223–
    224
  environment for creative writing, 2
  experiences provided by, 18–23
  guidance in developing writing skills, 1–7
  helping child plan assignments, 63–71
  language skills books for, 245–248
  positive responses to child's writing, 62–63
  praising child's efforts, 61
  role in school assignments, 63–71, 207–208,
    222
  tips and pointers for, 65–71
  ways to assist children, 2–17, 207–208, 222
"Peanuts" book (Schulz), 53
Pen pals, letters to, 168–169
  sources of names, 169–170
Pennsylvania State University, 5

Pens and pencils, 10
Period (.), 234
  at end of sentence, 30, 44, 124
Personification, 52–53, 194
  adds liveliness to writing, 156–157
  imaginative writing and, 156–159
  poems, 200–201
  "Pretend-You-Are" writing, 157–159
  report writing, 220–222
  riddle game, 149–150
Persons, descriptive writing, 118–130
  models and examples, 128
  one-sentence descriptions, 118–119
  party riddles, 119–120
  photo into words, 120–121
  relative or friend, 127–130
  self-portraits, 121–127
Phonetic spelling, 125
Photo essays, 33–34, 116–117, 153
  written words to explain each picture, 117
Photographs: descriptive writing, 120–121
  imaginative writing, 153
Pictures: building complete sentences, 29–33,
  35
  captions, 29–33, 35
  making collages, 33
  making connections between words and,
    25–27, 35, 153
  photo essays, 33–34, 116–117, 153
  words and sentences, 24–36, 45–46, 116–
    117
Places, descriptive writing, 108–117
  list of sense words, 110, 137–138
  opinions in focus, 112–114
  sensory language, 137–138
  subjective responses to details, 114–116
Places I Like, 117
Play-acting, 143
Play-writing, 221
Plurals, formation of, 238
Poet-in-the-Classroom Program, 186, 191
Poetry writing, 186–205
  avoid jingling, 191–193
  choosing words, 194
  cinquains (five-line poems), 203
  definitions of poetry, 191
  forms, 201
  guidelines, for, 194
  importance of writing, 204–205
  Japanese *haikus,* 201–202
  language singing, 193–201
  limericks, 203–205
  nature poems, 199–200
  nonsense and make-believe, 200
  personification poems, 200–201
  poetry workshops, 186
  reading poems aloud, 186–187, 193
  repetition of sounds and words, 194, 196–
    199
  rhyme and image, 191–193, 201–205
  rhymes and rhyming, 187–190
    "If I Were" rhyming poems, 188
    with sensory language, 189–190
    silly rhymes, 187–188
    "Talk-to-Me" rhymes, 188
    three-line rhymes, 187
    word groups, 189
    Word Whackies, 188
  selection of words, 191–194
  sense poems, 195–196

sentence-building games, 46
source of ideas, 196
teaching, 5
use of comparison, 196–199
use of similes, 194, 195
Portraits, word, 120–127
  attitude toward subject, 128–129
  collages, 125–127
  in particular time and place, 127–130
  self-portraits, 121–127
  sense impressions, 128–129
Possessives, use of apostrophe, 236–240
Praising child's efforts, 61–63
Precise words, use of, 39, 85–86, 113–114
Prefixes, suffixes, and roots, 87–88
  table of fourteen master words, 89–90
Prepositions, 43
"Pretend-You-Are" writing, 157–159
Professional careers, writing skills required,
  6–7
Pronouns, 153
Proofreading, 71–74
  final copy, 72
  hedge against errors, 71–74
  techniques, 73–74
Punctuation, 234–240
  correcting errors, 74
  periods, 30, 44, 124, 234
  sentences, 28, 30, 148, 229–230
  use of commas, 62

Question mark (?), 234
Questions and questioning, 21–22
  encouraging child's questions, 83
  to expand details, 24
  full-sentence responses to, 29
Quotations, 129
  picking meaningful, 221
  quotation marks, 129, 142–143, 236–240

"Re-" as a prefix, 88–89
Reading and writing, 17
  sequence in word and sentence recognition,
    74
  word books, 10–11
Realistic touches in writing, 147
Reinforcement, writing, 16–17
Report writing, 113–114, 206–222
  book reports, 206, 209, 219–220
  data collection, 208, 211–216
  encyclopedias and other source books, 211–
    216
  final writing, 218–222
  grouping data, 216–218
  limiting topic, 207, 209–211
  note-taking, 208, 212–216
  organizing material, 216–218
  outlines, 208, 216–218
  parent's role, 207, 222
  personification in, 220–222
  quotations in, 221
  science reports, 206, 219
  understanding assigned topic, 207, 208–209
Rewriting drafts, 61
Rhetoric (*see* Composition skills)
Rhymes and rhyming, 187–190
  avoid jingling, 191–193
  sensory details, 46
Riddles, 49–50
  complete sentences and, 149

Riddles (cont.):
    describing person, 119–120
    drawings to illustrate, 150
    two-sentence riddles, 148–150
    using sensory detail, 49
Roget's Thesaurus, 7, 11, 92–95
Roots or stems of words, 88
Rosetti, Christina, 189
Rough writing, 61, 65–67
    reading rough copy, 66–67
Rubber stamps and pads, 11
Ruffins, Reynolds, 148

"Sabbath Breakers, The," 145–146
Sarnoff, Jane, 148
Schulz, Charles M., 53
Science reports, 132, 219
Self-portraits, 121–127
Sense impressions: drawings and, 24–25
    game for recording, 110
    table of, 110–111, 127, 137, 213, 217
Sense words, 37–55, 117
    comparisons and, 51
    to expand sentences, 45
    list of, 110
    personification and, 52–53
    word-equivalents for real sensations, 37
Sensory details, 45–49
    "Build and Image" game, 43
    to expand sentences, 45–49
    "Sentence Staircase" game, 47–48
    writing riddles game, 49
Sensory experiences, 21–22
Sensory language, 117
    building image definitions, 54–55
    describing places, 137–138
    narrations, 137–142
    responses to experiences, 19–20
    rhyming exercises with, 189–190
    table of senses, 110–111, 127, 137, 213, 217
"Sentence Building" games, 44–49
"Sentence Staircase" game, 47–48
Sentences, 3
    capital letter at beginning, 30, 44, 148
    combining techniques, 102–107
        embedding, 102
        Jigsaw Sentence game, 104–106
    completeness, 27–29, 34, 44, 47, 148–149,
        229–231
    connecting words, 230
    correctness, 148
    cut-and-paste activities, 33–34
    end marks, 148
    establishing "sentence sense," 27–29, 55
    first, 115
    fragments, 28–29, 206, 149, 230–231
    full-sentence responses, 29
    image-building games, 44–49
    incomplete, 44
    incorrect, 106–107
    mature construction, 57, 101–102
    punctuation, 30, 44, 124, 148
    run together, 229–230
    shifting and expanding parts of, 45–47,
        105–106
    structuring, 100–107
    syntax, 100
    topic, 5
    transformations, 102–103

Sequence of events, 135–137, 147
    sense of, 135–137
Seuss, Dr., 83
Shakespeare, William, 61
Shaughnessy, Mina, 83, 89, 98
Shopping lists, 7, 12, 217
Shopping-trip excursions, 86
Short-story writing, 144–146
    dilemma and conflict, 144
Signs and sign-making, 14–15
    to reinforce reading skills, 25
Similes, 51
    in poems, 194, 195
Slang terms, 51
Slaughter, William, 191
Sound words, 37, 45, 123
Speaking skills, use of complete sentences,
    29–33
Spelling: correcting errors, 58, 62, 74, 95–98,
        124–125
    phonetic, 125
    problem words, 95–100, 231–232
        hot spots, 97
        memory tricks for, 97
    tests, 58
    use of dictionary, 98–99
    word often confused, 232–234
    writing activities and, 16
Stamps and stamp pads, 11
Stationery for letter-writing, 9
Storytelling, 22–23
Style of writing, 3
Subjective writing, 113–114
Suffixes, 87–88
SUNY Stony Brook, writing courses, 5
Syntax, 100

"Talk-to-Me" rhymes, 188
Taste words, 45
Teachers: ability to teach writing skills, 2–7
    instruction and evaluation of writing, 2, 4–7
    lack of instruction in how to teach com-
        position, 4–7
    marginal comments by, 2–3
    overburdened, 2, 4, 223–224
Teaching writing, college programs for
    teachers, 5
Television and radio programs, 6, 147
There, their, and *they're,* 233
Thesaurus, 11, 92–95, 175
    language games, 95
Time and place: identifying, 135, 137, 147
    sequences in narrations, 135–137
Titles, 30
    capitals used in, 30
Tolstoy, Count Leo, 18–19, 146
Too, to, and *two,* 232–233
Tools, writing, 9–12
    chalkboard and chalk, 10
    word books, 10–11
    writing implements, 10
Touch sensations, words for, 37
Transition words, 136
Typewriters for children, 8, 11

"un-" words, 89
University of California, Los Angeles, 5
University of Southern California, 5

Verbs, tense of, 5
Vocabulary-building, 83–86
  based on child's experience, 83
  dictionary use, 91–95
  games, 83–84
    "free association" game, 55–56
    "Name the Action," 41–42
    "What's the Best Word?," 40–41
  guessing meaning of words, 91–95
  list of new words, 177–178
  parent's role, 83–85
  precise words, 39, 85–86, 113–114
  prefixes, suffixes, and roots, 87–90
  sight vocabulary, 25
  sign-making, 14–15
  table of fourteen master words, 89–90
  use of thesaurus, 11
  word changes, 86–88
  writing clear definitions, 178–182

Weisinger, Mort, 172
"What's the Best Word?" game, 40–41
Who's and *whose,* 234
Wiener, Melissa: pictures and sentences, 31–35
  self-portrait, 121–125
  swimming lesson, 133–135
Wishes, Lies, and Dreams (Koch), 186
Wolfe, Don, 117, 125, 132, 136, 189, 192, 220
Word-attack skills for reading, 88
Word books, 10–11
  (*See also* Dictionaries)
Words:
  abstract, 183
  action words, 123
  alphabetizing, 177
  changes to mean different things, 86–90
  concept words, 183–184
  concrete sensory detail, 38–39
  concreteness, 37–39
  creative definitions, 174–185
    collage of meanings, 183
    denotation and connotation, 174–175

    extended, 181–182, 185
    home-made dictionaries, 177–178
    models for, 179–180
    multiple definitions, 176
    one-sentence, 181
    personal meanings, personal words, 182–185
    suggestions and feelings about words, 175–176
    use of dictionary or thesaurus, 175
    visual techniques, 183
    writing clear definitions, 178–182
  games and activities, 174–178
    "Build an Image" game, 42–44
    "What's the Best Word?," 40–41
    word associations, 175–178
  list of new words, 177–178
  making connections between pictures and, 25–27
  meanings, 84, 176, 182–185
    guessing, 91–95
    shades of, 176
  nonsense words, 83
  opposites, 84
  personalized meanings, 182–185
  precise expressions, 39, 85–86, 113–114
  prefixes, suffixes, and roots, 87–88
  pronunciation of, 178
  sense words, 37–39
  sound words, 123
  word parts, 87–88
Writing implements, 10
Writing paper, 9
Writing programs, 76–81
  language skills, 76–80
  writing exercises and composition skills, 76–81

"*-y*" words, 89
Yearbooks, 4
Your and *you're,* 233

About the Author

Harvey S. Wiener was born in Brooklyn, graduated from Brooklyn College, and taught in New York City's public schools before receiving his doctorate from Fordham University. As a teacher and father he has worked with young writers of all ages. An associate professor of English, he currently teaches writing and literature at La Guardia Community College of the City University of New York, having administered the writing program there for a number of years. In 1973 he spent several months in England on a grant from the National Endowment for the Humanities. Last year he directed the basic writing program at Pennsylvania State University. In addition to *Any Child Can Write* he is the author of several writing textbooks, including *Creating Compositions* (now in its second edition), *The Writing Lab* (with Rose Palmer), and *The English Skills Handbook* (with Charles Bazerman). He lives with his wife and two children in Massapequa, New York.